English Trader, Indian Maid

Edited by Frank Felsenstein

ENGLISH TRADER, INDIAN MAID

Representing Gender, Race, and Slavery in the New World

An Inkle and Yarico Reader

THE JOHNS HOPKINS UNIVERSITY PRESS

Baltimore and London

© 1999 The Johns Hopkins University Press
All rights reserved. Published 1999
Printed in the United States of America on acid-free paper
9 8 7 6 5 4 3 2 1

The Johns Hopkins University Press
2715 North Charles Street, Baltimore, Maryland 21218-4363
www.press.jhu.edu

Frontispiece. *Inkle and Yarico*. Engraving by Johann Wilhelm Meil (1733–1805). From C. F. Gellert, *Sämmtliche Fabeln und Erzählungen* (Leipzig, 1810), plate 2, Inkle selling Yarico into slavery. (Courtesy of the Brotherton Collection, University of Leeds.)

Library of Congress Cataloging-in-Publication Data will
be found at the end of this book.
A catalog record for this book is available from
the British Library.

ISBN 0-8018-6105-5
ISBN 0-8018-6106-3 (pbk.)

FOR KENNY AND FOR JOANNA

Contents

Illustrations

Preface and Acknowledgments

When the comic opera *Inkle and Yarico* was first mounted by George Colman at the Little Theatre in the Haymarket, London, in August 1787, an anonymous critic expressed his unfeigned surprise that a fable that was "originally very slender" could have been "expanded with ingenuity" into a full-length drama. What is more, he remarked, it was "received, by a very full house, with the strongest tokens of approbation" (*New London Magazine* 3 [1787]: 438–39). The plaudits of the audience owed not a little to the young dramatist's deft invigoration of a well-known tale, yet they were hugely enhanced by the play's sentient appeal to a subject that was becoming every day more topical. At the onset of the age of abolition, here was a musical extravaganza that touchingly personalized the dilemmas of slavery by dramatizing the romantic tryst or alliance between a beautiful noble savage and an emotionally wayward white merchant. As a recent commentator points out, the story "became a touchstone for the complicated dealings between black and white, where love and honour—all the finer instincts so dear to the public—were pitted against social and commercial gain" (Gerzina, *Black England,* 8).

More than two hundred years later, the renewed interest in this once famous tale of slavery and miscegenation has been spurred by the exponential advance of gender and postcolonial studies as academic disciplines that cross traditional subject boundaries. "Inkle and Yarico" has begun to be recognized once again as one of the great folk epics of its age, an intertextual narrative that draws simultaneously from sources that are as much noncanonical as canonical. Its anecdotal simplicity helps to explain its extraordinary ductility, and its opaque but seamless fusion of fact and fiction may be invoked to account for its potency as a defining myth of the Enlightenment. Its radical blending of the exotic with the familiar is yet another ample reason for the tale's enduring attraction.

Although many distinguished critics have written on the theme of Inkle and Yarico, there exists only one other full-length study. That is Lawrence Marsden Price's pioneering *Inkle and Yarico Album,* published more than sixty years ago. An extraordinary labor of love, Price's work was the first to systematically draw attention to the extensive use of the story by a diversity of writers in France and Germany, where Inkle and Yarico had its vogue no less than in England. His study examined its occurrence in the writings, among others, of Boulanger de Rivery, Claude Dorat, Chamfort, Gellert, Gessner, and Johann Heinrich Faber. Price's studious digging revealed that during the eighteenth century the story appeared in eight European languages. "Of 45 original works," he concluded, "21 are of German origin, 16 are English, and 8 are French" (138).

In revisiting many of the same works that captivated Price in the 1930s, I have benefited considerably from the rich fruits of scholarly endeavor of more recent vintage. In addition, digital databases such as the *Eighteenth-Century Short-Title Catalogue* and the search facilities of the Internet have thrown up diverse material that lay concealed until such resources became available. Whereas Price was able to identify sixteen works of English origin, this book virtually doubles that number. Given this wealth of new material, I made a conscious decision early on to concentrate in this volume exclusively on versions of the tale in English, though also including contemporary translations of a few German and French works. I echo Price in pointing out that the examples of the tale assembled here should be regarded as representative rather than all-inclusive, since like him I have not "undertaken to search all the magazines and all the collected poems of the eighteenth century for treatments of the theme" (31).

One of the most exciting results of examining in the widest sense "English" manifestations of Inkle and Yarico is the discovery that, whereas Price had assumed that the tale all but disappeared after the slave trade was abolished from Great Britain in 1807, it continued to flourish in the literature of the Caribbean. Its links with colonialist and postcolonialist discourse become clear once we trace examples of its appearance in English writing from the West Indies and, most particularly, from Barbados. I have included here three such examples, all ostensibly from the nineteenth century. The publication in 1996 of a fine novel on the theme by the Guyanese writer Beryl Gilroy is prime evidence that the story still holds its legendary fascination. A reviewer of an English version that saw the light of day in the final year of the eighteenth century percipiently remarked that "no story has ever taken so firm a hold on the public attention as this now before us" (*European Magazine* 35 [1799]: 256). Given recent interest, it is perhaps not too zealous an aspiration to hope that two centuries later on Inkle and Yarico will regain that regard.

Among institutions whose research facilities I used in preparing this work, I thank the following: American Antiquarian Society, Worcester, Massachusetts; National Library Service, Bridgetown, Barbados; Birmingham City Reference Library; British Library; Department of Prints and Drawings, British Museum; Cambridge University Library; Henry E. Huntington Library, San Marino, California; Drew University Library; Brotherton Library, University of Leeds; Leeds City Reference Library; McLennan Library, McGill University, Montreal; New York Public Library; Charles Deering McCormick Library of Special Collections at Northwestern University, Evanston, Illinois; Bodleian Library, University of Oxford; Rhodes House Library, Oxford; Royal Humane Society; Historical Society of Pennsylvania Library; Harry Ransom Humanities Research Center, University of Texas at Austin; Special Collections, Alderman Library, University of Virginia; Pollack Library, Yeshiva University.

On a more personal note, I have benefited considerably from the generous help and advice of many individuals, including Lee Arnold, Martin Banham, Alice Bennett, Dominic Berry, Paul-Gabriel Boucé, Vincent Carretta, Valerie Clarke, David Coward, Christina M. Deane, Carole Felsenstein, Antonia Forster, Mick Gidley, John Gilmore, Sara S. Hodson, Marie E. Lamoureux, Allan Lodge, Ronald Martin, R. Russell Maylone, Richard W. Oram, Elizabeth Paget, Wayne Paton, Oliver Pickering, Neil Plummer, Jeremy Poynting, Judith Priestman, Willis G. Regier, Tony St. Quintin, Julia Swindells, Andrea Verhoeven, and Richard Virr.

A Note on Texts

Many of the early texts of Inkle and Yarico are less than easily accessible. In transcribing the present collection, I have endeavored to locate those versions of particular texts that are likely to have had the greatest currency. In many cases, though not always, this has tended to be the first edition. As an editor, I have undertaken no more than discreet modernization.

Since the selections included here are not intended to be facsimiles, I have not reproduced the typography used in the original versions. Although spelling only rarely has been emended, capitalization and punctuation in the titles have been modernized, and emphasis in the text has been expressed through current conventions.

Cross-references to texts included in the reader are by bracketed numbers (e.g. [1]), with page or line numbers as appropriate. The following abbreviations refer to works that are widely employed in the introduction or commentary to the texts: *DNB, Dictionary of National Biography; ODEP, Oxford Dictionary of English Proverbs; OED, Oxford English Dictionary;* Price, *Inkle and Yarico Album.* Full references are given in the bibliography.

Editorial commentary to the texts is aimed to encompass the needs of students no less than those of specialist readers.

English Trader, Indian Maid

Introduction

Contexts

George Philpot. I shall never forget the story you recommended to my earliest
  notice, sir.
Old Philpot. What was that George? It is quite out of my head.
G. Phil. It intimated, sir, how Mr. Thomas Inkle of London, merchant, was cast
  away, and was afterwards protected by a young lady, who grew in love with him,
  and how he afterwards bargained with a planter to sell her for a slave.
Old Phil. Ay, ay, [*Laughs.*] I recollect it now.
G. Phil. And when she pleaded being with child by him, he was no otherwise
  moved than to raise his price, and make her turn to better account.
Old. Phil. [*Bursts into a laugh.*] I remember it—ha, ha, there was the very spirit
  of trade! ay, ay, ha, ha!
G. Phil. That was calculation for you. . . . That was a hit, sir!
Old Phil. Ay, ay!
G. Phil. That was having his wits about him.
Old Phil. Ay, ay! it is a lesson for all young men. It was a hit indeed, ha, ha!
(Arthur Murphy, The Citizen, 1761)¹

To the present-day reader, the linked names of Inkle and Yarico (the "young
lady, who grew in love with him") sound less than familiar and even rather
exotic. During the eighteenth century their names were no less exotic, but
their story was among the most popular and widely retold within its country of origin, Great Britain, as well as elsewhere across Europe and into
North America. It was, to adopt a phrase out of the dialogue between Old
Philpot and his son in Arthur Murphy's dramatic afterpiece, "a hit indeed."
A conservative estimate indicates that, drawing upon the century from 1711
to 1810 and the resources of at least ten European languages, well over sixty

discrete versions and a sizable number of translations of the tale have been preserved in print. Each of these surviving versions is distinct, though most share certain common or key elements. Almost all are to a greater or lesser extent indebted to Richard Steele's imaginative reclamation of the tale [2] in number 11 of *The Spectator* (13 March 1711), incontestably its century's most influential and widely read series of prose moral essays in English. The following is a brief synopsis of Steele's deceptively simple narrative, which provides the "main" version of the tale:

Mr. Thomas Inkle, an ambitious young English trader cast ashore in the Americas, is saved from violent death at the hands of savages by the endearments of Yarico, a beautiful Indian maiden. Their romantic intimacy in the forest moves Inkle to pledge that, were his life to be preserved, he would return with her to England, supposedly as his wife. The lovers' tender liaison progresses over several months until she succeeds in signaling a passing English ship. They are rescued by the crew, and with vows to each other intact, they embark for Barbados. Yet when they reach the island Inkle's former mercantile instincts are callously revived, for he sells her into slavery, at once raising the price he demands when he learns that Yarico is carrying his child.

The melodramatic outline given here (with its casual foreshadowings of *Madama Butterfly*) could easily be taken as the sketch for a libretto, and it is perhaps not surprising that one of the most important later renditions of the tale was as a three-act operatic drama. In an age that was capriciously poised between a still resonant oral tradition and an increasingly ubiquitous print culture, the celebrity of the tale is entirely owing to Steele. Its roots, however, must be traced to oral history, through parallel tales that go back as far as classical times, though the closest we can come to a specific source is Richard Ligon's discursive profile of "the unfortunate *Yarico,* an *Indian* woman" in his *History of the Island of Barbadoes* (1657; [1], 80). Its later development in a variety of narrative forms owes not a little to the exceptional plasticity of the story as popular anecdote rather than to empirical history based on verifiable fact. Current critical interest in the tale reflects a growing awareness of the value of studying the often intangible points of contact between oral traditions and written or printed cultures. Described by David Brion Davis as one of the great folk epics of its age, "Inkle and Yarico" provides just such a site of mediation between the oral and the literate.[2]

Walter Ong's observation that "oral expression can exist and mostly has existed without any writing at all, writing never without orality," expresses well a fundamental distinction between the two forms.[3] The recurrence throughout the eighteenth century of the tale of Inkle and Yarico suggests that it existed as a vibrant oral narrative, but inevitably for an epoch well before the technology of sound recording, it survives only as "writing," or rather as printed text. Yet as a relatively uncomplicated extended anecdote existing in many versions, it shows all the flexibility one might expect of an oral narrative that is sufficiently well known to flourish and to be kept alive in the collective consciousness of the age that fabricated it. It is significant that almost all extant versions retain enough of the key elements of the tale to make it distinct and recognizable.

However, we should also understand that a crucial mediation of a different kind between orality and literacy takes place within the story itself that dramatically captures a momentary rendezvous of the so-called civilized or literate world with the "unlettered" or primitive. In Steele's seminal version, Inkle's equivocal cultural superiority is defined through language. With the utter charm of an Englishman, he can pledge to Yarico "how happy he should be to have her in his country, where she should be clothed in such silks as his waistcoat was made of, and be carried in houses drawn by horses, without being exposed to wind or weather." Here Inkle's singular ease with what is culturally familiar to him depends on a shared response from the reader, who will be equally versed in recognizing silk waistcoats or horse-drawn carriages as signifiers of a fashionable English lifestyle that to Yarico is entirely exotic and fabulous. That Inkle should choose these rather superficial and specious signifiers as representative of things English divulges something of the shallowness of his false promises. Equally, the humorous yet memorable delineation of carriages as "houses drawn by horses" suggests that Inkle deliberately talks down or pidginizes language to make himself understood by Yarico. In his desire to flatter her, he conveniently forgets that such European accoutrements as waistcoats and carriages are entirely redundant to Yarico's seminaked world. The exoticism of the tale is in the conjunction within it of Yarico's primitivism and the "literate" European perspective that is the shared patrimony of Inkle and the reader.

Among the principal spheres of activity explored by postcolonial critics in recent years has been the often crude contradictions in European attitudes and reactions to primitivity. Whether consciously or otherwise, such attitudes commonly express a fundamental dualism by which primitive natives are represented as barbaric man-eaters lurking in the jungle and simultaneously as natural innocents living an Edenesque existence in a world uncontaminated by the fallen values of a "civilized" society. According to the American cultural critic Hayden White, the metaphors of "Wild Man" and "Noble Savage," in common currency in early modern European thought, may be said to represent "two moments necessary for the projection of the negative and positive poles" of a larger dialectic.[4] These contradictory impulses can be found in many texts treating of European encounters with the native, including within our period works of such prominence as Mrs. Aphra Behn's *Oroonoko* (ca. 1678) and Daniel Defoe's *Robinson Crusoe* (1719).

In Steele's version of Inkle and Yarico, although there is no direct mention of cannibalism, the English who went ashore are observed from their first landing "by a party of *Indians* . . . [who] intercepted . . . [and] slew the greatest number of them." Tracing the story on, in one of the sundry later poetical versions the attackers have progressed into a "savage people, greedy for your blood" ([6], line 32); in another, "a swarthy crowd / In quest of prey" ([8], lines 88–89); and in a third, most explicitly, they have become "men who thirst for human blood," viciously enacting their monstrous deed of ritual sacrifice:

Distrest, he [Inkle] landed on this fatal shore,
With some companions, which were soon no more;
The savage race their trembling flesh devour,
Off'ring oblations to th'infernal power.
Dreadfully suppliant, human limbs they tore,
(Accursed rites!) and quaft their streaming gore.   ([5], lines 17, 21–26)

The changes we witness through these different versions not only exemplify the extraordinary ductility of the tale but, more important, show how deeply ingrained in the European consciousness is the perception of primitive natives as lethal man-eaters.

Indeed, it is generally accepted that the term Carib used by Ligon and others to describe "the native race which occupied the southern islands of the West Indies at their discovery" (*Oxford English Dictionary*), furnishes the origin of the word cannibal. Among apt historical quotations given in *OED* under "Carib" are examples from Richard Eden (1555), "The wylde and myscheuous people called *Canibales* or *caribes,* whiche were accustomed to eate mannes flesche" (*The Decades of the New Worlde or West India*), and Thomas Nicholas's translation (1578) of Hernando Cortés's *Pleasant Historie of the Conquest of the Weast India,* "Others . . . looking for death, and to be eaten of the Cariues." The early seventeenth-century French traveler Jean Mocquet, whose work provides a striking analogue to our tale (see appendix B), describes the Caribs as "Man-Eaters" and recounts with horror how "an Indian woman offered a roasted Hand to our General, but he angrily refused it."[5] Even John Locke, a founding father of English empirical thought, accepts as proven fact their cannibalistic (or anthropophagic) tendencies when he remarks in his *Essay concerning Human Understanding* (1690) that "the *Caribes* were wont to geld their Children, on purpose to fat and eat them."[6] Eighteenth-century versions of Inkle and Yarico subscribe to the belief in the cannibalism and savagery of the Caribs no less than these earlier examples.[7] As Stephen Greenblatt has reminded us, "Europeans had long identified cannibalism as an emblem of extreme horror."[8] Yet recent inquiry has demonstrated that the case for the historical existence of cannibalism as an omnipresent rite among the Caribs—let alone many other "primitive" people—is far from proved and (if we postulate that the best witnesses would most likely have been eaten!) distinctly lacking in reliable prima facie evidence.[9] Instead it is powerfully apparent that the abiding *fear* rather than the absolute *fact* of cannibalism as supposedly practiced by many primitive societies is what remains most firmly implanted in the European or Occidental imagination.

The root causes of our fascinated fear of cannibalism are far too complex to be adequately dealt with here, but if we accept that its imaginative hold is far greater than its putative practice, we can at least begin to justify the validity of studying its representation in literary texts. For it becomes apparent that the recurrent textual assumption of cannibalistic practices by savage people may be read as an integral part of a larger Eurocentric discourse that helps to define the hegemonic relationship between colonizer and colonized. The insistence on its own superiority by a culture that condemns cannibalism as a savage practice simultaneously diverts attention from or even conceals the barbarisms it perpetrates in the name of civilization. European massacres of native Indians in the Americas (alas, too common in an age of territorial expansion) can conveniently be forgotten or forgiven as a just defense against the predatory instincts of primitive cannibals. Equally, the forced enslavement of the savages can be justified as a means to prevent them from engaging in further cannibalistic acts and to protect them from themselves.[10] It is surely far from an accidental irony that the unworthy Inkle resorts to slavery as a crudely effective means of disposing of Yarico at the end of Steele's tale.

1. *Natives of the Caribee Islands Feasting on Human Flesh*. Engraving. From William Hurd, *A New Universal History of the Religious Rites, Ceremonies, and Customs of the Whole World* (London, [ca. 1788]), opposite 432. (Private collection.)

Yarico herself, in conspicuous contrast to the anthropophagic appetite attributed to her people, emerges in the pages of *The Spectator* as "a person of distinction," soon further elevated to a young woman of "noble birth" ([5], line 38) and later—perhaps by percolation from the related story of Pocahontas—to a princess who voluntarily forsakes her throne for her love ([10], line 18). The cultural inferiority ascribed to the native is supplanted by an intrinsic nobility. Yarico's guileless love for Inkle, so cruelly cashed in on by his heartless mercantilism, may be a prime marker of her moral elevation, but inherent in the tale is a sense that her world (for all its primitivism) preserves elements of a prelapsarian golden age that has long since been lost to Europeans. In her presentation to us by Steele and others, she embodies strong aspects of one of the most potent of eighteenth-century urban myths, that of the Noble Savage.[11] Inkle's intrusion into her "lost" world is at once an apt metaphor for European conquest of the primordial native and also a temporary release for him from the social taboos and inhibitions that belong to his own culture. In the ideal country of the Noble Savage, nakedness and sexual freedom not only are subject to no restraint but are indicative of a return to a state of nature unknown since the Garden of Eden. Locked in each other's arms in a demiparadise that is harmonized by waterfalls and the melody of nightingales, Inkle and Yarico replicate the situation of mankind before the Fall as exemplified most famously by Milton in book 4 of *Paradise Lost* (1667), where to the sound of "heav'nly Quires," Adam partakes of Eve's "naked beauty" (4.711, 713).[12] Implicit both in the telling of Milton's great epic and in the tale of Inkle and Yarico is the knowledge that a dramatic ejection or departure from this ideal world is inevitable.

It should be apparent that the peculiar inversion (or more properly oxymoron) contained in the epithet Noble Savage is indicative of an inherent self-contradiction within the term itself. Hayden White has cogently argued that the oppositional force at the heart of the concept is not actually that of nobility over savagery, of giving an anomalous dignity to the Wild Man, but of ironically undercutting the very notion of "civilized" man. Rather than an endeavor to refine the Wild Man, the rendezvous of the sophisticated European with the Noble Savage represents an opportunity to satirize or demote the putative nobility of humanity in general and of the European in particular. For White, the Noble Savage should be viewed as the fetishistic invention of an acquisitive European culture intent on possessing for itself, by whatever means, the tribal patrimony of the prim-

2. *Inkle and Yarico.* Engraving by Johann Wilhelm Meil (1733–1805). From C. F. Gellert, *Sämmtliche Fabeln und Erzählungen* (Leipzig, 1810), plate 1, Yarico succoring Inkle after his shipwreck. (Courtesy of the Brotherton Collection, University of Leeds.)

itive native. Whether by destruction or by sublimation, he writes, "Europeans tended to fetishize the native peoples with whom they came into contact by viewing them simultaneously as monstrous forms of humanity and as quintessential objects of desire." In this view, destruction and consumption may be seen as primary metaphors of European engagement with the savage or primitive.[13]

Certainly, in Steele's description Yarico has all the physical appearance of a fetish, attiring herself before Inkle "every day . . . in a different dress, of the most beautiful shells, bugles, and bredes." She is represented displaying the portable commodities of the colonized as she reveals herself so enticingly to the colonizer. Her sexual desirability is enhanced by ornaments that elsewhere would be employed by primitive people as bartering counters in their trading with Europeans. But, ironically, it is only Inkle who descends to using her as a figure of trade by unpityingly selling her into slavery. As a fetishized native, a Noble Savage reduced to a mere possession, Yarico is perhaps unique among such figures in being given the opportunity to answer back. The popularity throughout most of the eighteenth century of poetic epistles written from Yarico to Inkle suggests a desire to explore the fetishized from within, the oralizing of her predicament (by English poets) perhaps representing the ultimate captivity of the native. Sexualized and then enslaved, Yarico comes to embody deeper discourses that emerge spontaneously from the tale's conjunction of savagery and nobility.

Gender, Race, and Slavery

In its multiple forms, the tale of Inkle and Yarico offers an intriguing paradigm for inquiry into eighteenth-century perceptions of gender and racial difference. It was primarily as a kind of debating piece "upon the old topic, of constancy in love" between the sexes that Steele first interpolated it into *The Spectator*, no. 11. In his essay, Steele imagines that Mr. Spectator, a shy and extremely taciturn observer of human behavior, is introduced into the salon of Arietta, "a woman of . . . taste and understanding," by his friend Will Honeycomb, "a well-bred fine gentleman" for whom "all . . . conversation and knowledge has been in the female world" (*Spectator*, no. 2). Arietta's salon is frequented, we are assured, "by all persons of both sexes, who have any pretence to wit and gallantry," but it is Mr. Spectator's misfortune that his visit coincides with that of a conceited loudmouth, "a commonplace talker," who rattles off an embarrassing catalog of allusions in plays and songs to "the perjuries of the fair [sex], and the general levity of women." "Methought," remarks Mr. Spectator in a wonderful flight of humorous deprecation, "he strove to shine more than ordinarily in his talkative way, that he might insult my silence, and distinguish himself before a woman of *Arietta's* taste and understanding." Despite Arietta's very best endeavors to interrupt him, there is no way he can be stopped until finally he has "repeated and murdered the celebrated story of the *Ephesian* Matron." Only after hearing this and to offset the charge of female falseheartedness does Arietta introduce the tale of Inkle and Yarico.

However poorly told, the story of the matron or widow of Ephesus that the unnamed loudmouthed boor employs to crown his spiteful litany remains among the best-known illustrations from classical times of the alleged fickleness of womankind. It is the most famous single story (appendix A) in the writings of Petronius (d. A.D.66), the sardonic chronicler of the sexual mores of the age of Nero, whose *Satyricon* enjoyed a scandalous reputation in the eighteenth century. Petronius's work is an episodic prose fiction designed as a loose dialogue interspersed with verse. Within it, the story of the widow of Ephesus is told by Eumolpus, a "disreputable hypocrite,"[14] as a "merry" illustration of his belief that women's lusts are uncontrollable. It has been described by one modern commentator as "the classic anti-woman libel."[15] In the *Satyricon,* as with Inkle and Yarico, it is presented as part of a similar debate on inconstancy between the sexes.

Steele assumes a knowledge of the story by his more literate reader, yet (in allowing it to be "murdered" out of the mouth of the misogynist commonplace talker) he refrains from retelling it himself. By simply alluding to it, he shows an awareness of its notoriety as a tale that is in common currency as a popular exemplum of female inconstancy but that would be considered by many as perhaps too lewd or risqué for polite ears. Steele seems to acknowledge the inherent gender bias to the story of the Ephesian matron by invoking its reputation as a tale that exalts masculine virility while simultaneously denigrating female frailty. By deliberately juxtaposing it with the story of Inkle and Yarico, he is consciously reopening what Arietta laconically describes as "this question between the sexes, which has been either a point of dispute or raillery ever since there were men and women." As a counterpart to Inkle and Yarico, Petronius's story of the Ephesian matron needs to be spelled out, particularly to a present-day audience, in order to contextualize the wider discussion at the heart of Steele's essay. Here is a synopsis:

A young soldier is deputed to guard several crucified bodies close to some catacombs. From inside, he hears sobbing and discovers a ravishingly beautiful woman (the Ephesian matron) weeping over the body of her husband who has just died. In short, he is immediately sexually attracted to her and, after some initial hesitation, this is reciprocated. For three days and three nights they make urgent physical love with each other within the catacomb. When finally the soldier emerges, he discovers that one of the crucified bodies he was supposed to have been guarding has been stolen, and he knows that the penalty for his neglect will be his own death. However, his quick-witted mistress instantly comes up with the optimal solution. "Take the corpse of my late husband," she says, "and let it replace the stolen one. Why should I be forced to lose two good men in the space of less than a week?"

At first glance, the story of the Ephesian matron appears as a strange mismatch alongside that of Inkle and Yarico. Does the matron's consent to the soldier's advances, almost before her dead husband's body is cold, make her comparable to Inkle? In her instinct to preserve the life of her new lover, is she really as unworthy as one who willfully sells his mistress into bondage? In many ways the two tales seem quite discrepant. Yet Mr. Spectator is strongly of the opinion that they should be regarded as counterparts. It can be argued, I think, that Steele's paralleling these anecdotal tales within the essay problematizes several important contemporary issues of gender and sexuality. Both pieces address from different gender perspectives an otherwise taboo subject, that of sexual relations outside marriage, with neither outwardly condemning such behavior. An open eroticism is condoned by locating it in distant climes, whether in the degenerate age of Nero or in a kind of prelapsarian sexual innocence of the New World. Both tales raise questions of fidelity and fickleness in love, though Petronius's tale does so in a manner that is palpably more double-edged. Their juxtaposition within the essay represents a conscious challenge by Steele to received wisdom that (in Arietta's words) "hypocrisy is the very foundation of our [female] education; and that an ability to dissemble our affections, is a professed part of our breeding." Even before considering its multiple derivations in other forms, *The Spectator*, no. 11, provides for us a highly effective initiation into eighteenth-century male discourse on women.

In aligning himself on the side of Arietta (as surely he does), Steele creates in Yarico what Kathryn Shevelow has described as a Noble Savage who "behaves very much like the virtuous and domestic English middle-class wife whose husband's needs and comforts are her primary study." In the essay, having saved Inkle from the savages, Yarico "conveyed him to a cave, where she gave him a delicious repast of fruits, and led him to a stream to slake his thirst. . . . Her part was to watch and hold him in her arms, for fear of her country-men, and wake him on occasions to consult his safety." Yarico reveals here, comments Shevelow, "an impulse toward domestication figured as innately female," of which we can catch many later glimpses in the eighteenth-century novel.[16] Almost unconsciously, the unraveling of the tale seems to sentimentalize the self-sacrifice of the female on the altar of masculine egotism. Certainly, in some of the later poetic versions, Yarico's tearful pleas to Inkle to release her from her slavery and take her back to him, for all their intended pathos, veer horrendously close to embarrassment. Yarico's nobility seems to be considerably more threatened by these pathetic gestures than by her unsought enslavement.

Yarico may indeed behave (as Shevelow suggests) in the manner of a "domestic English middle-class wife," but if so, it comes as a telling irony that she and Inkle remain *unmarried.* In a recent discussion, Felicity Nussbaum has stressed that although "Inkle promises Yarico the luxury and ease of a future life in England," the exchange is at once heavily weighted against the Native American on account of her racial difference. In her sexual freedom, the primitive Yarico teaches the prudish Inkle the secrets of her land, though, remarks Nussbaum, the inevitable consequence of this "tale of masculine advantage" is that "the Indian maiden is denied the anticipated European acculturation as the permanent idyllic union between the civilized and the savage evaporates. Instead Inkle, the disempowered third son in his native England, exercises his colonial and racial power, previously forgotten in the heat of love, over the body of the pregnant Indian Yarico whom he enslaves and abandons." For Nussbaum, the narrator of *The Spectator,* no. 11, by juxtaposing Inkle and Yarico with the Ephesian matron and then remaining silent, strives to achieve a kind of "neutral history" in the depiction of relations between the genders, but it is ostensible that both he and Arietta take "the unspoken component" of European racial privilege for granted.[17]

Curiously, for all Steele's virtuous (if unavoidably masculinized) endeavors to promote debate on gender by comparing the two tales, later versions of Inkle and Yarico unshackle themselves completely from the story of the Ephesian matron, which was to develop its own distinct and equally interesting later history.[18] After its publication in *The Spectator,* the tale of Inkle and Yarico became so well known in its own right that its framing as a counterpart within a larger debate on sexuality was soon forgotten. There is no longer a place for Arietta or for the nameless loudmouth as a fore-ground to a tale that stands so well on its own. Certainly Mary Wollstone-craft, among others, thought sufficiently well of it to extract it as "The History of Inkle and Yarico" for inclusion among the narrative pieces in *The Female Reader* (1789), a compilation explicitly intended for the improvement of young women.[19]

But despite its not uncommon appearance in this way, in many of its later adaptations the burden of the tale shifts increasingly from gender to slavery. In its main source, *A True and Exact History of the Island of Barbadoes*, Richard Ligon had represented Yarico as "an *Indian* woman, a slave in the house," who, some while before his encounter with her, had saved an unnamed English youth from being intercepted and killed by the savages but "for her love, lost her liberty" ([1], 73–74). In *The Spectator*, however, Steele commits her enslavement to the dramatic climax of the tale as a means of passing ironic comment on the mercenary disposition of "the prudent and frugal young man [who] sold *Yarico* to a *Barbadian* merchant." In Ligon's account, Yarico had "chanc'd to be with child" not by Inkle but by a Christian servant. Steele's brilliant elision by which Yarico becomes impregnated by Inkle is intended more to underscore the wanton treachery and feckless ease of the male sex than to pass judgment on the iniquities of the slave trade. For all that, there is much to be said in favor of David Dabydeen's view that Yarico, no less than the pregnant black woman in plate 4 of Hogarth's *A Harlot's Progress* (1732), with whom he accords comparison, should be seen as a victim both of sexual and economic exploitation. Dabydeen writes that "Hogarth would have known . . . of the enhanced economic value of pregnant slavewomen in the colonies. The female slaves were 'breeder women'; the slave-owner had his fun of them secure in the knowledge that his sexual recreation was profitable since it led to an increase in the stock of slaves."[20] There is every reason to assume that Steele would have been similarly informed.

Steele's own knowledge of British involvement in the Atlantic slave trade during the early eighteenth century may not have been extensive, but his interest in Barbados was certainly more than academic, for in 1706, on the death of his first wife, he had inherited the freehold of a considerable sugar plantation there. The property, which was let at £850 per annum, consisted of some seven hundred acres and included as chattels several white servants and two hundred Negro slaves. Although by the time Steele came to coauthor *The Spectator* the plantation had some while before been sold, it is most likely that his attention would have first been drawn to Richard Ligon as a result of his inheritance. As Rae Blanchard suggests, his "sugar plantation in Barbados . . . stirred his imagination, and thus our storehouse of tales was enriched by Inkle and Yarico."[21] Perhaps because of his own earlier involvement but more so because the circumstances were not yet propitious, Steele shows little inclination openly to indict slavery, which was not in any case the intended target of his essay. When he penned the tale, the abolition of the Atlantic slave trade had so far not really entered the political agenda, though even from reading Inkle and Yarico it is evident that the practice already inspired deeply ambivalent attitudes, being at the same time valued for its economic advantages and condemned for its sheer inhumanity and cruelty.

The appropriation of the tale by the antislavery lobby during the eighteenth century allowed writers to present in literary form a compelling (if inevitably sanitized and sentimentalized) critique of the horrors of the transatlantic slave trade and of British attitudes as the preeminent slaving nation. It is ironic that in Ligon's seminal account, describing his extended visit to Barbados in the late 1640s, on which Steele was to base his tale, the practice of keeping slaves is close to being condoned, perhaps even celebrated. Ligon regards Negro slaves as less than human, "as near beasts as may be, setting their souls aside," to be chosen out of the ships by the Barbadian planters "as they do horses in a market; the strongest, youthfullest, and most beautiful, yield[ing] the greatest prices" ([1], 63). The rarer native or Amerindian slaves are prized as "very active . . . and apt to learn any thing, sooner than the *negroes*" yet are, warns Ligon, "much craftier, and subtiler then the negroes; and in their nature falser." Physiognomically, they are preferred too, the men being "very broad shoulder'd, deep breasted, with large heads, and . . . their skins some of them brown, some a bright bay," and the women, seminaked except for a girdle "to cover their privities," displaying "very small breasts, and . . . more of the shape of the *Europeans* than the *negroes*" ([1], 73). In his fetishized ogling of slave women's breasts, Ligon shows all the male voyeurism of a class of European colonizer for whom there seems to exist little more than the vaguest distinction between proprietorship and sexual possession. He rarely misses the chance, remarks Peter Hulme, "to add to his collection of native breasts, of which he was a tireless admirer."[22] His own ocular rapacity stands in striking contrast to that of the African slaves themselves, whom he describes as "chaste . . . as any people under the sun; for, when the men and women are together naked, they never cast their eyes towards the parts that ought to be covered; and those [slaves] amongst us, that have breeches and petticoats, I never saw so much as a kiss, or embrace, or a wanton glance with their eyes between them" ([1], 64). Almost unconsciously, the narrative encapsulates the first phase of an inevitable erosion of ingrained native codes and values before the intrusive gaze of the European.

For all its racialized overtones, Ligon's stated preference for the American Indian over the African slave at least reveals an eyewitness's ability to discriminate between the two. A significant aspect of later English renditions of the Inkle and Yarico tale, composed in most cases by armchair literati who may never have traveled far, is that they reveal a repeated ineptitude or inability in distinguishing one group from the other. In its revisions during the middle years of the eighteenth century from a primarily gendered discourse to one that is also concerned with the issues of race and slavery, the story may have been deemed more applicable to the plight of the African than to the Carib or American Indian. At the zenith of British involvement in the Atlantic slave trade, it is perhaps not surprising to discover that Yarico commences her translation by appearing [3A] in a poem of 1725 (now identified as the work of Frances Seymour, Countess of Hertford) as a hybridized figure who is indistinguishably African/American Indian. When Inkle is cast among the cannibals "on a barb'rous coast," he is saved from "threat'ning danger" by "A negroe virgin [who] chanc'd to pass that way." Yet no sooner has she taken him to the safety of her bower than she reverts to being an "*Indian* virgin"! The confusion is sustained toward the climax of the poem when

> The ship arriv'd on the *Barbadian* coast;
> Immediately the planters from the town
> To trade for goods and negroe slaves came down;
> And now his mind, by sordid interest sway'd,
> Resolv'd to sell his faithful *Indian* Maid.   (lines 83–87)

By 1734, when the tale resurfaces [5] in the *London Magazine* as "The Story of Inkle and Yarico, from the Eleventh *Spectator*," Yarico has been fully translated into "a negro virgin,"

> Whose glitt'ring shells and elegant undress,
> With various plumes, a noble birth confess.   (lines 37–38)

Here the anonymous author, traditionally identified as a woman, remains otherwise relatively true to her source even to the extent that she is concerned, like Steele before her, to expose "the dire arts of faithless man" while showing little more than an incidental interest in the topic of slavery.[23] It is, however, as a "negroe slave" and not as an Indian that Yarico is purchased by a Barbadian planter.[24]

The progressive distancing of Yarico from her American Indian origins continues in "Yarico to Inkle: An Epistle" of 1736 [6], sometimes attributed to Edward Moore, which justifiably became the most popular poetic rendition of the tale, appearing in at least eleven separate imprints during the eighteenth century. Here the poet gives equal weighting to the twin themes of sexual betrayal and physical bondage. Yarico pens her heroic epistle from "the sad place, where . . . / hopeless wretches groan beneath their chains" (lines 1–2), but through her bitter reproaches ("make me yours, if I must be a slave!" [line 38]) she pathetically links her own enslavement to her love for Inkle. The single specific clue to Yarico's new racial identity is a reference in the invocation to the poem, addressed to Miss Arabella Saintloe, to "the Negro's cause." It is perhaps appropriate that a poem that contains a clear indictment of slavery should point in the direction of the transatlantic trade.

By the time of Edward Jerningham's identically named [10] though considerably more cumbersome *Yarico to Inkle: An Epistle* (1766), racial demarcations have become ever more polarized. Yarico has undergone yet a further mutation, appearing here as "a Nubian dame" (line 50) with "woolly hair" (line 181), whose "sable breast" (line 68) is betrayed by the falsehood of a "Christian, . . . Albion's son" (lines 3, 13). Jerningham endeavors to underline her Africanizing by emphasizing her regal status and pagan nobility. By contrast, Inkle is portrayed as an almost godlike Englishman ("form'd by nature in her choicest mould" [line 96]), utterly irresistible in his seductive beauty and charm. Fated by "love's decree" (line 17) to spurn the Nubian throne for him, Yarico is shown to have sorely failed to heed the lesson of former European incursions that had led to the merciless killing of her own father. After Inkle has so unceremoniously reduced her to a vendible commodity, her haughty refusal to submit to future enslavement by "low-born traders" (line 101) leads her to a final contemplation of suicide. Like Virgil's Dido, on whom she seems to be partly modeled, she prefers self-sacrifice to enduring unhappiness.

For all its righteous intentions, the epistle seems to encapsulate many of the contradictory impulses inherent in liberal perceptions of the relationship of colonizer and colonized. Jerningham valorizes the nobility of Yarico's primitivism but remains oddly blind to the extent to which he ventriloquizes through his heroine a desire for those very aspects of European mercantilism the poem denounces elsewhere. This is most apparent when she is given latitude to imagine the fulfillment of Inkle's vain promises to bring her home as his lawful wife:

> I hop'd, alas! to breathe thy native air,
> And vie in splendor with the British fair:
> Ascend the speedy car enchas'd with gold,
> With robes of silk this pearl-deck'd form infold:
> Bid on this jetty hand the diamond glow,
> And chosen rubies sparkle from my brow.   (lines 83–88)

By commodifying her in this way, Jerningham invests Yarico with all the qualities of the fetishized female, but his substitution of gold and diamonds for shells and beads rings false. It appears that if only she could be allowed to share those material riches prized by the colonizing culture, Yarico would be perfectly happy. She becomes a voice that is morally no longer trustworthy, a figure who appears more ridiculous in her vanity than pathetic in her loss. Jerningham's Yarico, comments Wylie Sypher, is "a 'Nubian' maiden who dwells in a pseudo-African, pseudo-American world and behaves like a Roman vestal virgin." In remarking how poetry can often be far more sensitive than either history or ethnography in capturing such inherent contradictions, Sypher concludes that the antislavery movement found in the literary texts of the age a symbol that was "ready for its purposes . . . , the African who united the traits of the white man, so that he might not be repulsive; the traits of the Indian, so that he might not seem base; and the traits of the Negro, so that he might rouse pity." In her piecemeal transformation from Indian to "noble Negress," says Sypher, Yarico risks being perceived as "all things to all poets."[25]

The growing uncertainty as to Yarico's racial ancestry that develops so conspicuously in poetic renditions of the tale may reflect a wider public distaste at British involvement in the cruel and immoral transatlantic trade of Africans to the Americas. As Douglas Grant remarks, Steele's "Yarico is an Indian, not an African; but as Inkle sells her into slavery in the West Indies where only Africans were slaves—the native Indians earlier enslaved having failed to survive—her story hinted at the desperate condition of the Negroes and directed sympathy where it could still be useful."[26] This may be so, but one can argue no less cogently that the discrepancies we have examined are indicative of a colossal ignorance by the British public at large of the racial and geographical parameters (not to mention the real horrors) of the slave trade. If we combine this with the same public's seemingly insatiable hunger for exotic tales set in faraway climes, it is not difficult to see why the racialized "Otherness" of a semifictive figure like Yarico could so easily be transferred from America to Africa or vice versa. It is more than a poignant reminder of their pitiful fate that in a large number of English tales depicting blacks or deracinated slaves they are represented as being without or having lost family ties. "Since Yarico is without family," points out Joan Hamilton, "it is fairly easy for Inkle to take Yarico to Barbados with him. And when he decides he no longer wants or needs her, *no one* considers returning her. Without family context, she belongs nowhere."[27] As a figure alone here, the racialized "Other" has little choice but to submit to an inevitable destiny.

George Colman the Younger

The confusion as to Yarico's racial or geographical identity can be illustrated once again when we turn our attention to George Colman's three-act comic opera (or, more accurately, play with songs interspersed), *Inkle and Yarico* [12], first performed to great acclaim at the Theatre Royal in the Haymarket, London, on 4 August 1787. The stage directions are abundantly clear in specifying that the first act is to take place "*on the Main of America*," whereas the setting for the final two acts is "*in Barbadoes*." The play opens with Inkle's cockney servant, Trudge, and Medium, the hero's uncle, lost deep in the middle of an American forest, which they graphically imagine to be crawling with hostile natives at the ready to "take off heads like hats, and hang 'em on pegs, in their parlours" ([12], 174). The complexion of "every inhabitant" of the dark forest is enhanced into being "not only as black as a pepper-corn, but as hot into the bargain" (175). Among the array of natives arraigned as wanton savages by the English characters in the play are naked headhunters "dancing about in black buff" (175), "old hairy negroes" (178), "a fleet of black devils" (180), "Hottypots" (Hottentots) (211) and "Black-a-moor ladies" (214). This almost impromptu array of native peoples led one of the play's early editors, Elizabeth Inchbald, to enumerate among its "trivial faults" that "the scene at the commencement of the opera, instead of Africa, is placed in America." In a dramatic work intended to champion the abolitionist cause, contends Mrs. Inchbald (disregarding Ligon and Steele), should not the playwright have recalled that "slaves are imported from Africa, and never from America"? Evidently, as Wylie Sypher points out, "Yarico is, to her [Mrs. Inchbald] mind's eye, a Negress." The racial imprecision that dogs the portrayal of Yarico after Steele is all too apparent in the inaccuracy of Mrs. Inchbald's observations.[28]

It is specifically this supreme ineptitude of the colonizing English in differentiating one racial group from another and the simultaneous tendency, conscious or otherwise, to barbarize the native that are the targets of Colman's lighthearted satire. To Medium (whose very name suggests the average Englishman), the mere mention of natives conjures up in his head paranoiac fears of being "eat[en] up by the black devils" (205) or being cut up and "ate raw by an inky commoner" (178). Within the comic idiom of his parodic exposure of English attitudes, Colman lards the text of *Inkle and Yarico* with what a contemporary reviewer describes well as "geographical trespasses." By introducing into the opera countless situational inaccuracies or blunders, such as "converting America into Africa, and peopling her forests with lions, where no lion was ever seen," Colman illustrates the appalling ease with which English perceptions of the world of savages become blurred and monstrous. At worst these introductions are unconscious on the part of the author and (in the words of the same reviewer) "very flagrant mistakes," but a more generous interpretation would suggest that their inclusion is entirely deliberate and the very essence of the drama.[29]

Throughout the opera, Colman uses every opportunity to deprecate and make fun of the assumption by the white characters of an innate racial superiority over the native black. To do this, initially he draws on the traditional story of Inkle and Yarico in which the "comely copper" (213) heroine is inherently the moral superior to her fair-skinned yet false lover. But the writer also invents a further twosome, whose chief function is to act as a dramatic foil to the main characters, for Trudge falls incurably in love with Wowski, Yarico's maid and companion, described in flippant contrast to her beautiful mistress as "an angel of rather a darker sort" (184). And unlike Inkle, Trudge remains resolutely true to his promises. When Inkle endeavors to sell Yarico to one of the Barbadian planters, Trudge virtuously defends his pledge to marry Wowski. "Dam'me," he swears to the white planter who wishes to buy her, "if ever I do any thing to make me asham'd of showing my own." Her complexion may indeed be dark, but says Trudge to the planter, "if your head and heart were to change places I've a notion you'd be as black in the face as an ink-bottle" (201). Later, when challenged by

3. James Gillray, *Philanthropic Consolations, after the Loss of the Slave-Bill*. Engraving, 4 April 1796 (BM Cat. no. 8793). Gillray's satirical print shows William Wilberforce and Bishop Horsley reveling indecorously with two black women after a motion to abolish the slave trade had been defeated in the House of Commons. Above Wilberforce's head is a picture, *Inkle and Yarico*. (Courtesy of the Department of Prints and Drawings, British Museum, London.)

Patty, a hoity-toity English maid who had once been the object of his affection, that kissing a black will "make [your] face all smutty," the undaunted Trudge responds: "I'd have you to know, Madam Patty, that Black-a-moor ladies, as you call 'em, are some of the very few whose complexions never rub off! 'Sbud, if they did, Wows[ki] and I should have changed faces by this time" (214).[30]

Surviving stage anecdote suggests that the players who performed in Colman's *Inkle and Yarico* resorted to liberal use of theatrical makeup as a visual means of capitalizing the moral message that racial difference should be viewed as no more than skin deep. When Fanny Kelly, a much loved early nineteenth-century Yarico, toured the provinces in the opera, the property master produced a length of hessian liberally spotted with black paint for her to wear as a "leopard skin." In the meantime, Inkle as her opposite had appeared in the opening scene "in elegant white drill" but—to the considerable amusement of the audience—was to emerge piebald out of the lovers' first passionate embrace.[31] Similarly, a well-known habit of the comedian John Liston, who took the part of Trudge in the early 1820s, was to wipe the coloring off Wowski's face and rub it on to his own,[32] a comic practice that was subsequently to become near routine in the vaudeville acts of black and white minstrel players.[33] Both of these are late examples and possibly reflect stage conventions that developed with the popularity of the play, but they do help to illustrate how slapstick or farcical elements could help to focus attention on the serious issues of race that, however crudely, Colman was endeavoring to address.[34]

In its treatment of the love of a white man for a savage woman and in its stand against slavery, *Inkle and Yarico* has been singled out as "one of our first problem plays."[35] According to Linda V. Troost, it is almost unique among comic operas of the late eighteenth century in consciously handling such socially laden "topics as the possible superiority of the natural man to the civilised man, the evils of slavery, and the problem of inter-racial romances."[36] Within the immediate context of its time, these social aspects have a particular resonance. In April 1787, just four months before the first performance of Colman's play, Granville Sharp and a group of like-minded emancipators had established the Society for the Abolition of the Slave Trade. Two rising young politicians, William Pitt and William Wilberforce—like Colman, still in their twenties—had earlier in the year begun the parliamentary campaign, persuading the House of Commons in May 1787 to commit, come the following session, to a full debate on the slavery question. In the same year, Thomas Clarkson published his highly influential tract *A Summary View of the Slave Trade and of the Possible Consequences of Its Abolition.* As Roger Anstey remarks, in the history of British abolition, "1787 was the year of real decision."[37] The enthusiastic reception that greeted *Inkle and Yarico* owes not a little to this coincidence.

Colman's major departure from the story he inherited from Steele is to endow the opera with a happy ending. As well as his serendipitous invention of Trudge and Wowski, Colman also contrives a parallel plot in which, before being rescued from the savages by Yarico, Inkle had been en route to Barbados, where he was to marry Narcissa, the daughter of Sir Christopher Curry, the island's governor. On her own voyage from England, however, Narcissa had fallen in love with a fellow passenger, the gallant Captain Campley, and by the end of the play, through the shifts and complications of the plot, Colman is able to bring all three couples together in marriage. The main dramatic device employed to precipitate this is mistaken identity whereby Sir Christopher takes Campley for Inkle, willingly offering the captain his daughter's hand, and in turn, Inkle mistakes the governor for a slave buyer and shames himself by attempting to sell Yarico to him. Colman employs Sir Christopher to voice the play's antislavery sentiments, his normative role as a true Englishman being "to speak the dictates of his heart" (206). "I can't help thinking," maintains the worthy Sir Christopher in response to Inkle, that "the only excuse for buying our fellow creatures, is to rescue them from the hands of those who are unfeeling enough to bring them to market" (221). If the sentimental stance adopted here comes perilously close to implying that slaves are necessary in order that a freeborn Englishman might give expression to his finer feelings by liberating them, at least the intention is to demonstrate that Sir Christopher's heart is in the right place. Contemporary audiences certainly thought so, applauding the play as (in Mrs. Inchbald's words) "the bright forerunner of alleviation to the hardships of slavery." For all its inherent moral ambivalences and patriarchal biases that may seem offensive to the modern reader, *Inkle and Yarico* gave expression in its day to sentiments that struck a peculiar chord in the hearts of its audience. Its curious mixture of pathos and laughter, of moral seriousness and irreverent farce, awakened many of them to the iniquity of slavery. "It was popular," reveals Mrs. Inchbald, "before the subject of the abolition of the slave trade was popular. It has the peculiar honour of preceding that great question."[38]

Modern critical interpretations are divided down the middle between those who dismiss Colman's play as "little more than farce and ephemeral entertainment," a work that evades rather than explores moral questions, and those who commend it in historical terms as one of the first dramatic works actually to engage in a meaningful way in the crucial debate on the ethics of slavery.[39] Part of the problem of interpretation is that Colman's personal position on the question of slavery remains so unclear. Barry Sutcliffe has argued that Colman's long career in the theater shows no evidence that his attitude to social issues was anything other than conservative. For Colman, he writes, "any overt challenge to legitimacy, either in the theatre or in any other aspect of life, would simply have been inconceivable."

Certainly the happy ending to the play and the conspicuous omission of Yarico's pregnancy might be construed as the author's attempts to gloss over difficult issues. "On the basic level of the creative process," comments Sutcliffe, "it would almost seem that Colman has sold out his subject matter to the prevailing conventions of sentimental drama."[40]

Yet the few details that are known suggest that it was in the process of writing the play and producing it for the first time on stage that the traditional storyline became transformed. In his incomplete autobiographical excursus, titled *Random Records,* Colman inserts the following illustration as testimony of what can "sometimes [be] happily produced from the spur of the moment":

> Criticks have been pleased to observe, that, it was a good hit when I made Inkle offer Yarico for sale to the person whom he afterwards discovers to be his intended father-in-law;—The hit, good or bad, only occurr'd to me when I came to that part of the Piece in which it is introduced, and arose from the accidental turn which I had given the previous scenes;—as it is not in the original story, it would, in all probability, *not* have occurr'd to me while coldly preparing an elaborate prospectus;—and such a prospectus once made, it is ten to one that I should have follow'd it mechanically.[41]

That Colman did not produce a mechanical reiteration of the original story may owe as much to the fact that he studiously rehearsed the idea of the play with a number of his friends. During the process of writing, he tells us that he read large parts to his friend Joseph Jekyll and that "I profited much by his criticism."[42] Jekyll (1754–1837) was celebrated in his day as one of the foremost London wits—by profession he was a lawyer and politician—and is remembered now only because of the *Letters of the Late Ignatius Sancho, an African* (1782), to which he penned a brief prefatory memoir of its author. The sensation of Sancho's *Letters* had been in introducing to an incredulous public the seeming contradiction of a literate African, a black man who was sufficiently cultured to have corresponded, among others, with the great Laurence Sterne. Jekyll's relationship to Sancho (1729–80) remains unclear, but his memoir is a conscious effort to exonerate black people at large from the accusations of those who had endeavored to degrade them "as a deterioration of the human." In turn, Colman does not tell us exactly how he profited from Jekyll's advice, though it seems reasonable to assume that the bias of the play could only have been positively influenced by one who had written eloquently in favor of the nobility and mental abilities of the black man at liberty in his native Africa over "the ignorance and grossness of slaves in the sugar-islands, expatriated in infancy, and brutalized under the whip and the task-master."[43]

If Jekyll was Colman's unsung moral mentor, there is enough piecemeal evidence to suggest that the final shaping of the play (and reshaping of the story) before its first performance owed a great deal to last-minute dramatic improvisation. *Inkle and Yarico* was Colman's fourth play but his first outstanding success on stage. As son of the manager at the Haymarket Theatre, he was intimate with the actors and, at this juncture in his dramatic career, singularly responsive to their advice. In rehearsal, it was soon apparent that Jack Bannister, the leading actor of the company who had been chosen to play Inkle, was far from comfortable with a part that—following the original storyline—was destined to climax with an exhibition of callous indifference in the act of selling Yarico into slavery. His biographer, John Adolphus, describes well Bannister's undeniable anguish and perplexity in engaging with the role during rehearsals, altogether unused as a comic actor to giving dramatic credence to such an unfeeling action:

[The] genuine traces of the performer were lost; his real powers were buried; he struggled under a load of formality and dulness. To see Bannister playing a character in which his large eye never cast forth a beam of benevolence,—in which his countenance never expanded for a moment to express the impulse of a humane heart, . . . —was indeed to see him driven from the fair fields in which Nature had destined him to dwell. . . . To hear him calculating the probable value of uncultivated land on the American continent, and the possible produce of free men "in their native confines hunted down," enslaved and sold in a market, and all without a syllable of compunction or compassion, . . . was to suppose a greater change than the general course of dramatic representation implies. . . . I have heard him say, that the thought of Inkle's repentance, which brings the piece to a satisfactory, if an awkward conclusion, was suggested by him. "But after all," said Colman, "what are we to do with Inkle?" "Oh!" said Bannister, "let him repent"; and so it was settled.[44]

A scribal copy of the play, submitted for formal approval to John Larpent, the examiner of plays, only ten days before the first performance and now preserved in the Huntington Library, San Marino, California, provides by far the most significant documentary corroboration of Bannister's claim that at his behest Colman altered the original ending. At the critical moment in the scene (3.3), just when Sir Christopher Curry calls Inkle to account for the heartless ease with which he was willing to abandon Yarico, the final section of the text has been extracted and a revised ending supplied in a different scribal hand. However, a single extant leaf of the rejected version gives us an intriguing glimpse into the original direction of the play. In response to Sir Christopher's rebuke of Inkle, the following dialogue ensues:

Inkle.   This is too much. I can bear this place no longer. [*going*]

Yarico.   Stay, Oh Stay! Or take me with you. Remember your oaths of eternal constancy, your earnest promises, that even if you return'd to your own country, Yarico shou'd be your companion.

Inkle.   No more! I cannot answer you. This is no time or place for remonstrance, or expostulation.

Yarico.   No time, or place, can ever change your Yarico: Did she not before she left home risk every danger to preserve your life? And she will follow you and still watch over you, go where you will, till she gives up her own.

Inkle.   Oh heaven! Where shall I turn myself? Such affection and fidelity strikes deeper than the bitterest reproaches. But Oh! remorse and penitence may cut me to the heart, yet never can restore my own peace or retrieve the good opinion of others.

Sir Christopher.   Why, you'll find it a pretty hard task, Master Inkle, that's the truth on't; and yet the worse you speak or think of yourself, the better we and the rest of the world shall speak and think of you.—What have you to say?

Inkle's answer to Sir Christopher's question and the rest of Colman's original ending to the opera have not been preserved in the Larpent manuscript, and one can only speculate as to what had initially been intended. Sutcliffe plausibly surmises that it "might have been a much more harrowing ending of the play . . . [with an] emotional temperature, . . . clearly in the process of . . . boiling over into . . . melodrama." He remarks further that "this was an area of theatrical potential which Colman lacked the confidence to share with his audiences."[45] However, a hitherto unpublished verse "Prologue to Inkle and Yarico" (included with the Larpent manuscript of the play) alludes specifically to Colman's alteration by forewarning the audience that the traditional tale is about to receive an unaccustomed final twist:

Yet you'll behold to night—nor think it strange!
Before the piece concludes some little change. . . .

Here, first, not following the stale narration,
In Inkle's heart was wrought a reformation.
But how shou'd he, all guilt, for pardon plead?
How prove his penitence sincere indeed?

If the rhetorical questions proffered here remain unanswered, at least the prologue implies that Colman's revisions are consonant with a recognition of what works best in the theater and what is most likely to appeal didactically and emotionally to the audience of his day:

No! we but claim the charter of the stage,
'Gainst vice and folly constant war to wage;
To teach young poets the first rule of art,
To charm the fancy, and improve the heart.[46]

Whether shaped by Bannister's apprehensions or by other causes, the newly supplied "happy ending" in which Inkle and Yarico are reunited became hugely popular from its first performance. Blithely unaware of the changes wrought late in rehearsal, audiences responded by shedding profuse tears both in sympathy for Yarico and at the final reunion of the lovers. Colman's friend and fellow dramatist John O'Keefe pays amusing tribute to the phenomenal success of *Inkle and Yarico* as a sentimental tearjerker when he introduces into one of his own plays a brewer's wife who complains bitterly to her husband of being dispatched to the theater "only t'other night without a pocket handkerchief, . . . when all the boxes were in tears for the sorrows of Yarico." Instead of a handkerchief, quips her sarcastic husband, she "was fain to twitch the tears from off [her moistened cheek] with her white kid-gloves, so that the finger and thumb look'd as if she had been taking brazil snuff."[47]

Colman's abandonment of the original ending leads inexorably to a heart-heaving sentimentality. As awkward and stilted as we may find the hero's repentance, there seems little doubt of its appeal to contemporary taste. "Mr. Colman, junior," remarks a contemporary reviewer, "has judiciously conceived that the reformation of his hero would be agreeable to an English audience."[48] In the revised text, Inkle's inner struggle ends with the following maladroit effusion:

Ill-founded precept too long has steeled my breast—but still 'tis vulnerable—this trial was too much—Nature, 'gainst habit combating within me, has penetrated to my heart; a heart, I own, long callous to the feelings of sensibility; but now it

bleeds—and bleeds for my poor Yarico. Oh, let me clasp her to it, while 'tis glowing, and mingle tears of love and penitence. [*Embraces her.*] (3.3, [12], 228)

Peter Thomson is surely right to question here "whether Colman's sentimental writing is ever free from flippancy."[49] For an actor like Bannister,
the comic and burlesque possibilities of such a speech must have far outweighed any desire to play it literally. Yet by so clearly inducing the audience to reach for their handkerchiefs, Colman was simultaneously endeavoring to promote the abolitionist cause by tugging at people's heartstrings.
As Paul Langford has argued, when "viewed against the sentimental background in which it belongs, abolition takes its place among the manifold
expressions of the new sensibility."[50] In the case of Inkle and Yarico, its sentimentality is crucial to its political impact. The revised version with its
sentimental finale has come down to us as the printed text of *Inkle and
Yarico*. Ironically, after only a few performances, Jack Bannister, after apparently prompting Colman to change the ending, relinquished the part of
Inkle in favor of that of Trudge.

Even if from our perspective it has not withstood the test of time, Colman's comic opera remained a favorite part of the English theatrical reper-
toire until well into the nineteenth century. Paradoxically, however, its later
popularity coincides with the gradual demise of the legend it is based on.
The tale of Inkle and Yarico, which had epitomized so many facets of its
age, proved oddly ill founded to flourish far beyond the century that had
engendered it. The impulse to overwork its sentimental aspect, which is
such a prominent feature in the revised ending to the play, meant that the
story was not equipped to cope with the cultural backlash against sensibility that set in during the early years of the new century. In addition, the
abolition of the British slave trade in 1807 took away at a stroke what had
become the story's most topical component. Yet, as I shall argue, certain sa-
lient features of the tale were able to survive by becoming subsumed within
the larger ideology of a nascent Romanticism.

Influence

To explain how the fickle gauge of popular taste came to relegate Inkle and
Yarico to comparative obscurity, it is necessary to reexamine the roots of
the story in the eighteenth century. The factors that caused it to lose its
appeal during the early to middle nineteenth century may be educed from
a reconsideration of its very ability to translate itself into a variety of dif-

ferent forms and to blend disparate elements that derive eclectically from oral and literary sources. What is remarkable about the various manifestations of the tale in the eighteenth century is the sheer energy and inventiveness with which it could be recast into so many discrete forms in prose and verse, whether moral essay, heroic epistle, comic opera, ballad, or pantomime. Equally remarkable is its thematic spectrum, which can involve such major social and political issues as gender, race, miscegenation, and slavery. With the advantage of hindsight, it must be apparent that the resources of a short and fairly simple anecdotal tale would eventually be exhausted, there being a limit to how far it could be reused without becoming totally clichéd or stretched without losing its identity. In reviewing its incredible range, we should not lose sight of the fact that (with the notable exception of Steele's moral essay) it failed to outlive its century, which Samuel Johnson considered to be the ultimate test of literary merit. Yet merely to dismiss the versions of the tale after *The Spectator* as inconsequential or trivial is to ignore their capacity to be interpreted as decipherable cultural markers of the age that created them.

In his pioneering *Inkle and Yarico Album,* published in 1937, Lawrence Marsden Price explored the extraordinary popularity of the legend across Europe through the eighteenth century. Toward the end of his study he contends that "as the century wore on in England, a new public developed side by side with the older, a public which read not to improve its mind and edify its soul, but more and more from a frivolous desire for light entertainment." Price dismisses Colman's opera as a work that panders to this new public, diluting the original legend in order to cater to a changing taste. What the story of Inkle and Yarico "gained in breadth," says Price, "it lost in depth and after a century of praise the name of Yarico was rarely heard again."[51] In accounting for its demise, Price resorts to a kind of nostalgic pleading for the tale in its original form without perhaps sufficiently appreciating that the flexibility of the legend was always its greatest strength. From its earliest manifestation following Steele, the tale is nothing less than pliable. This becomes particularly apparent when we employ the resources of recent scholarship, which allow us to see that adaptations and reworkings of the story occurred distinctly before the first example cited by Price. Its influence is far more widespread and deep-rooted than even he allows.

The earliest example Price lists of an English adaptation of Steele's tale is "The Story of Inkle and Yarico, from the Eleventh *Spectator,*" an anonymous poetical rendition that appeared in the *London Magazine* of May

1734. At the time of its publication, Steele had already been dead for five years. Given the innumerable impressions of *The Spectator*, which never went out of print during the whole of the eighteenth century, was there really no attempt during its author's lifetime to recast its first and best-known fictive tale in any other form? If the appeal of Inkle and Yarico was as ubiquitous as Price has claimed, it seems peculiar that almost a quarter of a century should have elapsed before its earliest imitation. In fact, recent scholarship has shown that the fashion for penning verses about Inkle and Yarico had started more or less a decade earlier, in the mid-1720s.

By the end of 1725, at least two poems on the theme had been written. They can now be identified as the compositions of Frances Seymour, Countess of Hertford (1699–1754), and were published in an undated collection of poetic pieces, known as the Tunbridge Miscellany (ca. 1726), which also included the first printing of John Dyer's well-known poem *Grongar Hill*.[52] The second of Lady Hertford's poems is titled "An Epistle from Yarico to Inkle, after He Had Sold Her for a Slave" [3B], and it initiates a strain of similar heroic epistles written from the perspective of the abandoned mistress that were attempted by different authors throughout the century. Among these are the 1736 poem once attributed to Edward Moore and another by Edward Jerningham that have already been discussed. To the group may be added inter alia an incomplete fragment by the Cambridge poet William Pattison (1706–27), posthumously published in 1728 [4], John Winstanley's "Yarico's Epistle to Inkle" of 1751 [8], and "Yarico to Inkle," pseudonymously ascribed to "Amicus" [16], which made its appearance in the *American Museum*, published at Philadelphia in 1792.[53]

The distinction of all these verses is that they can claim an important classical precedent, in that they are consciously written in the style of heroic epistle invented by the Roman poet Ovid (43 B.C.–A.D. 17). His *Heroides*, though the creation of a male author, are principally poems of persuasion that adopt the voices of forsaken women vainly endeavoring to woo back their former lovers. In the genre of heroic epistle, the emotions articulated by the disempowered female contain the potential to disturb because of the pendular process by which they reflect extremes of passion and hope in tandem with the most rankling despair. "The quasi-historical fiction of Yarico," writes Gillian Beer, "is a particularly striking example of the way heroic epistle could disturb, and could claim space for those whose experience was usually brushed aside." The peculiar strength of the genre, which is evident in the best of the poems penned by Yarico to Inkle, is in their poignant combination of the elements of tragedy and romance as a means of expressing "the experience of the slighted, the abandoned, the powerless." "The black slave-woman," comments Beer, "is left with nothing but the white man's language; and with that she can protest, but not find freedom."[54]

If the heroic epistles of Lady Hertford and others represent an early manifestation of the creative influence of the tale, Catherine E. Moore has argued that an even earlier echo of Inkle and Yarico is apparent in Daniel Defoe's *Robinson Crusoe* (1719). Toward the beginning of Defoe's well-known narrative, the hero escapes from slavery with the help of Xury, a Moorish boy, whose menial devotion to the Englishman is callously rewarded when Crusoe sells him to a Portuguese sea captain for sixty pieces of eight. By way of parallels between the two stories, Moore argues that both Inkle and Crusoe are young merchant adventurers, motivated by a love of gain. Each is "the third son of an eminent father," and each goes to sea "to improve his fortune by trade and merchandise" (*Spectator*). Yarico and Xury, though differing in race and gender, are both treated by their respective companions as simple savages who can be sold into slavery without compunction, despite each one's having been instrumental in preserving the life of a Christian Englishman. As Moore notes, the major dissimilarity is the absence in *Robinson Crusoe* of a romantic element, though she contends that this "makes no difference with respect to the similarity of theme" shared by the two tales. Although she is unable to prove beyond reasonable doubt that the account of Crusoe's relationship with Xury was definitely influenced by Inkle and Yarico, she marshals sufficient evidence to suggest that "it seems not unlikely that Defoe's imagination would have responded to and his memory stored away the little anecdote which appeared in the *Spectator* . . . eight years before the publication of *Robinson Crusoe*."[55]

In arguing her case, Moore remarks on the instant popularity of Inkle and Yarico as anecdote and its ready availability to readers in the pages of *The Spectator*. If she is correct in believing that the influence of the story was already so pervasive such a short time after its first appearance, it becomes easier to comprehend its widening popularity in the middle years of the century. The translation and publication of *The Spectator* in all the major European languages served to disseminate the tale across the Continent. Price devotes a large part of his study to its replication in German and French literature. As a consequence of his scholarship, we now know that across the English Channel its appeal was if anything even more extensive than in its country of origin. To cite only some of its most significant renderings, it is illuminating to discover the young Goethe writing in sanguine mood to his sister Cornelia from Leipzig in October 1766 of his plan—alas, never achieved—to compose a drama on the subject of Inkle and Yarico.[56] Goethe would most probably have been aware of the work of other German writers, such as Christian Gellert and Salomon Gessner, who had already written on the theme. Gessner's popular continuation to the story, among the most maudlin of sequels, is included here [9] in one of its later English translations.

Goethe may also have known the most famous French dramatic adaptation of the tale, *La jeune Indienne,* written by Sébastian-Roch Nicolas Chamfort (1740–94), which was first put on to great acclaim at the Comedie-Française on 30 April 1764. Though the setting was transferred to the English colony of Charlestown (Charleston, South Carolina) and the names of the protagonists were altered to Belton and Betti, the indebtedness of the play to Inkle and Yarico was at once recognized by the public and never denied by its author. Chamfort's one-act verse comedy was translated and successfully performed in a number of European languages but (perhaps because of an incipient bias against things French in the wake of the Seven Years' War) not in English. Gilbert Chinard has claimed that Colman's decision to modify the ending of his comic opera by reuniting Yarico and Inkle may have been influenced by a similar stratagem in *La jeune Indienne,* but direct evidence that the English dramatist was familiar with Chamfort's play has not been found.[57]

However, a later French transformation of the tale into the realm of pantomime, though not well received in England, found sufficient favor to be rendered into English and published in the United States. Jean-François Arnould-Mussot's mime in three acts, *L'héroine américaine,* first performed at the Ambigu-Comique in Paris in 1786, was translated out of the French by Samuel Chandler and printed in Philadelphia in 1797 as *The American Heroine* [13]. Quite unlike *La jeune Indienne,* with its sentimental closure, *The American Heroine* reads as a crude but effective depiction of colonial cruelty in which (by a sudden metamorphosis that some may construe as long overdue poetic justice) Yarico ends up experiencing total revulsion toward the faithless Inkle, whose hand she finally rejects in favor of the noble generosity of an Indian chief. By sensationally gutting the tale of its pathos and its romantic expectation, Arnould introduces to his mime a needed note of realism. A dramatic afterpiece, in all probability a version of Arnould's pantomime, titled *The American Heroine, or Ingratitude Punished*, was performed on a single occasion at Drury Lane in March 1792, but it met with disapprobation. Its failure may have been owing to its unedifying representation of an Englishman, but more pertinent, it would have stood little chance of success on the London stage in the shadow of Colman's comic opera (with its romantic ending) that was so much in vogue.[58]

The conspicuous ease with which the story could be adapted to arbitrary employment in different forms in other languages is also evident in its ongoing flexibility in eighteenth-century English oral culture as a topical anecdote firmly embedded in the popular memory. Its status as a tale that is so commonly known that it has taken on an aura of veracity is evident from a reference in an anonymous essay of 1758 titled "A Short Account of the British Colonies, in the Islands of America, Commonly Called the West-Indies," that made its appearance in the *London Magazine*. As a prelude to attacking the practice of keeping slaves, the author draws attention to "that infamous and cruel affair of Inkle and Yarico, which I shall not presume to repeat . . . ; but I must add, that besides being a reproach to the man who was guilty of it, it is a reproach upon all those who were then the inhabitants of Barbadoes, for suffering such a piece of ingratitude and cruelty to be perpetrated in their island, and which certainly they would not have suffered, if they had not been hardened in barbarity by the long use of slaves."[59] In similar fashion, without naming the tale, it is unquestionably Inkle and Yarico that Dr. William Alexander alludes to in *The History of Women* (1779) when disputing that the surfeit of human greed is proportional between the sexes:

Avarice, sordid avarice, seems alone to have occupied the breasts of the greatest part of these who have travelled from Europe to the Indies; and from so fruitful a source has sprung up almost every other crime. An Englishman who was shipwrecked on the coast of Africa, being taken and condemned to death by the natives, was saved by a woman of some distinction in the country; who, on a promise he would marry her, contrived to escape along with him. The wretch had no sooner arrived in an European settlement, than he sold his deliverer for a slave, and abandoned her for ever. But the vices are not solely attached to the man who had left Europe in pursuit of gain: even the women who have accompanied them, leaving behind the gentleness of European manners and of female nature, have been often hardly less distinguished for debauchery and cruelty than the men. A virago of this sort in the East or West-Indies, seldom meeting with any opposition to her whim and caprice, assumes at last a spirit of presumption and tyranny; and lost to feeling and humanity, wields the whip with such dexterity, as to fetch at every stroke blood from the back of the naked and unresisting slave; whose only fault was, that he did not anticipate the wishes of his mistress, or because he let fall some hints, that he was a creature of the same genus as herself.[60]

Both examples serve to show once again how the tale has moved from its original intention as a counterpart in an age-old debate about gender to a more specific case history that is illustrative of the iniquities of the slave trade. But the passages also endorse our sense of Inkle and Yarico as a factual fiction deeply rooted in the public consciousness, an exemplary fable that may be randomly invoked for a whole variety of purposes.

The particular aspect of the tale that arguably contributed most to its popular appeal throughout the long eighteenth century was its relatively uncurbed expression of human passion. Here it was able to arouse in its auditors sensations and feelings that they might in other circumstances be only too inclined to suppress. It was acceptable to weep at the plight of Yarico, whereas elsewhere such venting of emotion would risk being condemned as unmanly or overdelicate. We have the witness among others of Robert Burns, William Hazlitt, and Charles Lamb as to the acute emotional effect on each of Colman's dramatization of the situation. Fresh from seeing Mrs. Elizabeth Kemble (Colman's original stage Yarico) playing the part in a touring production at Dumfries in October 1794, Burns addressed and presented to her a lachrymose eulogium of the sensations awakened in him:

> *Kemble,* thou cur'st my unbelief
>   Of Moses and his rod:
> At Yarico's sweet notes of grief
>   The rocks with *tears* had flow'd.[61]

A few years later, after watching Fanny Kelly play Yarico, Hazlitt appears to be biting hard on his nether lip when remarking that "critics, as it has been said of judges, must not give way to their feelings." Yet, casting restraint aside, he cannot defer from observing, "Ah! there were tones, and looks, and piercing sighs in her representation of the fond, injured, sunburnt Indian maid."[62] Similarly, and even more remarkably, Charles Lamb's comments on the same performer are charged with emotional fervor:

Her Yarico is the most intense piece of acting which I ever witnessed, the most heart-rending spectacle. To see her leaning upon that wretched reed, her lover— the very exhibition of whose character would be a moral offence, but for her cling-

ing and noble credulity—to see her lean upon that flint, and by the strong workings of passion, imagine it a god, is one of the most afflicting lessons of the yearn-
ings of the human heart, and its mistakes, that was ever read upon a stage. The
whole performance is everywhere African, fervid, glowing.[63]

By attributing to Fanny Kelly's acting the ability to emulate passions that
he views as intrinsically "African," Lamb infers a line of demarcation between the "fervid, glowing" exoticism of a far continent and the pallid un-
emotionalism of things English. As a tale, Inkle and Yarico dramatically reenacts such a distinction while simultaneously confuting it by making the
audience side with the emotional sufferings of the victim. In sentimentally
allying with Yarico, the listeners are made to acknowledge in themselves and
openly express (if only through weeping) what Lamb felicitously describes
as "the strong workings of passion."

    Given the almost universal knowledge of the tale and its employment by
so many writers, it is somewhat surprising that no direct allusion to it has
been discovered in the works of William Wordsworth. The poet's own preoccupation with what has been termed "the poetry of passion" is well
known, and bearing in mind his enthusiastic pursuit of oral literature and
its traditions, the tale could be construed as an ideal source for Wordsworth's art. If (as I suspect) he was familiar with Inkle and Yarico, it would
have been as a tale that belonged as much to his subconscious recollection
as to a direct awareness of its popularity in the theater and in poetic form
in journals such as the *Gentleman's Magazine* or the *London Magazine*.
In his study of the poet's extensive reading, Duncan Wu has noted that
Wordsworth would have first read *The Spectator* as early as 1773–76 when
he was an infant at Ann Birkett's dame school. During his time at Cambridge (1788–89) his continuing regard for the periodical prompted him to
assay as an academic exercise a translation into Italian of several of its
papers, including the "Vision of Mirza" (*Spectator*, no. 159), a short fiction
by Addison that he was later to applaud as "a sublime allegory."[64] The ori-
ental setting of the "Vision of Mirza" is a far cry from the American context of Inkle and Yarico, yet both share an exoticism that would have appealed to Wordsworth.

    In *Lyrical Ballads* (1798), the particular poem that is often cited as most
closely reflecting Wordsworth's creative infatuation with the primitive customs and mores of the Native American is "The Complaint of a Forsaken
Indian." In it Wordsworth reenacts in her own voice the last struggles of an
Indian woman, too sick to travel and finally left to die by her tribe. A brief

authorial note at the head of the poem acknowledges Wordsworth's indebtedness to a descriptive passage from Samuel Hearne's *Journey from Prince of Wales's Fort in Hudson's Bay to the Northern Ocean* (1795), a fine example of the poet's imaginative sourcing out of his wider reading. Critics have drawn parallels between this poem and what Mary Jacobus describes as "a thriving [contemporary] tradition of 'Indian' poetry . . . showing alien customs strikingly superimposed on a common humanity."[65] The pathos of the Indian woman's dying lament is augmented here by her traumatic expressions of grief at the loss of her child, who has been taken from her arms by her companions as they left her on her own to perish:

> My poor forsaken child! if I
> For once could have thee close to me,
> With happy heart I then should die.
> And my last thoughts would happy be.   (lines 65–68)

By accentuating her isolation, the poem registers an empathy for human suffering and loss that, through the simple voice of the dying woman, is shared dramatically with the reader.

"The Complaint of a Forsaken Indian Woman" is often coupled with another famous poem in *Lyrical Ballads,* "The Mad Mother," also known as "Her Eyes Are Wild" (Appendix C). Written at about the same time, it employs the former's unusual stanza arrangement and is also an acute expression of what Wordsworth described as "the maternal passion." The precise racial identity of the mad mother is unspecified, though her familiarity with their customs ("I'll build an Indian bower" [line 55], etc.) suggests that she too was originally conceived by Wordsworth as a Native American. In this case the poet provided no headnote acknowledgment of a specific source, though modern scholars have uncovered remarkable similarities between "The Mad Mother" and a medieval Scottish ballad, "Lady Anne Bothwell's Lament," which Bishop Percy had restored to public attention in his influential *Reliques of Ancient English Poetry* (1765). Recent editors of *Lyrical Ballads* concur that "The Mad Mother" is "unmistakably modelled" on the Scottish poem and, in so doing, have unwittingly drawn attention away from its corresponding indebtedness to contemporary representations of American Indians. The situation is not helped by Wordsworth's own statements on the poem, which are characteristically opaque. When dictating comments on his poems to Isabella Fenwick in 1843, the venerable poet recalled that "the subject [of "The Mad Mother"] was re-

ported to me by a lady of Bristol who had seen the poor creature," pointing apparently toward a rather specific local source as his inspiration. When
questioned several years earlier (September 1836) by his friend John Kenyon, however, Wordsworth contended far less precisely that "though she
came from far, English was her native tongue—which shows her either to
be of these Islands, or a North American."[66] The two statements do not
necessarily contradict one another, though they do provide handy testament to the creative enhancement of empirical observation that distinguishes so much of Wordsworth's best poetry.

Among Wordsworth scholars, Robert Mayo was probably the first to
demonstrate what he called the "contemporaneity" of the *Lyrical Ballads.*
Mayo was able to show that the figures of humanity Wordsworth employed
may also be found in profusion in late eighteenth-century magazine poetry,
which commonly features (among others) songs and ballads from women
abandoned by their husbands and from homeless wanderers with babes in
arms.[67] More recently, Alan Bewell has concentrated on Wordsworth's ob-
session with figures on the margins of society, and for many of them we
may trace their imaginative origin in the poet's favorite reading of travel
narratives. In *Lyrical Ballads,* argues Bewell, such figures are made to undergo a process of displacement whereby they are transferred from exotic
to familiar settings. "Many of these figures," writes Bewell, undertake or
have undergone some kind of journey, often a transatlantic crossing. . . .
The narrator of 'The Mad Mother' tells us that 'she came far from over the
main' and attests that she speaks 'in the English tongue.' Yet our need for
such reassurance suggests that this woman, herself a figure of displacement,
has far more exotic origins than one might initially assume."[68]

Of all the exotic figures of transatlantic origin in the public domain and
readily accessible to the Wordsworthian imagination, by far the most uni-
versally known would have been Yarico, the prototypical female Noble Savage of the Enlightenment. Her situation, it has to be said, is not exactly
parallel to that of the mad mother, and we must caution ourselves against
reading the story of Inkle and Yarico as an explicit source. In fact, there are
substantial differences between the two narratives that need to be spelled
out before any attempt at demonstrating semblance. Insanity (so vital to
the representation of the mad mother) does not feature as a prominent
trope in Inkle and Yarico, nor does the topical subject of slavery impinge
on *Lyrical Ballads.*[69] The single aspect central to both narratives is that of
the faithful woman jilted by a false husband or lover—as we have seen, a

common enough motif in the magazine poetry of the period. In Wordsworth's poem the reader becomes literally enmeshed in a process of reconstruction by being obliged to piece together the private history of the mother's abandonment by her husband from casual hints and allusions scattered through her semicoherent address to her suckling baby boy. If there are affinities here with Inkle and Yarico, it is as a story brought forward from the moment of abandonment (with which Steele's version ends) to that of the jilted woman now advanced into early motherhood. As a kind of unconscious sequel, the poem records willy-nilly the history of the mother's abandonment but achieves its power through its evocation of the maternal passion in which the defenseless baby at her breast has displaced his father in the mother's affections:

> Suck, little babe, oh suck again!
> It cools my blood; it cools my brain;
> Thy lips I feel them, baby! they
> Draw from my heart the pain away. . . .
>
> Thy father cares not for my breast,
> 'Tis thine sweet baby there to rest:
> 'Tis all thine own!   (lines 31–34, 61–63)

Although it appears highly improbable that Wordsworth was directly aware of it, at least one earlier poem written in the popular mode as a verse epistle from Yarico to Inkle is contrived in a manner that strikingly anticipates "The Mad Mother." In John Winstanley's "Yarico's Epistle to Inkle," composed before the middle of the century but published only in 1751 [8], the poet also projects forward to the birth of the child, a "sad *pledge* . . . / Torn from my Womb" (lines 130–31), who becomes momentarily the object of his mother's address:

> O thou dear *partner* of my grief, I'll find
> In thee a *child,* a *husband* and a *friend.*
> While yet, *sweet babe,* to my fond bosom prest,
> Thou like a *pearl* hang'st pendant on my breast,
> Thy soul with early courage I'll inspire,
> To brave the insults of a treach'rous *sire;*
> In spite of scorn and cruelties, we'll live,
> And lost in sympathy forget to grieve.   (lines 138–45)

The malleability of the tale of Inkle and Yarico allows Winstanley to create a poem that (in Price's words) "is less pictorial than its predecessors and is reflective rather than narrative."[70] Although lacking the subtlety and close psychological insight that characterize "The Mad Mother," Winstanley's verse epistle indicates an inherent potential to address through dramatic soliloquy inner thought processes but rarely explored earlier by English poets. Fifty years on, it became the distinction of Wordsworth and of his fellow poets of the Romantic school to have responded to this potential by creating poems that subjectively interiorize and probe the subtle workings of the female mind. Critical comparison of the delineation of Yarico in her various epistles to her lover with the kindred portrayal of the mad mother provides an almost unparalleled insight into the handling of a "feminized" sensibility in English poetry from the age of Pope through that of Wordsworth.

In tracing what may still be no more than a subconscious influence, I should mention at least two other factors that help link Inkle and Yarico to "The Mad Mother." Wordsworth's poem ends with the mother's avowal to her babe of an escape from abandonment and personal suffering in the world of the woods:

Then, pretty dear, be not afraid;
We'll find thy father in the wood.
Now laugh and be gay, to the woods away!
And there, my babe, we'll live for aye.   (lines 97–100)

It is at once a conventional balladic "happy" ending and also an ironic restatement of the pathos of her situation and the precariousness of both her own sad existence and that of the child. Significantly, at a climactic moment in the final act of Colman's comic opera, Yarico vainly appeals to Inkle to pursue a similar course in place of abandoning her:

Come, come, let's go. I always feared these cities. Let's fly and seek the woods; and there we'll wander hand in hand together. No cares shall vex us then. . . . and we'll live cheerily I warrant—In the fresh, early morning, you shall hunt down our game, and I will pick you berries—and then at night I'll trim our bed of leaves and lie me down in peace—Oh! we shall be so happy! (3.3 [12], 224).

Eleven years after, Wordsworth's distracted mother shows herself no less familiar than Colman's Yarico with Indian lore or, more properly, with life in the woods, telling us, "I know / The leaves that make the softest bed" (line 56) and "I know the earth-nuts fit for food" (line 96). The similarities are sufficient to suggest some recollection of Yarico's dramatic plea in the recesses of Wordsworth's creative imagination.[71]

We have already seen that the narrator's assertion at the beginning of "The Mad Mother" that "She talked and sung the woods among; / And it was in the English tongue" troubled Wordsworth's friend John Kenyon and prompted a written response from the poet. It is the closest Wordsworth comes outside the poem itself to a specific acknowledgment of a Native American origin for his protagonist. If we are to suppose her a North American, he remarks, "While the distance removes her from us, the fact of her speaking our language brings us at once into close sympathy with her."[72] That the mother is not English poses no more than a minor technical obstacle to the poet, for he allows her to speak the language with a facility that might otherwise be unexpected in an American Indian. An element of suspension of poetic disbelief is necessary for us to accept her ease with English. However, this becomes far less of a problem if we accept that as dramatic monologue "The Mad Mother" derives much of its impetus from the strong eighteenth-century tradition of verse epistles penned by Yarico to Inkle, in which it had long been conventional for the heroine to address her unfaithful lover in a polite form of poetic English. All the heroic epistles addressed from Yarico to Inkle tacitly authorize the suppression of the American Indian's native tongue in favor of the language of her unfaithful lover. It prompts an implicit concession or surrender by the woman to thought processes and a value system of which she is inevitably the victim. In Steele's seminal version, in which "the lovers . . . learn'd a language of their own," it had remained intriguingly unverifiable whether this should be understood as English. By their choice of English as her language of communication, later poets (for all the sympathy they may show) unconsciously conspire in Yarico's entrapment. Wordsworth is possibly unique in apparently recognizing that there is much that is aberrant in giving an Indian woman a language other than her own.

The affinities we have uncovered suggest that "The Mad Mother" rather than "The Complaint of the Forsaken Indian" provides the closest approximation in the Wordsworthian canon to the tale of Inkle and Yarico. Even if it proves impossible on present evidence to establish direct indebtedness, a reading of poetic renderings of the tale in conjunction with Wordsworth's poem serves to show the far greater intensity and subtlety of the latter in its delineation of human passion. The simple but powerful language of the poem is far more responsive to psychological nuance and depth of feeling than any of the Ovidian heroic epistles written from Yarico to Inkle. By spurning conventional poetic English, Wordsworth endows "The Mad

Mother" with what he describes in his 1800 preface to the *Lyrical Ballads* as a "language somewhat more appropriate . . . to follow the fluxes and refluxes of the mind when agitated by the great and simple affections of our nature." The result is a poem of extraordinary poignancy and power in its complex treatment of insanity and abandonment. On one level, we may simply be arguing in favor of Wordsworth's creative mastery as a poet, but the singular combination of insight and empathy he achieves simultaneously reveals the inadequacy of Inkle and Yarico—by the late eighteenth century a more than clichéd anecdotal tale—to treat such complex emotional issues. Wordsworth's isolation of the Indian woman's abandonment as the single narrative aspect that interests him anticipates the fragmentation and eventual demise of the tale. By translating the Noble Savage to a localized environment and presenting her without loss of dignity as the sympathetic victim of a culture to which she is extrinsic, Wordsworth ensures that the ideologies of the tale are inscribed into the poetry of passion that constitutes the new Romanticism.[73]

Endings

Many years ago, Paul Hazard offered an appealing taxonomy to Inkle and Yarico by which he expounded the tale as a diptych. "In one panel," he explains, "was the traitor, the scoundrel, the villain; in the other, the noble but ill-fated soul. And the former was the European, the latter, the child of Nature!"[74] The history of European expansionism into the New World is replete with similar examples of the rendezvous of the perfidious "civilized" man with the guileless "primitive" savage. Inkle and Yarico functions as a compelling textual paradigm of an often repeated geographical process. That its prominence as anecdote diminished after the beginning of the nineteenth century suggests that its appeal is primarily as a myth of the Enlightenment, in which the empirical observation of savage peoples was often ruthlessly coupled with a cynical predilection to undermine endemic beliefs in European superiority.

If, as several scholars have assumed, the abolition of the British slave trade may have contributed to a terminal decline in the tale's popularity, it is significant that its period of greatest currency was when the issue was so much the subject of national debate. Here it is more than happy coincidence that the leading Whig politician who was to introduce into the House of Commons in June 1806 the successful motion that led to abolition's finally being enacted had himself only a few years earlier composed a verse rendering of

4. *Am I Not a Man and a Brother.* Wood engraved replica of Wedgwood seal. From Thomas Clarkson, *The History of the Rise, Progress, and Accomplishment of the Abolition of the African Slave-Trade by the British Parliament,* 2 vols. (London, 1808), 1:450. (Courtesy of the Brotherton Collection, University of Leeds.)

the tale. Charles James Fox's rediscovered "Yarico to Inkle" of 1802 [14] presents us with an enticing link between a topical tale and the endeavors of the abolitionists. After the legislation, despite still being replicated among others by Paul Methuen in his pedestrian "Epistle from Yarico to Incle" (1810) and again by Anna Maria Porter in a similarly titled poem of 1811 [15], the vein was exhausted almost exactly a hundred years after Steele had so auspiciously opened it.[75] Though the tale continued to resurface desultorily in print and though for some fair while performances of Colman's play continued to hold the stage, it no longer appealed spontaneously to the creative imagination of a new generation of writers. It is a curious generalization that in place of the sentimental nobility of a generous Yarico willing to yield to her false lover, the female icon that excited male poets after Wordsworth became what Barbara Fass has described as "the unattainable temptress who keeps her admirer in a perpetual state of longing, or the frequently faithless partner of a destructive love affair"—in short, the counterfigure of La Belle Dame sans Merci.[76] The Romantic passion to probe private agony and the consequent internalization of suffering meant that instead of the narrative heroine as victim, it was the first-person poet or his fictitious alter ego who visibly stood as the injured party. Such a compelling discourse, with its outright reversal of previously allotted gender roles, was to leave the myth of Inkle and Yarico in precious limbo.

Our own interest in reclaiming the myth two centuries on presupposes its new validity as an important source in colonial and postcolonial polemic. In a widely discussed analysis, Edward Said has controversially reminded us that Inkle and Yarico should be read as one of several inaugural fables "that stand guard over the Imagination of the New World," mentally fortifying the cultural hegemony of the colonial past. For Said, "European geographical centrality . . . is buttressed by a cultural discourse relegating or confining the non-European to a secondary, racial, cultural, ontological status. Yet this secondariness is, paradoxically, essential to the primariness of the European." Notwithstanding, says Said, "for natives to want to lay claim to that terrain is, for many Westerners, an intolerable effrontery, for them actually to repossess it unthinkable." He claims that "it is a measure of how embattled this matter of 'inaugural figures' has become that it is now virtually impossible to say anything simple about any of them."[77] Whether or not we concur with all the implications of this assessment, the experience of reading Inkle and Yarico in its multifarious forms helps at least to support Said's final point.

The complexity of the myth can be shown to reveal itself in a number of other ways. Peter Hulme has argued that as an autonomous narrative, "the product of no single authorial consciousness," Inkle and Yarico lends itself, at least in theory, to psychoanalysis as a representation of the collective consciousness of the age that chose persistently to retell it.[78] Certainly, in postmodern critical thinking, much lip service has been paid to notions of intertextuality. In Inkle and Yarico we have that rare entity, a perfect example of an intertextual discourse that reflects so much of the diversity and contradictions of the age that fostered it. If, two centuries after, there is something hybridized about collecting between two covers sundry models of the tale that may never have been intended to appear together, it is a qualification no different from that for any other anthology. Inkle and Yarico not only is intertextual, it is also intergeneric, permitting us to move with ease from travel discourse through such forms as periodical essay, heroic epistle, comic opera, pantomime, ballad, and popular anecdote. As a narrative that survives as text, it replicates an important factual fiction of communal memory that belonged in its day as much to oral as to written culture. At least in my own experience, its diverse handling of issues of gender and race makes it a lively and highly topical discussion piece in the classroom. Equally, given the regrettable (and actually surprising) shortfall of prominent eighteenth-century literary texts that treat of the subject of slavery, Inkle and Yarico fills a highly significant gap.

Finally, in its portrayal of the Noble Savage and of the American Indian (as well as in its relation to the well-known tale of Pocahontas), Inkle and Yarico is an important point of reference in early modern cultural representations of the New World. It is not without interest that the tale continued to find creative expression in early nineteenth-century America [16 and 17] when its popularity in England had already begun to wane. At a shrewd guess, the story of Inkle and Yarico in the United States was eventually submerged by the native myth of Pocahontas, which (according to Philip Young) was reconstituted from its early origins "about the start of the nineteenth century [when] Americans began to search intensely for their history." As Young argues well, by embodying for America the spirit of wildness (as Yarico had before her for eighteenth-century European sensibility), Pocahontas became the "progenitress of all the 'Dark Ladies' of our culture . . . whom our civilization . . . has summoned up only to repress."[79]

I have spoken earlier of England as the country of origin of a tale that, at its greatest currency, had a standing that delved deep into the European popular consciousness. Perhaps the assertion is a tad misleading, particularly in the light of postcolonial endeavors (as enunciated by Said and others) to reclaim cultural artifacts that are imaginatively sited in former imperial possessions. As a Caribbean legend, Inkle and Yarico is as much a part of the mislaid patrimony of the West Indies as it is an English and European folktale. Ironically, the English have lost this particular piece of cultural plunder, for Inkle and Yarico, once so extraordinarily popular, is now neglected and largely forgotten. However, in Barbados, where the unfortunate Yarico lost her freedom because of the treachery of her white lover, the story thrives as a local folk song that tells of the fate of the beautiful Amerindian [18–20]. Close to where she once toiled, one of the springs that is still used to provide drinking water and to irrigate the adjacent fields of sugarcane even bears the name "Yarico's pond." According to a recent standard history of the island, after she had been betrayed "Yarico joined the other Amerindians who were then enslaved in Barbados . . . and, when her time was come, she walked to the edge of a pond where she was delivered of 'a lusty boy, frolick and lively,' . . . , while Inkle died of yellow fever soon after his return to England."[80]

Notes

1. Arthur Murphy, *The Citizen* (1.2), in *The Modern British Drama,* 5 vols. (London, 1811), 5;469.

2. David Brion Davis, *The Problem of Slavery in Western Culture* (1966; New York, 1988), 10–11.

3. Walter J. Ong, *Orality and Literacy: The Technologizing of the Word* (London, 1982), 8.

4. Hayden White, *Tropics of Discourse: Essays in Cultural Criticism* (Baltimore, 1978), chap. 8, "The Noble Savage Theme as Fetish," 187.

5. Jean Mocquet, *Travels and Voyages into Africa, Asia, America, the East and West-Indies,* trans. Nathaniel Pullen (London, 1696), 78, 80.

6. John Locke, *An Essay concerning Human Understanding,* ed. Peter Nidditch (Oxford, 1979), 71 (1.3.9). Locke derived this information from his reading of Peter Martyr (Petrus Martyr d'Anghiera), *De Orbe Novo Decades Octo,* bk. 1.

7. See, for instance:
The cruel natives thirsted for their blood,
And issu'd furious from a neighbouring wood.
His friends all fell, by brutal rage o'er-power'd,
Their flesh the horrid *cannibals* devour'd.   ([3A], lines 15–18)

8. Stephen Greenblatt, *Marvelous Possessions: The Wonder of the New World* (Oxford, 1991), 136. Elsewhere in the same work, Greenblatt proposes a post-Freudian thesis that "the parabolic quality of otherness" invested in cannibalism may be witnessed through "its inverted, metaphoric representation" of one of the central rituals of Christian worship, the

"eucharist piety that ardently celebrated the eating of the sacred flesh and the drinking of the sacred blood" (45).

9. See particularly W. Arens, *The Man-Eating Myth: Anthropology and Anthropophagy* (New York, 1979), passim. So seriously were Arens's doubts concerning the veracity of cannibalism taken that the American Anthropological Association set up a special panel to audit its methods of research. After rigorous inquiry, most of the procedures that Arens attacked were vindicated (see Paula Brown and Donald Tuzin, eds., *The Ethnography of Cannibalism* [Washington, D.C., 1983]; also see Mary Douglas, *Risk and Blame: Essays in Cultural Theory* [London, 1992], 306–7). As Brown and Tuzin admit, however, such an investigation could not possibly validate the accuracy of historical claims, many of which will have been prone to exaggeration and embellishment, "the common *attribution* of cannibalism [being a plausible] . . . rhetorical device used ideologically by one group to assert its moral superiority over another" (3). Of particular interest in Arens's argument is his comparison of man-eating myths with parallel tales (which may appear easier to refute nowadays) concerning the putative engagement of Jews in ritual acts of child sacrifice. On the persistence of such myths concerning the Jews in eighteenth-century England, see my own *Anti-Semitic Stereotypes: A Paradigm of Otherness in English Popular Culture, 1660–1830* (Baltimore, 1995), 147–57.

10. Recognition of the inequities in European perceptions of the savage may be found as early as the sixteenth century, most notably in Michel de Montaigne's essay "Of Cannibals," which has long been claimed as a focal point for topical debate on the issue. Montaigne's contention that we commonly tend to consider barbaric anyone or anything that appears to us as alien or unfamiliar expresses well the one-sided nature of a Eurocentric discourse that consigns the native savage to the bestial while at the same moment implicitly condoning our own wretched and inhuman behavior. In addition to John Florio's famous translation (1603) of Montaigne, thought to have been tapped by Shakespeare as a source for *The Tempest,* Charles Cotton's frequently reprinted English rendition of 1685 will have been readily available to Steele and his contemporaries. There are many modern translations.

Similar views are expressed in the eighteenth century by, among others, William Hurd, *A New Universal History of the Religious Rites, Ceremonies, and Customs of the Whole World* (London, [ca. 1780]), 430, who blames "the almost total extirpation of the Caribbees" on the greed of European conquerors: "They seem to have been destroyed with a more violent spirit of fury than the rest of the Americans; and one would think that their conquerors, in order to palliate their [own] inhuman butcheries, had endeavoured to make them [Caribs] pass for the most unnatural monsters, who had neither law, nor religion; and, in a word, who had nothing human about them but their shape." Despite an impassioned defense of "the poor Caribbee," Hurd also includes a print titled "Natives of the Caribee Islands Feasting on Human Flesh" (fig. 1).

11. See Hoxie Neale Fairchild, *The Noble Savage: A Study in Romantic Naturalism* (New York, 1928), 80–86. Also Stelio Cro, *The Noble Savage: Allegory of Freedom* (Waterloo, Canada, 1990), and Gordon M. Sayre, *Les Sauvages Américains: Representations of Native Americans in French and English Colonial Literature* (Chapel Hill, N.C., 1997), 123–43, though neither author treats of Inkle and Yarico.

12. It should, of course, be noted that Milton stresses the connubial nature of Adam and Eve's lovemaking, whereas the relationship of Inkle and Yarico is extramarital.

13. White, *Tropics of Discourse,* particularly 188–94. See also Edward Dudley and Maximilian E. Novak, eds., *The Wild Man Within* (Pittsburgh, 1972).

14. He is so dubbed by H. D. Rankin, *Petronius the Artist* (The Hague, 1971), 39.

15. G. Legman, *The Horn Book: Studies in Erotic Folklore and Bibliography* (New York, 1964), 105.

16. Kathryn Shevelow, *Women and Print Culture: The Construction of Femininity in the Early Periodical* (London, 1989), 144.

17. Felicity Nussbaum, "The Politics of Difference," *Eighteenth-Century Studies* 23, no. 4 (1990): 375–76.

18. The story of the Ephesian matron was particularly popular in France, where it was frequently adapted. Laclos is said to have written a drama on the theme, though the text has not survived. Among English adaptations "had . . . from Petronius," Christopher Fry's verse drama *A Phoenix Too Frequent* (1946), should be mentioned. D. H. Greene casts serious doubt on claims that J. M. Synge's play *The Shadow of the Glen* (1903) was also indebted to Petronius's tale (see Greene, "The Shadow of the Glen and the Widow of Ephesus," *PMLA* 62 [1947]: 233–38). Its ostensible influence on James Joyce is explored by Jean Kimball, "An Ambiguous Faithlessness: Molly Bloom and the Widow of Ephesus," *James Joyce Quarterly* 31 (1994): 455–72.

19. Mary Wollstonecraft, *The Female Reader, or Miscellaneous Pieces, in Prose and Verse; Selected from the Best Writers, and Disposed under Proper Heads; for the Improvement of Young Women* (1789), reprinted in *The Works of Mary Wollstonecraft,* ed. Janet Todd and Marilyn Butler, 7 vols. (London, 1989), 4:97–99 (see also 5:179). Wollstonecraft's use of Inkle and Yarico as "a paradigm of slavery" is discussed by Moira Ferguson, *Colonialism and Gender Relations from Mary Wollstonecraft to Jamaica Kincaid* (New York, 1993), 11, 27.

20. David Dabydeen, *Hogarth's Blacks: Images of Blacks in Eighteenth Century Art* (Mundelstrup, Denmark, 1985), 108.

21. Rae Blanchard, "Richard Steele's West Indian Plantation," *Modern Philology* 39 (1942): 281–85. For some more recently discovered evidence of Steele's affairs in Barbados, see James Alsop, "Richard Steele and Barbados: Further Evidence," *Eighteenth-Century Life* 6, pt. 1 (1981): 21–28.

22. Peter Hulme, *Colonial Encounters: Europe and the Native Caribbean, 1492–1797* (London, 1986), 237.

23. The assumption that the author of this poem was a woman is made by Lawrence Marsden Price, *Inkle and Yarico Album* (Berkeley, Calif., 1937), 9, and accepted by most other critics (see, for instance, Moira Ferguson, *Subject to Others: British Women Writers and Colonial Slavery, 1670–1834* (London, 1992), 85–90). The evidence for this is that its invocation reads:

Ye virgin train, an artless *dame* inspire,
Unlearnt in schools, unblest with natal fire,
To save this story from devouring fate,
And the dire arts of faithless man relate.

Recently Martin Wechselblatt, "Gender and Race in Yarico's Epistles to Inkle: Voicing the Feminine/Slave," *Studies in Eighteenth-Century Culture* 19 (1989): 201, has questioned Price's conclusion by arguing that "the invocation may suggest that a male author has taken up Steele's strategy of placing Yarico's story in the mouth of a woman."

24. Another important example that illustrates well the facility with which English

writers randomly shuffled racial types is Stephen Duck's long poem *Avaro and Amanda; A Poem in Four Canto's, Taken from "The Spectator," Vol. I, No. XI* (first published in his *Poems on Several Occasions* [London, 1736]) [7]. In it Amanda (Duck's Yarico) is simultaneously represented as "An *Indian* princess" (157), "a *Moor*" (552) and "a doating *negro*" (556)!

25. Wylie Sypher, *Guinea's Captive Kings: British Anti-slavery Literature of the Eighteenth Century* (1942; reprinted New York, 1969), 129, 131.

26. Douglas Grant, *The Fortunate Slave: An Illustration of African Slavery in the Early Eighteenth Century* (Oxford, 1968), 122.

27. Joan Hamilton, "Inkle and Yarico and the Discourse of Slavery," *Restoration and Eighteenth Century Theatre Research* 9, no. 1 (1994): 22.

28. Prefatory remarks by Mrs. Inchbald to George Colman the Younger, *Inkle and Yarico; An Opera in Three Acts, British Theatre* 20 (1808). A rather acrimonious correspondence between Colman and Elizabeth Inchbald concerning her publication of his plays is found in Richard Brinsley Peake, *Memoirs of the Colman Family*, 2 vols. (London, 1841), 2:316–23. Colman picks up Mrs. Inchbald's error concerning the setting of Inkle and Yarico and remarks sarcastically that "it would be well for [her] to reflect that it may sometimes be necessary for a critic on one book to have read another" (318n).

29. *Monthly Review* 77 (1787): 389. In his overall estimation of the play, the reviewer finds "much more reason to applaud than to censure."

30. Black (or as they became known, "burnt cork") roles were almost invariably played by white actors. Very little evidence has been collected in support of more than the occasional presence, typically in minor roles, of genuine black actors on the eighteenth-century stage. Errol Hill cites Ignatius Sancho's aspiration to become an actor, a desire curtailed by a speech defect. "Of utmost significance," remarks Hill, "is the fact that in eighteenth-century England a black would-be actor could hope to be employed in an all-white company. . . . No such option existed in America at that time, nor would it exist for almost another two hundred years" (*Shakespeare in Sable: A History of Black Shakespearean Actors* [Amherst, Mass., 1984], 10). However, when the English clothier Henry Wansey attended a production of *Inkle and Yarico* before an audience of twelve hundred persons at Boston, Massachusetts, he was sufficiently struck to record that "one of the dramatis personae, was a negro, and he filled his character with great propriety" (*The Journal of an Excursion to the United States of North America, in the Summer of 1794* [Salisbury, 1796], 42). Clifford Ashby, who first drew theater historians to this account, remarks that "Wansey's comment indicates that the role was more than that of a supernumerary; . . . either the speaking role of "Dirty Runner" or that of "Servant" might well have been filled by a black without jarring the sensibilities of a white audience" ("A Black Actor on the Eighteenth Century Boston Stage?" *Theatre Survey: The American Journal of Theatre History* 28, no. 2 [1987]: 101–2).

31. Basil Francis, *Fanny Kelly of Drury Lane* (London, 1950), 42, 150. Cumberland's edition of Colman's *Inkle and Yarico* describes the costume worn by Inkle as "nankeen trowsers and jacket, white waistcoat, light hat, white stockings, black belt and hanger." By contrast, Yarico is exotically garbed in "white and coloured striped muslin dress, with coloured feathers and ornaments, leopard's skin drapery across one shoulder, dark flesh-coloured stockings and arms, sandals, various coloured feathers in head, a quantity of beads around the head, neck, wrists, arms, and ancles" (Cumberland's British Theatre, no. 111, n.d., c. 1827, p. 7).

32. Jim Davis, *John Liston, Comedian* (London, 1985), 55.

33. See Dale Cockrell, *Demons of Disorder: Early Blackface Minstrels and Their World* (Cambridge, 1997).

34. The contemporary popularity of exhibiting "piebalds" as curiosities of nature may also have encouraged stage practice. The best-known example was Primrose, "the Celebrated Piebald Boy," also known as "the Spotted Indian Youth." Born in St. Lucia in 1773, he was widely exhibited, including to the royal family at Windsor. An advertisement of 1795 describes this "most astonishing and wonderful Production of Human Nature": "His Head is covered with black and white Wool, his Breast, Arms, Legs, &c., are of a delicate white, equal to any Europeans, spotted and intermixed with black, resembling a beautiful Leopard, and in short, it is impossible to give the human imagination an adequate Idea of so matchless a rarity" (*A Biographical Dictionary of Actors, Actresses, Musicians, Dancers, Managers and Other Stage Personnel in London, 1660–1800*, ed. Philip H. Highfill Jr., Kalman A. Burnim, and Edward Langhans, 16 vols. (Carbondale, Ill., 1973–93), 12:163–64).

35. Roger Fiske, *English Theatre Music in the Eighteenth Century* (Oxford, 1973), 477. See also Phyllis T. Dircks, "London's Stepchild Finds a Home," in *Musical Theatre in America*, ed. Glenn Loney (Westport, Conn., 1984), 31–32.

36. Linda V. Troost, "Social Reform in Comic Opera: Colman's *Inkle and Yarico*," *Studies on Voltaire and the Eighteenth Century* 305 (1992): 1428.

37. Roger Anstey, *The Atlantic Slave Trade and British Abolition, 1760–1810* (London, 1975), 251. See also, inter alia, James Walvin, *England, Slaves and Freedom, 1776–1838* (Jackson, Miss., 1986); Anthony J. Barker, *The African Link: British Attitudes to the Negro in the Era of the Atlantic Slave Trade, 1550–1805* (London, 1978); and Folarin Shyllon, *Black Slaves in Britain* (London, 1974).

38. Mrs. Inchbald, prefatory remarks, 3.

39. Davis, *Problem of Slavery*, 12–13; Fiske, *English Theatre Music*, 477.

40. George Colman the Younger, *Plays by George Colman the Younger and Thomas Morton*, ed. Barry Sutcliffe (Cambridge, 1983), 14, 22.

41. George Colman the Younger, *Random Records*, 2 vols. (London, 1830), 2:180.

42. Peake, *Memoirs of the Colman Family*, 2:211. Details of Jekyll's life are given in the *Dictionary of National Biography* and in R. G. Thorne, *The House of Commons, 1790–1820*, 5 vols. (London, 1986), 4:296–99. Among others, Colman also read the play to Dr. Benjamin Moseley, an authority on the West Indies (see note 94 to the text of the play [12]).

43. Joseph Jekyll, "The Life of Ignatius Sancho," in *Letters of the Late Ignatius Sancho, an African*, 5th ed. (1803); facsimile edition with an introduction by Paul Edwards (London, 1968), vii–viii.

44. John Adolphus, *Memoirs of John Bannister, Comedian*, 2 vols. (London, 1839), 1:167–68.

45. Colman, *Plays by George Colman the Younger*, 23–24.

46. Prologue to *Inkle and Yarico*, Larpent manuscript, Huntington Library, no. LA 782. The prologue is dated 1789 but appears to refer to the first production of the play.

47. John O'Keefe, *The World in a Village* (London, 1793), 1.2.

48. *Monthly Review* 77 (1787): 389.

49. See Peter Thomson, "The Early Career of George Colman the Younger," in *Essays on Nineteenth Century British Theatre*, ed. Kenneth Richards and Peter Thomson (London, 1971), 73.

50. Paul Langford, *A Polite and Commercial People: England 1727–1783* (Oxford, 1989),

516. Langford sees sensibility as having more effect than economic arguments in bringing about the eventual abolition of the slave trade. More recently, G. J. Barker-Benfield, *The Culture of Sensibility: Sex and Society in Eighteenth-Century Britain* (Chicago, 1992), 224, citing Langford's linkage of sentimentalism and slavery, has written that a fundamental meaning of sensibility requires "a heightened awareness of suffering" and that "sensibility's galvanizing of 'public opinion' was fundamental to the remarkable legislative initiatives aimed at humanitarian reform during the last third of the century."

51. Price, 136, 138.

52. Price, 17–18, incorrectly cites the later publication in 1738 of these two poems in a separate volume as their first appearance. Of their author, "The Right Hon. the Countess of ****," he states that "nothing further is known." On the author's identification, see D. F. Foxon, *English Verse, 1701–1750*, 2 vols. (Cambridge, 1975), 1:723; Helen Sard Hughes, *The Gentle Hertford: Her Life and Letters* (New York, 1940), 419–20; and Roger Lonsdale, ed., *Eighteenth Century Women Poets: An Oxford Anthology* (Oxford, 1989), 105–9, 521. The 1738 volume contains some minor revisions to the poems.

53. Yet another poem that may belong to the same group is "Inkle and Yarico," written by James Cawthorne (1719–61) at Kirkby Londsdale in 1735, of which no copy has been traced. Based on this poem, Cawthorne is supposed to have composed *The Perjur'd Lover, or Tragical Adventure of Alexis and Boroina; in Heroic Verse, from the Story of Inkle and Yarico* (Sheffield, 1736). The book has the distinction of being considered the first Sheffield imprint, but again no copy has been located. Neither work appears in Cawthorne's *Poems* of 1771. See Alexander Chalmers, ed., *The Works of the English Poets*, 21 vols. (London, 1810), 14:229; *Gentleman's Magazine* 7 (1737): 578, and 59, no. 2 (1791): 1081–83; William Glasby, ed., *The Sheffield Miscellany*, 6 pts. (Sheffield, 1897), 5:187; Robert Eadon Leader, *Sheffield in the Eighteenth Century* (Sheffield, 1901), 121, 314; and Enid Gilberthorpe, *Books Printed by John Garnet, Sheffield's First Known Printer*, Sheffield City Libraries Local History Leaflets 13 (Sheffield, 1969), 2–3.

54. Gillian Beer, "'Our Unnatural No-Voice': The Heroic Epistle, Pope, and Women's Gothic," *Yearbook of English Studies* 12 (1982): 129–30.

55. Catherine E. Moore, "Robinson and Xury and Inkle and Yarico," *Modern Language Notes* 19 (1981): 24–29.

56. Hanna Fischer-Lamberg, ed., *Der junge Goethe*, 5 vols. (Berlin, 1963–74), 1:122: "J'ai commencé de former le Sujet d'Ynkle et d'Jariko pour le Theatre, mais j'y ai trouvé beaucoup plus de difficultés, que je ne croiois, et je n'espere pas d'en venir a bout." See also Price, 97–100; Ernst Beutler, *Essays um Goethe* (Leipzig, [1941]), 430–38.

57. See the introduction to Sébastian-Roch Nicolas Chamfort, *La jeune Indienne*, ed. Gilbert Chinard (Princeton, N.J., 1945), 30; Claude Arnaud, *Chamfort: A Biography*, trans. Deke Dusinberre (Chicago, 1992), 11–14; and Price, 57–59.

58. Price, 69–72; Charles Beecher Hogen, ed., *The London Stage, 1660–1800*, part 5, *1776–1800* (Carbondale, Ill., 1968), 1438. Among other versions of the tale in French, mention should be made of *La tribu indienne, ou Edouard et Stellina*, 2 vols. (Paris, 1799), written by Lucien Bonaparte, the brother of Napoleon. Price records (68–69, 162–63) that the work went through at least three editions in French and was twice translated into German.

59. *London Magazine* 27 (1758): 168.

60. William Alexander, M.D., *The History of Women*, 2 vols. (London, 1779), 1:291.

61. Robert Burns, "On Seeing M^rs. Kemble in Yarico—," in *The Poems and Songs of*

Robert Burns, ed. James Kinsley, 3 vols. (Oxford, 1968), 2:746. As Kinsley notes, "the allusion . . . is to Moses, who struck the rock in Horeb to give the Israelites water (Exod. xvii)." See also *The Letters of Robert Burns,* 2d ed., ed. G. Ross Roy, 2 vols. (Oxford, 1985), 2:314, 321.

The ongoing popularity through the lowlands of Scotland of touring productions of *Inkle and Yarico* is attested by an early memory of the encyclopedist Robert Chambers (1802–71), who recalled as a child accompanying his elder brother, William, to see a strolling company perform the play in his native Peebles. The play was given a makeshift but enthusiastic performance in the cramped upper room of a public house after the acting chief magistrate, an eccentric old Calvinist known as Tammas, refused permission to use the town hall as a theater. "I'll oppose it with all the means in my poo'er, sir!" responded Tammas fiercely to the actor making the solicitation. "Not with the hatchet, I hope, sir," retorted the nonchalant thespian (John Lehmann, *Ancestors and Friends* [London, 1962], 99; *Man of Letters: The Early Life and Love Letters of Robert Chambers* [Edinburgh, 1990], 20).

62. William Hazlitt, *The Complete Works of William Hazlitt,* ed. P. P. Howe, 21 vols. (London, 1930–34), 18:354 (review from *London Magazine,* August 1820).

63. Charles Lamb, "Miss Kelly at Bath," 7 February 1819, in *The Life, Letters and Writings of Charles Lamb,* ed. Percy Fitzgerald, 6 vols. (London, n.d.), 6:207–8.

64. Duncan Wu, *Wordsworth's Reading, 1770–1799* (Cambridge, 1993), 131.

65. Mary Jacobus, *Tradition and Experiment in Wordsworth's Lyrical Ballads (1798)* (Oxford, 1976), 193. See also Hulme, *Colonial Encounters,* 229 and Wechselblatt, "Gender and Race," 223n.

66. See William Wordsworth, *Lyrical Ballads,* ed. Michael Mason (London, 1992), 173–76, 376, 386–87.

67. Robert Mayo, "The Contemporaneity of the 'Lyrical Ballads,'" *Publications of the Modern Language Association of America* 69 (1954): 486–522.

68. Alan Bewell, *Wordsworth and the Enlightenment* (New Haven, Conn., 1989), 31–32.

69. Mary Jacobus, *Romanticism, Writing and Sexual Difference* (Oxford, 1989), has remarked (chap. 3) on the virtual absence of reference to the slave trade in *The Prelude* (1805), completed just two years before the British abolition. A single explicit passage attacking "the traffickers in Negro blood" (10.206) accentuates the near audible detachment from the subject in the rest of the poem. Jacobus notes that "the history of Wordsworth's relations towards the slave-trade is complicated by the fact that he numbered among his friends the sons of prominent Bristol sugar merchants and wealthy Nevis plantation owners . . . ; Bristol was at this point Britain's second largest slaving port as well as closely tied by its mercantile economy to the sugar-producing West Indian colonies." Paradoxically, in an accompanying note to a copy of the second edition of *Lyrical Ballads* (1800) given to the abolitionist William Wilberforce, Wordsworth inscribed himself as "a Fellow-labourer . . . in the same Vineyard" (Jacobus, 72–73n). The omission in *Lyrical Ballads* of any direct allusion to slavery, one of the most topical issues in the 1790s, raises important questions concerning Wordsworth's radicalism.

70. Price, 19.

71. Wu, *Wordsworth's Reading,* 34–35, lists Colman's later play *The Iron Chest* (1796) in his catalog of Wordsworth's reading but makes no reference to *Inkle and Yarico.*

72. Wordsworth, *Lyrical Ballads,* ed. Mason, 376.

73. For a listing of further connections of the idea of the Noble Savage in Wordsworth, see Fairchild, *Noble Savage,* 172–91.

74. Paul Hazard, *European Thought in the Eighteenth Century* (1946; London, 1973), 366.

75. Among early nineteenth-century versions, Price, 159, cites the *Lady's Magazine* 33 (1802): 215–16, 436–37, 495–96, and 714–15, containing verses by W. Smith and John Webb, constituting a two-way correspondence between Inkle and Yarico. Price fails to mention either Paul Methuen's *An Epistle from Yarico to Incle, and Other Poems* (London, 1810), a copy of which may be consulted in the British Library, or Anna Maria Porter's "Epistle from Yarico to Inkle," included in *Ballad Romances and Other Poems* (London, 1811), 101–19 (15).

A much later prose fiction—also omitted from consideration by Price—which shows a strong measure of indebtedness to Inkle and Yarico is George Eliot's neglected short story "Brother Jacob" (1860). After buying "the story of "Inkle and Yarico, which made him feel sorry for poor Mr Inkle," the unscrupulous pastry cook in Eliot's ironic moral fable dreams of sailing to the West Indies, where he believes it "probable that some Princess Yarico would want him to marry her, and make him presents of very large jewels" (Blackwood edition [Edinburgh, n.d.], 309, 319). He steals from his mother to pay for his passage to Jamaica, discovers after six years that no "gullible princess awaited him" there (324), and receives his true comeuppance only after his return to England. The appropriation of the eighteenth-century tale as an exemplum of the excesses of economic individualism is discussed by Peter Allan Dale in "George Eliot's 'Brother Jacob': Fables and the Physiology of Common Life," *Philological Quarterly* 64 (1985): 17–35.

76. Barbara Fass, *La Belle Dame sans Merci and the Aesthetics of Romanticism* (Detroit, 1974), 22.

77. Edward W. Said, *Culture and Imperialism* (London, 1993), 70, 256.

78. Hulme, *Colonial Encounters,* 228.

79. Philip Young, "The Mother of Us All: Pocahontas," in *Three Bags Full: Essays in American Fiction* (New York, 1967), 175–203. For a fuller study of the myth, see Robert S. Tilton, *Pocahontas: The Evolution of an American Narrative* (Cambridge, 1994). Neither work extends to a discussion of Inkle and Yarico.

80. F. A. Hoyos, *Barbados: A History from the Amerindians to Independence* (London, 1978), 39. The quotation is taken from Richard Ligon's account, and it seems likely that Inkle's putative ending has been erroneously confused with that of Ligon, who returned to England because of ill health. The account given by Hoyos accords with Ligon in ascribing the boy's paternity to a household servant rather than to Inkle.

ENGLISH VERSIONS
and Some Translations

I

Richard Ligon, *A True and Exact History of the Island of Barbadoes* (Extracts)

From the second edition (1673), 43–59, 65.[1]

Two short paragraphs in Richard Ligon's personal and historical memoir of Barbados provide the kernel from which Steele came to fashion the tale of Inkle and Yarico. According to Ligon, Yarico was a beautiful freeborn Indian slave at the plantation house where he dwelled. He divulges that she had become pregnant by an unidentified white servant and gave birth to "a lusty boy, frolick and lively." Ligon details the circumstance of her enslavement by recounting that she had been brought to Barbados from the mainland by a nameless young Englishman, whose life she had preserved when he and his companions had been attacked by Indians. By way of reward for her love, upon reaching Barbados he had nonchalantly sold her into slavery, and "so poor *Yarico* . . . lost her liberty." Later, in describing the painful effect of chiggers, a particularly nasty tropical mite, Ligon briefly records that Yarico removed ten from his foot in a morning.

Richard Ligon (ca. 1589–1662) visited the English colony of Barbados between 1647 and 1650, at a critical time in the development of the transatlantic slave trade. From being a tobacco island in the early years of its settlement, Barbados was undergoing a rapid but uneasy transition to the far more labor-intensive cultivation of sugarcane. Where tobacco had chiefly been grown on smallholdings, sugarcane necessitated large plantations. A system of labor that in the past had relied on indentured servants mainly from the British isles was no longer providing an adequate number of work-

---

1. In this selection, the page numbers cited in the headnote and footnotes refer to the 1673 text of Ligon's work.

ers for the far more complex process of running the sugar plantations. Because Caribs were in short supply, traders turned increasingly to the coast of West Africa as an abundant source for the lucrative traffic in slaves. Despite Ligon's higher tally of the number of blacks, it has been estimated that when he visited Barbados the white population still exceeded the aggregate of slaves, but by the early eighteenth century transported Africans had outstripped the total of Europeans by about three to one (see Dunn, *Sugar and Slaves*, 87).

Of Richard Ligon himself comparatively little is known. The *History* is his sole published work, and from it we can glean only meager facts about him. A man of genteel background, he appears to have suffered in his personal life as a consequence of the Civil War in England. At the time of his visit to Barbados, he records that he was "above sixty years" and that he had escaped from his native land after "having lost (by a barbarous riot) all that I had gotten by the painful travels and cares of my youth; by which means I was stript and rifled of all I had, left destitute of a subsistence, and brought to such an exigent, as I must famish or fly" (1). In the company of a royalist friend, Colonel Thomas Modyford, he set sail for the West Indies "on the good ship called the *Achilles*, a vessel of 350 tons," diverting to the coast of Africa "to trade for *negroes*, horses and cattle; which we were to sell at the *Barbadoes*" (1–2).

Shortly after their arrival, Modyford bought into the five-hundred-acre plantation estate of Major William Hilliard, which Ligon enumerates as being populated by "*negroes* and *Indian* slaves, with 96 *negroes*, and three *Indian* women, with their children; 28 Christians [white servants], 45 cattle for work, 8 milch cows, a dozen horses, and mares, 16 assinigoes" (22). Many of Ligon's most vivid observations are based on his experience at this plantation, though his eyewitness account ranges freely from a natural history of the island to remarks on the architecture and design of plantation houses, and from the economics of growing sugar cane to the cadences of music as practiced by black slaves. Modyford remained in the Caribbean, being elevated to the rank of governor of Jamaica in 1664 (see *DNB*), but after suffering a severe deterioration in his health, Ligon was to sail home to England in 1660. There he was summarily incarcerated in London's Upper Bench prison "by the subtle practices of some, whom I have formerly called friends" (121), and it was in jail that he was to write his *History . . . of Barbadoes*. Though he is believed to have been released, his latter days are shrouded in obscurity.

It is Ligon's distinct achievement to have chronicled an important stage in the advent of British dominance of the transatlantic slave trade. The decline of indentured servitude after the 1640s was more than matched by the exponential increase in the number of black slaves shipped over from Africa. The cruelties inflicted on white servants were indiscriminately transferred to these blacks, but too often they were endorsed by a common assumption that as savages, who were less than human and devoid of human souls, they were unworthy of better treatment. The mythical status with which the sensibility of the Enlightenment was to endow the story of Inkle and Yarico makes far greater sense if we are to see it as an emotional response to the iniquities of slavery as witnessed, among others, by Ligon. The extracts chosen here provide a graphic description of a culture in which white servants, black slaves, native American Indians, and plantation owners were thrown together cheek by jowl in response to an increasing European demand for a single commodity. Yarico's enslavement (emblematic as it became of the tragic predicament of countless others) was the bittersweet offering so casually surrendered for the taste of sugar.

The fullest and most reliable account of Richard Ligon is Campbell, "Richard Ligon." See also Morgan, "'Some Could Suckle over Their Shoulder.'"

Ligon's *History* was first published in 1657 and reprinted in 1673. A French translation appeared in 1674. The text reproduced here is taken from the second edition of 1673. It has been collated with the 1657 text, and several minor corrections have been silently incorporated.

The Number and Nature of the Inhabitants

It were somewhat difficult, to give you an exact account, of the number of persons upon the island; there being such store of shipping that brings passengers daily to the place, but it has been conjectur'd, by those that are long acquainted, and best seen in the knowledge of the island, that there are not less than 50 thousand souls, besides[2] *negroes;* and some of them who began upon small fortunes, are now risen to very great and vast estates.

The island is divided into three sorts of men, *viz.* masters, servants, and slaves. The slaves and their posterity, being subject to their masters for ever,

2. *besides* Other than, excepting.

are kept and preserv'd with greater care than the servants, who are theirs
but for five years, according to the law of the island. So that for the time,
the servants have the worser lives, for they are put to very hard labour, ill
lodging, and their diet very slight. When we came first on the island, some
planters themselves did not eat bone meat, above twice a week: the rest of
the seven days, potatoes, loblolly,[3] and bonavist.[4] But the servants no bone
meat at all, unless an oxe died: and then they were feasted, as long as that
lasted. And till they had planted good store of plantines,[5] the *negroes* were
fed with this kind of food; but most of it bonavist, and loblolly, with some
ears of maize toasted, which food (especially loblolly,) gave them much discontent: But when they had plantines enough to serve them, they were
heard no more to complain; for 'tis a food they take great delight in, and
their manner of dressing, and eating it, is this: 'tis gathered for them (somewhat before it be ripe, for so they desire to have it,) upon *Saturday,* by the
keeper of the plantine grove; who is an able *negro,* and knows well the number of those that are to be fed with this fruit; and as he gathers, lays them
all together, till they fetch them away, which is about five a clock in the
afternoon, for that day they break off work sooner by an hour: partly for
this purpose, and partly for that the fire in the furnaces is to be put out,
and the ingenio[6] and the rooms made clean; besides they are to wash, shave
and trim themselves against *Sunday.* But 'tis a lovely sight to see a hundred
handsome *negroes,* men and women, with every one a grass-green bunch of
these fruits on their heads, every bunch twice as big as their heads, all coming in a train one after another, the black and green so well becoming one
another. Having brought this fruit home to their own houses, and pilling[7]
off the skin of so much as they will use, they boil it in water, making it into
balls, and so they eat it. One bunch a week is a *negro*'s allowance. To this,
no bread nor drink, but water. Their lodging at night a board, with noth-

---

3. *loblolly* A thick gruel made out of maize. Elsewhere Ligon remarks on how unpopu-
lar this was among the slaves: "The *negroes,* when they come to be fed with this, are much
discontented, and cry out, *O! O! no more lob-lob*" (31).

4. *bonavist* "A species of tropical pulse" (*OED*).

5. *plantines* Plantains, "tree-like tropical herbaceous plant . . . closely allied to the Banana" (*OED*). Ligon later notes that "the bonano differs nothing from the plantine, in the
body and leaves, but only this, that the leaves are somewhat less, and the body has here and
there some blackish spots. . . . This tree wants a little of the beauty of the plantine" (81–82).

6. *ingenio* The term used for a sugar mill in the West Indies during the seventeenth and
early eighteenth centuries.

7. *pilling* Peeling.

ing under, nor any thing a top of them. They are happy people, whom so little contents. Very good servants, if they be not spoiled by the *English*. But more of them hereafter.

[Servants][8]

As for the usage of the servants, it is much as the master is, merciful or cruel. Those that are merciful, treat their servants well, both in their meat, drink, and lodging, and give them such work, as is not unfit for Christians to do. But if the masters be cruel, the servants have very wearisome and miserable lives. Upon the arrival of any ship, that brings servants to the island, the planters go aboard; and having bought such of them as they like, send them with a guide to his plantation; and being come, commands them instantly to make their cabins, which they not knowing how to do, are to be advised by other of their servants, that are their seniors; but, if they be churlish, and will not shew them, or if materials be wanting, to make them cabins, then they are to lie on the ground that night. These cabins are to be made of sticks, withes,[9] and plantine leaves, under some little shade that may keep the rain off; their suppers being a few potatoes for meat, and water or mobbie[10] for drink. The next day they are rung out with a bell to work, at six a clock in the morning, with a severe overseer to command them, till the bell ring again, which is at eleven a clock; and then they return, and are set to dinner, either with a mess[11] of loblolly, bonavist, or potatoes. At one a clock, they are rung out again to the field, there to work till six, and then home again, to a supper of the same. And if it chance to rain, and wet them

8. *Servants* Ligon refers in this section of his *History* to white indentured servants, in later years known commonly as redlegs. After their period of servitude, those who remained on Barbados came to constitute a disadvantaged underclass of poor whites. See Sheppard, *"Redlegs" of Barbados.*

9. *withes* Flexible stems taken from a West Indian creeping plant. Ligon describes the withe as "the harmfullest weed that can grow," yet one that can "serve for all uses where ropes or cords are required, as for binding our wood and canes into faggots, or what else ropes are needful for" (96–97).

10. *mobbie* Elsewhere Ligon describes this spirituous liquor as "the drink most generally used in the island." It is distilled, he says, "of [sweet] potatoes . . . the drink it self, being temperately made, does not at all fly up into the head, but is a sprightly thirst-quenching drink" (31). It should not be confused with its near homonym *mauby,* a bittersweet local drink still made today by boiling the bark of the mauby tree. Allsopp, *Dictionary of Caribbean English Usage,* 376, notes that "the transfer of the name to a drink made from a fermented bark . . . could have been a later folk adaptation in the slave era."

11. *mess* Meal, serving.

through, they have no shift, but must lie so all night. If they put off their clothes, the cold of the night will strike into them; and if they be not strong men, this ill lodging will put them into a sickness: if they complain, they are beaten by the overseer; if they resist, their time is doubled. I have seen an overseer beat a servant with a cane about the head, till the blood has followed, for a fault that is not worth the speaking of; and yet he must have patience, or worse will follow. Truly, I have seen such cruelty there done to servants, as I did not think one Christian could have done to another. But, as discreeter and better natur'd men have come to rule there, the servants' lives have been much bettered; for now, most of the servants lie in hammocks[12] and in warm rooms, and when they come in wet, have shift of shirts and drawers, which is all the clothes they wear, and are fed with *bone meat* twice or thrice a week. Colonel *Walrond*[13] seeing his servants when they came home, toiled with their labour, and wet through with their sweating, thought that shifting of their linen not sufficient refreshing, nor warmth for their bodies, their pores being much opened by their sweating; and therefore resolved to send into *England* for rug gowns, such as poor people wear in hospitals, that so when they had shifted themselves, they might put on those gowns, and lie down and rest them in their hammocks: For the hammocks being but thin, and they having nothing on but shirts and drawers, when they awak'd out of their sleeps, they found themselves very cold; and a cold taken there is harder to be recovered than in *England,* by how much the body is enfeebled by the great toil, and the sun's heat, which cannot but very much exhaust the spirits of bodies unaccustomed to it. But this care and charity of Colonel *Walrond's,* lost him nothing in the conclusion; for, he got such love of his servants; as they thought all too little they could do for him; and the love of the servants there, is of much concernment to the masters, not only in their diligent and painful labour, but in foreseeing and preventing mischiefs that often happen; by the carelessness

12. *hammocks* It deserves noting that the term (deriving as it does from the Spanish *hamiaca*) is of Caribbean origin, entering the English language about a century before Ligon. *OED* quotes Richard Eden, ca. 1555, "Theyr hangynge beddes whiche they caule *Hamacas*" (*Decades of the New Worlde or West India,* 200).

13. *Colonel Walrond* Humphrey Walrond (1600?–1670?) arrived in Barbados in 1649, having previously sided with the royalist cause in England. In 1653 he enlisted in the Spanish service, for which he was granted the title Marquess de Vallado. After the Restoration of Charles II, he was appointed deputy governor of Barbados but was summarily removed from office in 1663. When a revolt he led failed, he fled the island and is supposed to have died in some part of the West Indies under Spanish rule. See *DNB*

and slothfulness of retchless[14] servants; sometimes by laying fire so negligently, as whole lands of canes and houses too, are burnt down and consumed, to the utter ruin and undoing of their masters: For, the materials there being all combustible and apt to take fire, a little oversight, as the fire of a tobacco-pipe, being knocked out against a dry stump of a tree, has set it on fire, and the wind fanning that fire, if a land of canes be but near, and they once take fire, all that are down the wind will be burnt up. Water there is none to quench it, or if it were, a hundred *negroes* with buckets were not able to do it; so violent and spreading a fire this is, and such a noise it makes, as if two armies, with a thousand shot of either side, were continually giving fire, every knot of every cane, giving as great a report as a pistol. So that there is no way to stop the going on of this flame, but by cutting down and removing all the canes that grow before it, for the breadth of twenty or thirty foot down the wind, and there the *negroes* to stand and beat out the fire, as it creeps upon the ground, where the canes are cut down. And I have seen some *negroes* so earnest to stop this fire, as with their naked feet to tread, and with their naked bodies to tumble, and roll upon it; so little they regard their own smart[15] or safety, in respect of their master's benefit. The year before I came away, there were two eminent planters in the island, that with such an accident as this, lost at least 10000 l. sterling, in the value of the canes that were burnt; the one, Mr. *James Holduppe,* the other, Mr. *Constantine Silvester:* And the latter had not only his canes, but his house burnt down to the ground.[16] This, and much more mischief has been done, by the negligence and wilfulness of servants. And yet some cruel masters will provoke their servants so, by extreme ill usage, and often and cruel beating

14. *retchless* Reckless, "careless in respect of some duty or task" (*OED*).

15. *smart* Physical pain.

16. *James Holduppe . . . Constantine Silvester* Colonel James Holdip is credited with having been the first English settler in Barbados to establish a sugar plantation during the early 1640s. The attempt by disgruntled white servants to destroy his plantation by arson is one of the earliest recorded incidents of resistance against the system. According to Beckles, *White Servitude and Black Slavery,* 109–10, Holdip "bartered fifty acres of cleared land for twenty-five male servants. . . . Apparently he mistreated these servants, who . . . burned his house and crop." Dunn, *Sugar and Slaves,* 62n, remarks that the fire caused Holdip "a loss of £10,000, and thereafter he tried Surinam and Jamaica, but returned to England in 1658." Constantine Silvester, an active puritan, settled in Barbados rather later than Holdip and, although politically opposed to them, married into the pro-royalist Walrond family (see Bridenbaugh and Bridenbaugh, *No Peace beyond the Line,* 132). Silvester's plantation is not included under his own name on the map of Barbados that appeared as a frontispiece to Ligon's *History.*

them, as they grow desperate, and so join together to revenge themselves upon them.

A little before I came from thence, there was such a combination amongst them, as the like was never seen before. Their sufferings being grown to a great height, and their daily complainings to one another (of the intolerable burdens they labour'd under) being spread throughout the island; at the last, some amongst them, whose spirits were not able to endure such slavery, resolved to break through it, or die in the act; and so conspired with some others of their acquaintance, whose sufferings were equal, if not above theirs; and their spirits no way inferior, resolved to draw as many of the discontented party into this plot, as possibly they could; and those of this persuasion, were the greatest numbers of servants in the island. So that a day was appointed to fall upon their masters, and cut all their throats, and by that means, to make themselves not only freemen, but masters of the island. And so closely was this plot carried, as no discovery was made, till the day before they were to put it in act: And then one of them, either by the failing of his courage, or some new obligation from the love of his master, revealed this long plotted conspiracy; and so by this timely advertisement, the masters were saved: Justice *Hethersall*[17] (whose servant this was) sending letters to all his friends, and they to theirs, and so one to another, till they were all secured; and, by examination, found out the greatest part of them; whereof eighteen of the principal men in the conspiracy, and they the first leaders and contrivers of the plot, were put to death, for example to the rest. And the reason why they made examples of so many, was, they found these so haughty in their resolutions, and so incorrigible, as they were like enough to become actors in a second plot, and so they thought good to secure them; and for the rest, to have a special eye over them.

Negroes

It has been accounted a strange thing, that the *negroes,* being more than double the numbers of the Christians that are there, and they accounted a bloody people, where they think they have power or advantages; and the more bloody, by how much they are more fearful than others: that these

17. *Justice Hethersall* This seems to have been Thomas Hothersall, who owned a plantation of one thousand acres (see Beckles, *White Servitude and Black Slavery,* 20–22). Though the attempted rebellion of 1647 by white servants against the intolerable conditions in which they were kept was ruthlessly suppressed, their simmering discontent was probably behind the torching of the Holdip and Silvester plantations that Ligon records.

should not commit some horrid massacre upon the Christians, thereby to enfranchise themselves, and become masters of the island. But there are three reasons that take away this wonder; the one is, they are not suffered to touch or handle any weapons: The other, That they are held in such awe and slavery, as they are fearful to appear in any daring act; and seeing the mustering of our men, and hearing their gun-shot, (than which nothing is more terrible to them) their spirits are subjugated to so low a condition, as they dare not look up to any bold attempt. Besides these, there is a third reason, which stops all designs of that kind, and that is, They are fetch'd from several parts of *Africa,* who speak several languages, and by that means, one of them understands not another: For, some of them are fetch'd from *Guinny* and *Binny,* some from *Cutchew,* some from *Angola,* and some from the river of *Gambia.*[18] And in some of these places where petty kingdoms are, they sell their subjects, and such as they take in battle, whom they make slaves; and some mean men sell their servants, their children, and some-times their wives; and think all good traffic, for such commodities as our merchants send them.

When they are brought to us, the planters buy them out of the ship, where they find them stark naked, and therefore cannot be deceived in any outward infirmity. They choose them as they do horses in a market; the strongest, youthfullest, and most beautiful, yield the greatest prices. Thirty pound sterling is a price for the best man *negro;* and twenty five, twenty six, or twenty seven pound for a woman; the children are at easier rates. And we buy them so as the sexes may be equal; for, if they have more men than women, the men who are unmarried will come to their masters, and com-plain, that they cannot live without wives, and desire him, they may have wives. And he tells them, that the next ship that comes, he will buy them wives, which satisfies them for the present; and so they expect the good time: which the master performing with them, the bravest fellow is to choose first, and so in order, as they are in place; and every one of them knows his better, and gives him the precedence, as cows do one another, in passing through a narrow gate; for, the most of them are as near beasts as may be, setting their souls aside. Religion they know none; yet most of them

18. *Guinny . . . Gambia* In the period Ligon described, most slaves imported into Bar-bados were sold by Dutch merchants, who had taken them mainly from present-day Angola, Ghana, Togo, and Dahomey. Ligon's stated sources of the transatlantic slave trade cover much of the West African coast, including Guinea, Benin (Binny), and Cacheu in Portuguese Guinea (Cutchew).

acknowledge a God, as appears by their motions and gestures: For, if one of them do another wrong, and he cannot revenge himself, he looks up to heaven for vengeance, and holds up both his hands, as if the power must come from thence, that must do him right. Chaste they are as any people under the sun; for, when the men and women are together naked, they never cast their eyes towards the parts that ought to be covered; and those amongst us, that have breeches and petticoats, I never saw so much as a kiss, or embrace, or a wanton glance with their eyes between them. Jealous they are of their wives, and hold it for a great injury and scorn, if another man make the least courtship to his wife. And if any of their wives have two children at a birth, they conclude her false to his bed, and so no more ado but hang her.[19] We had an excellent *negro* in the plantation, whose name was *Macow*, and was our chief musician; a very valiant man; and was keeper of our plantine-grove. This *negro's* wife was brought to bed of two children and her husband, as their manner is, had provided a cord to hang her. But the overseer finding what he was about to do, informed the master of it, who sent for *Macow*, to dissuade him from this cruel act, of murdering his wife, and used all persuasions that possibly he could, to let him see, that such double births are in nature, and that diverse precedents were to be found amongst us of the like; so that we rather praised our wives, for their fertility, than blamed them for their falseness. But this prevailed little with him, upon whom custom had taken so deep an impression; but resolved, the next thing he did, should be to hang her. Which when the master perceived, and that the ignorance of the man, should take away the life of the woman, who was innocent of the crime her husband condemned her for, told him plainly, that if he hang'd her, he himself should be hang'd by[20] her, upon the same boughs and therefore wish'd him to consider what he did. This threatning wrought more with him than all the reasons of philosophy that could be given him; and so let her alone; but he never car'd much for her afterward, but chose another which he lik'd better. For the planters there

19. *And if . . . hang her* Before the mid-eighteenth century, it was a tribal belief among the (Nigerian) Yoruba people and some of their west African neighbors that the birth of twins was a monstrous aberration, commonly precipitating murder and infanticide. Later attitudes reversed this idea, however, making the birth of twins (*ibeji*) a particular blessing (see Fagg, Pemberton, and Holcombe, *Yoruba*, 80). African slaves taken to the West Indies brought many of their indigenous customs and beliefs with them.

20. *by* Alongside.

deny not a slave, that is a brave fellow, and one that has extraordinary qualities, two or three wives, and above that number they seldom go: But no woman is allowed above one husband.

At the time the wife is to be brought a bed, her husband removes his board, (which is his bed) to another room (for many several divisions they have, in their little houses, and none above six foot square) and leaves his wife to God, and her good fortune, in the room, and upon the board alone, and calls a neighbour to come to her, who gives little help to her delivery, but when the child is born, (which she calls her pickaninny)[21] she helps to make a little fire near her feet, and that serves instead of possets, broths, and caudles.[22] In a fortnight, this woman is at work with her pickaninny at her back, as merry a soul as any is there: If the overseer be discreet, she is suffer'd to rest her self a little more than ordinary; but if not, she is compelled to do as others do. Times they have of suckling their children in the fields, and refreshing themselves; and good reason, for they carry burthens on their backs; and yet work too. Some women, whose pickaninnies are three years old, will, as they work at weeding, which is a stooping work, suffer the he[23] pickaninny, to sit a stride upon their backs, like St. *George* a horse-back;[24] and there spur his mother with his heels, and sings and crows on her back, clapping his hands, as if he meant to fly; which the mother is so pleas'd with, as she continues her painful stooping posture, longer than she would do, rather than discompose her jovial pickaninny of his pleasure, so glad she is to see him merry. The work which the women do, is most of it weeding, a stooping and painful work; at noon and night they are call'd home by the ring of a bell, where they have two hours time for their repast at noon; and at night, they rest from six, till six a clock next morning.

On *Sunday* they rest, and have the whole day at their pleasure; and the

21. *pickaninny* "A little one, a child: commonly applied in the West Indies and America to negro and coloured children" (*OED*). Ligon provides here the earliest *OED* reference.

22. *possets . . . caudles* Warm drinks. A posset was "composed of hot milk curdled with . . . liquor, often with sugar, spices or other ingredients," and a caudle was "a warm drink consisting of thin gruel mixed with wine or ale, sweetened and spiced" (*OED*). As well as broths, these were among the more familiar English country remedies administered to mothers in childbirth.

23. *he* Boy.

24. *St. George a horse-back* St. George, the patron saint of England, is traditionally depicted on horseback.

most of them use it as a day of rest and pleasure; but some of them who will make benefit of that day's liberty, go where the mangrave trees[25] grow, and gather the bark, of which they make ropes, which they truck away[26] for other commodities, as shirts and drawers.

In the afternoons on *Sundays,* they have their music, which is of kettle drums, and those of several sizes; upon the smallest the best musician plays, and the other come in as choruses: the drum, all men know, has but one tone; and therefore variety of tunes have little to do in this music; and yet so strangely they vary their time, as 'tis a pleasure to the most curious ears, and it was to me one of the strangest noises that ever I heard made of one tone; and if they had the variety of tune, which gives the greater scope in music, as they have of time, they would do wonders in that art. And if I had not fallen sick before my coming away, at least seven months in one sickness, I had given them some hints of tunes, which being understood, would have serv'd as a great addition to their harmony; for time without tune, is not an eighth part of the science of music.

I found *Macow* very apt for it of himself, and one day coming into the house, (which none of the *negroes* used to do, unless an officer, as he was,) he found me playing on a theorbo,[27] and singing to it, which he hearkened very attentively to; and when I had done, he took the theorbo in his hand, and strook one string, stopping it by degrees upon every fret, and finding the notes to vary, till it came to the body of the instrument; and that the nearer the body of the instrument he stopped, the smaller or higher the sound was, which he found was by the shortening of the string, considered with himself, how he might make some trial of this experiment upon such an instrument as he could come by; having no hope ever to have any instrument of this kind to practise on. In a day or two after, walking in the plantine grove, to refresh me in that cool shade, and to delight myself with the sight of those plants, which are so beautiful, as though they left a fresh impression in me when I parted with them, yet upon a review, something is discern'd in their beauty more than I remembered at parting: which

25. *mangrave trees* Mangrove. "The mangrave is a tree of such note, as she must not be forgotten; . . . she is of great extent . . . that . . . may very well hide a troop of horse. The bark of this tree being well ordered, will make very strong ropes, and the *Indians* make it as fine as flax, and spin it into fine thread, whereof they make hammocks, and diverse other things they wear" (Ligon, 72).

26. *truck away* Exchange, barter.

27. *theorbo* "A large kind of lute . . . much in vogue in the 17th century" (*OED*).

caused me to make often repair thither, I found this *negro* (whose office it was to attend there) being the keeper of that grove, sitting on the ground, and before him a piece of large timber, upon which he had laid cross, six billets,[28] and having a handsaw and a hatchet by him, would cut the billets by little and little, till he had brought them to the tunes, he would fit them to; for the shorter they were, the higher the notes, which he tried by knocking upon the ends of them with a stick, which he had in his hand. When I found him at it, I took the stick out of his hand, and tried the sound, finding the six billets to have six distinct notes, one above another, which put me in a wonder, how he of himself, should without teaching do so much. I then shewed him the difference between flats and sharps, which he presently apprehended, as between *Fa,* and *Mi:* and he would have cut two more billets to those tunes, but I had then no time to see it done, and so left him to his own enquiries. I say thus much to let you see that some of these people are capable of learning arts.

Another, of another kind of speculation I found; but more ingenious than he: and this man with three or four more, were to attend me into the woods, to cut church ways,[29] for I was employed sometimes upon public works; and those men were excellent axe-men, and because there were many gullies in the way, which were impassable, and by that means I was compell'd to make traverses, up and down in the wood; and was by that in danger to miss of the point, to which I was to make my passage to the church, and therefore was fain to take a compass with me, which was a circumferenter,[30] to make my traverses the more exact, and indeed without which, it could not be done, setting up the circumferenter, and observing the needle: This *negro Sambo* comes to me, and seeing the needle wag, desired to know the reason of its stirring, and whether it were alive: I told him no, but it stood upon a point, and for a while it would stir, but by and by stand still, which he observ'd and found it to be true.

The next question was, why it stood one way, and would not remove to any other point. I told him that it would stand no way but north and south, and upon that shew'd him the four cardinal points of the compass, east, west, north, south, which he presently learnt by heart, and promis'd me never to forget it. His last question was, why it would stand north. I

28. *billets* Pieces of wood.
29. *church ways* Paths leading to the church.
30. *circumferenter* An instrument equipped with a magnetic needle for use in surveying, eventually superseded by the theodolite.

gave this reason, because of the huge rocks of loadstone that were in the north part of the world, which had a quality to draw iron to it; and this needle being of iron, and touch'd with a loadstone, it would always stand that way.

This point of philosophy was a little too hard for him, and so he stood in a strange muse; which to put him out of, I bade him reach his axe, and put it near to the compass, and remove it about; and as he did so, the needle turned with it, which put him in the greatest admiration that ever I saw a man, and so quite gave over his questions, and desired me, that he might be made a Christian; for, he thought to be a Christian, was to be endued with all those knowledges he wanted.

I promised to do my best endeavour; and when I came home, spoke to the master of the plantation, and told him, that poor *Sambo* desired much to be a Christian. But his answer was, That the people of that island were governed by the laws of *England,* and by those laws, we could not make a Christian a slave. I told him, my request was far different from that, for I desired him to make a slave a Christian. His answer was, That it was true, there was a great difference in that: But, being once a Christian, he could no more account him a slave, and so lose the hold they had of them as slaves, by making them Christians; and by that means should open such a gap, as all the planters in the island would curse him. So I was struck mute, and poor *Sambo* kept out of the Church; as ingenious, as honest, and as good a natur'd poor soul, as ever wore black, or ate green.

On *Sundayes* in the afternoon, their music plays, and to dancing they go, the men by themselves, and the women by themselves, no mixed dancing. Their motions are rather what they aim at, than what they do; and by that means, transgress the less upon the *Sunday;* their hands having more of motion than their feet, and their heads more than their hands. They may dance a whole day, and ne'er heat themselves; yet, now and then, one of the activest amongst them will leap bolt upright, and fall in his place again, but without cutting a caper. When they have danc'd an hour or two, the men fall to wrestle, (the music playing all the while) and their manner of wrestling is, to stand like two cocks, with heads as low as their hips; and thrusting their heads one against another, hoping to catch one another by the leg, which sometimes they do: But if both parties be weary, and that they cannot get that advantage, then they raise their heads, by pressing hard one against another, and so having nothing to take hold of but their bare flesh, they close, and grasp one another about the middle, and have one another in the hug, and then a fair fall is given on the back. And thus two or three couples of them are engaged at once, for an hour together, the women looking on: for when the men begin to wrestle, the women leave off their dancing, and come to be spectators of the sport.

When any of them die, they dig a grave, and at evening they bury him, clapping and wringing their hands, and making a doleful sound with their voices. They are a people of a timorous and fearful disposition, and consequently bloody, when they find advantages. If any of them commit a fault, give him present punishment, but do not threaten him; for if you do, it is an even lay,[31] he will go and hang himself, to avoid the punishment.

What their other opinions are in matter of religion, I know not; but certainly, they are not altogether of the sect of the *Sadducees*:[32] For, they believe a resurrection, and that they shall go into their own country again,[33] and have their youth renewed. And lodging this opinion in their hearts, they make it an ordinary practice, upon any great fright, or threatning of their masters, to hang themselves.

But Colonel *Walrond* having lost three or four of his best *negroes* this way, and in a very little time, caused one of their heads to be cut off, and set upon a pole a dozen foot high; and having done that, caused all his *negroes* to come forth, and march round about this head, and bid them look on it, whether this were not the head of such an one that hang'd himself. Which they acknowledging, he then told them, That they were in a main error, in thinking they went into their own countries, after they were dead; for, this man's head was here, as they all were witnesses of; and how was it possible, the body could go without a head. Being convinc'd by this sad, yet lively spectacle, they changed their opinions; and after that, no more hanged themselves.

When they are sick, there are two remedies that cure them; the one, an outward, the other, an inward medicine. The outward medicine is a thing they call *negro-oil*,[34] and 'tis made in *Barbary*, yellow it is as bees' wax, but soft as butter. When they feel themselves ill, they call for some of that, and anoint their bodies, as their breasts, bellies, and sides, and in two days they

31. *lay* Bet.

32. *Sadducees* Jewish sect at the time of Christ that disbelieved in the resurrection of the dead.

33. *go into their own country again* Return to their native lands in Africa.

34. *negro-oil* Probably a form of palm oil. *OED* cites Ephraim Chambers's *Cyclopaedia* (1753): "*Negro-oil*, a name by which the palma of botanists is sometimes called."

are perfectly well. But this does the greatest cures upon such, as have bruises or strains in their bodies. The inward medicine is taken, when they find any weakness or decay in their spirits and stomachs, and then a dram or two of *kill-devil*[35] revives and comforts them much.

I have been very strict, in observing the shapes of these people and for the men, they are very well timber'd, that is, broad between the shoulders, full breasted, well filletted,[36] and clean leg'd and may hold good with *Albert Durer's* rules, who allows *twice the length of the head,* to the breadth of the shoulders, and twice the *length of the face,* to the breadth of the hips, and according to this rule these men are shap'd. But the women not; for the same great master of proportions, allows to each woman, twice the length of the face to the breadth of the shoulders, and twice the length of her own head to the breadth of the hips.[37] And in that, these women are faulty; for I have seen very few of them, whose hips have been broader than their shoulders, unless they have been very fat. The young maids have ordinarily very large breasts, which stand strutting out so hard and firm, as no leaping, jumping, or stirring, will cause them to shake any more, than the brawns of their arms. But when they come to be old, and have had five or six children, their breasts hang down below their navels, so that when they stoop at their common work of weeding, they hang almost down to the ground, that at a distance, you would think they had six legs: And the reason of this is, they tie the clothes about their childrens' backs, which comes upon their breasts, which by pressing very hard, causes them to hang down to that length. Their children, when they are first born, have the palms of their

---

35. *kill-devil* "A West Indian name for rum" (*OED*). Earlier, Ligon comments that "the drink of the island, which is made of the skimmings of the coppers, that boil the sugar, . . . they call kill-devil" (27).

36. *filletted* Loined (according to *OED,* more commonly applied to an animal).

37. *Albrecht Durer's rules . . . of the hips* The set of artistic rules attributed to Albrecht Dürer in *A Book of Dravving, Limning, Washing or Colouring,* calls for "a sweet harmony in the parts of the body, that it may not have broad shoulders, and a thin slender waste [waist], a raw-bone arme, and a thick gouty leg, or any part disproportionable from the other" (10). The legend to an accompanying engraving states that "the Proportion & Measure of a woman . . . is like the Mans, excepting that yᵉ measure of the breadth between the shoulders of the woman containes but 2 lengths of the face . . . and you must make the Armes Thighes & Legges fatter and plumper then yᵉ mans." Ligon appears to be citing this from memory, though earlier in his *History of . . . Barbadoes,* he refers to Dürer as "the great master of proportion" (15).

hands and the soles of their feet, of a whitish colour, and the sight of their eyes of a blueish colour, not unlike the eyes of a young kitling;[38] but, as they grow older, they become black.

Their way of reckoning their ages, or any other notable accident they would remember, is by the moon; and so accounting from the time of their childrens' births, the time they were brought out of their own country, or the time of their being taken prisoners, by some prince or potentate of their own country, or any other notorious accidents, that they are resolved to re-member, they account by the moon; as, so many moons since one of these, and so many moons since another; and this account they keep as long as they can: But if any of them live long, their arithmetic fails them, and then they are at a dead fault, and so give over the chase, wanting the skill to hunt counter.[39] For what can poor people do, that are without letters and num-bers, which is the soul of all business that is acted by mortals, upon the globe of this world. . . .

Though there be a mark set upon these people, which will hardly ever be wip'd off, as of their cruelties when they have advantages, and of their fearfulness and falseness; yet no rule so general but hath his exception: for I believe, and I have strong motives to cause me to be of that persuasion, that there are as honest, faithful, and conscionable people amongst them, as amongst those of *Europe,* or any other part of the world.

A hint of this, I will give you in a lively example; and it was in a time when victuals were scarce, and plantines were not then so frequently planted, as to afford them enough. So that some of the high spirited and turbulent amongst them, began to mutiny, and had a plot, secretly to be reveng'd on their master; and one or two of these were firemen that made the fires in the furnaces, who were never without store of dry wood by them. These villains, were resolved to make fire to such part of the boiling-house, as they were sure would fire the rest; and so burn all, and yet seem ignorant of the fact, as a thing done by accident. But this plot was discovered, by some of the others who hated mischief, as much as they[40] lov'd it; and so traduc'd them to their master, and brought in so many witnesses against them, as they were forc'd to confess, what they meant should have been put in act

38. *kitling* Kitten.
39. *to hunt counter* To work backward (cf. *2 Henry IV,* 1.2.102).
40. *they* These villains.

the next night: so giving them condign punishment, the master gave order to the overseer that the rest should have a day's liberty to themselves and their wives, to do what they would; and withal to allow them a double proportion of victual for three days, both which they refus'd: which we all wonder'd at, knowing well how much they lov'd their liberties, and their meat, having been lately pinch'd of the one, and not having overmuch of the other; and therefore being doubtful what their meaning was in this, suspecting some discontent amongst them, sent for three or four of the best of them, and desir'd to know why they refus'd this favour that was offer'd them, but receiv'd such an answer as we little expected; for they told us, it was not sullenness, or slighting the gratuity their master bestow'd on them, but they would not accept any thing as a recompence for doing that which became them in their duties to do, nor would they have him think, it was hope of reward, that made them to accuse their fellow servants, but an act of justice, which they thought themselves bound in duty to do, and they thought themselves sufficiently rewarded in the act. The substance of this, in such language as they had, they delivered, and poor *Sambo* was the orator, by whose example the others were led both in the discovery of the plot, and refusal of the gratuity. And withall they said, that if it pleas'd their master, at any time, to bestow a voluntary boon upon them, be it never so slight, they would willingly and thankfully accept it: and this act might have beseem'd the best Christians, though some of them were denied Christianity, when they earnestly sought it. Let others have what opinion they please, yet I am of this belief; that there are to be found amongst them, some who are as morally honest, as conscionable, as humble, as loving to their friends, and as loyal to their masters, as any that live under the sun; and one reason they have to be so, is, they set no great value upon their lives: And this is all I can remember concerning the *negroes,* except of their games, which I could never learn, because they wanted language to teach me.

[Indians]

As for the *Indians,* we have but few, and those fetched from other countries; some from the neighbouring islands, some from the Main,[41] which we make slaves: the women who are better vers'd in ordering the cassavie[42]

41. *the Main* The mainland of America.
42. *cassavie* Cassava, A tropical plant whose roots are used for making Indian bread and also cassava farina (tapioca). Dr. John Gilmore, a leading expert on the Caribbean, informs

and making bread than the *negroes* we imploy for that purpose, as also for making mobbie:[43] the men we use for footmen and killing of fish, which they are good at; with their own bows and arrows they will go out; and in a day's time, kill as much fish, as will serve a family of a dozen persons, two or three days, if you can keep the fish so long. They are very active men, and apt to learn any thing, sooner than the *negroes;* and as different from them in shape, almost as in colour; the men very broad shoulder'd, deep breasted, with large heads, and their faces almost three square, broad about the eyes and temples, and sharp at the chin, their skins some of them brown, some a bright bay. They are much craftier, and subtiler then the *negroes,* and in their nature falser; but in their bodies more active. Their women have very small breasts, and have more of the shape of the *Europeans* than the *negroes,* their hair black and long, a great part whereof hangs down upon their backs, as low as their haunches, with a large lock hanging over either breast, which seldom or never curls: clothes they scorn to wear, especially if they be well shap'd; a girdle they use of tape, covered with little smooth shells of fishes, white, and from their flank of one side, to their flank on the other side, a fringe of blue *bugle;*[44] which hangs so low as to cover their privities. We had an *Indian* woman, a slave in the house, who was of excellent shape and colour, for it was a pure bright bay;[45] small breasts, with the niples of a porphyry colour, this woman would not be woo'd by any means to wear clothes. She chanc'd to be with child, by a Christian servant, and lodging in the *Indian*-house, amongst other women of her own country, where the Christian servants, both men and women came; and being very great, and that her time was come to be delivered, loath to fall in labour before the men, walk'd down to a wood, in which was a pond of water, and there by the side of the pond, brought her self a bed; and presently washing her child in some of the water of the pond, lap'd[46]

---

me that "the point about cassava (also known as *manioc* and in Hispanic countries, *yuca*) is that it was a major item of diet for the Amerindians throughout the Caribbean—roughly speaking the equivalent of maize in Mexico. Ligon's throwaway line disguises the important fact that the early English colonists found it hard to support life because they found most European staples would not grow satisfactorily in Barbados; they accordingly fetched Indians 'from the Main' for the express purpose of showing them how to grow indigenous food crops. The Indians went to Barbados voluntarily, but were later enslaved" (personal communication).

43. *mobbie* See note 10 above.   44. *bugle* Ornamental beads.
45. *bay* Reddish brown.   46. *lap'd* Folded, swaddled.

it up in such rags, as she had begg'd of the Christians; and in three hours time came home, with her child in her arms, a lusty boy, frolick and lively.

This *Indian* dwelling near the sea-coast, upon the Main, an *English* ship put in to a bay, and sent some of her men ashore, to try what victuals or water they could find, for in some distress they were: But the *Indians* perceiving them to go up so far into the country, as they were sure they could not make a safe retreat, intercepted them in their return and fell upon them, chasing them into a wood, and being dispersed there, some were taken, and some kill'd: but a young man amongst them straggling from the rest, was met by this *Indian* maid, who upon the first sight fell in love with him, and hid him close from her countrymen (the *Indians*) in a cave, and there fed him, till they could safely go down to the shore, where the ship lay at anchor, expecting the return of their friends. But at last, seeing them upon the shore, sent the long-boat for them, took them aboard, and brought them away. But the youth, when he came ashore in the *Barbadoes*, forgot the kindness of the poor maid, that had ventured her life for his safety, and sold her for a slave, who was as free born as he: And so poor *Yarico* for her love, lost her liberty.

[Masters]

Now for the masters, I have yet said but little, nor am able to say half of what they deserve. They are men of great abilities and parts, otherwise they could not go through, with such great works as they undertake; the managing of one of their plantations, being a work of such a latitude, as will require a very good head-piece,[47] to put in order, and continue it so.

I can name a planter there, that feeds daily two hundred mouths, and keeps them in such order, as there are no mutinies amongst them; and yet of several nations. All these are to be employed in their several abilities, so as no one be idle. The first work to be considered, is weeding, for unless that be done, all else (and the planter too) will be undone, and if that be neglected but a little time, it will be a hard matter to recover it again, so fast will the weeds grow there. But the ground being kept clean, 'tis fit to bear any thing that country will afford. After weeding comes planting, and they account two seasons in the year best and that is, *May* and *November;* but canes are to be planted at all times, that they may come in, one field after

---

47. *a very good head-piece* A very good intellect. *OED* quotes "1720 [John] Gay *Poems* (1745) I.226. Is not this Steward of mine a pure ingenious fellow now . . . a rare head-piece?"

another; otherwise the work will stand still. And commonly they have in a
field that is planted together, at one time, ten or a dozen acres. This work
of planting and weeding, the master himself is to see done; unless he have
a very trusty and able overseer; and without such a one, he will have too
much to do. The next thing he is to consider, is the ingenio, and what belongs to that; as, the ingenio it self, which is the *primum mobile*[48] of the
whole work, the boiling-house, with the coppers and furnaces, the filling
room, the still-house, and curing-house; and in all these, there are great
casualties. If any thing in the rollers, as the gouges, sockets, sweeps, cogs,
or braytrees,[49] be at fault, the whole work stands still; or in the boiling-
house, if the frame which holds the coppers, (and is made of clinkers,[50] fastened with plaster of *Paris*) if by the violence of the heat from the furnaces,
these frames crack or break, there is a stop in the work, till that be mended.
Or if any of the coppers have a mischance, and be burnt, a new one must
presently be had, or there is a stay in the work. Or if the mouths of the furnaces, (which are made of a sort of stone, which we have from *England,* and
we call it there, high gate[51] stone) if that, by the violence of the fire, be soft-
ened, that it moulder away, there must new be provided, and laid in with
much art, or it will not be. Or if the bars of iron, which are in the floor of
the furnace, when they are red hot (as continually they are) the fire-man,
throw great shides[52] of wood in the mouths of the furnaces, hard and
carelessly, the weight of those logs, will bend or break those bars, (though
strongly made) and there is no repairing them, without the work stand still;
for all these depend upon one another, as wheels in a clock. Or if the stills
be at fault, the *kill-devil* cannot be made. But the main impediment and
stop of all, is the loss of our cattle, and amongst them, there are such diseases, as I have known in one plantation, thirty that have died in two days.

48. *primum mobile* Mainspring.
49. *goudges . . . braytrees* In describing the manner of grinding sugarcane, Ligon writes
that "horses and cattle being put to their tackle, . . . go about, and by their force turn (by
the sweeps) the middle roller; which being cog'd to the other two, at both ends, turn them
about" (89). *OED,* quoting Ligon, explains *sweeps* (definition 25) as long bars "swept round
so as to turn a shaft." The description contains no further technical details on the employment of *gouges* (probably cutting tools) and *braytrees* (perhaps "brattices," wooden parapets
or planking).
50. *clinkers* Dutch bricks.
51. *high gate* Probably *highway,* for which this remained a synonym during the seventeenth century (see *OED*).
52. *shides* Pieces of wood used to build a fire.

And I have heard, that a planter, an eminent man there, that clear'd a dozen acres of ground, and rail'd it about for pasture, with intention, as soon as the grass was grown to a great height, to put in his working oxen; which accordingly he did, and in one night fifty of them died; so that such a loss as this, is able to undo a planter, that is not very well grounded. What it is that breeds these diseases, we cannot find, unless some of the plants have a poisonous quality; nor have we yet found out cures for these diseases. Chickens' guts being the best remedy was then known, and those being chop'd or minc'd, and given them in a horn, with some liquor mixed to moisten it, was thought the best remedy: yet it recovered very few. Our horses too have killing diseases amongst them, and some of them have been recovered by glisters,[53] which we give them in pipes, or large syringes made of wood, for the same purpose. For, the common diseases, both of cattle and horses, are obstructions and bindings in their bowels; and so lingering a disease it is, to those that recover, as they are almost worn to nothing before they get well. So that if any of these stops continue long, or the cattle cannot be recruited in a reasonable time, the work is at a stand; and by that means, the canes grow over ripe, and will in a very short time have their juice dried up, and will not be worth the grinding.

Now to recruit these cattle, horses, camels, and assinigos,[54] who are all liable to these mischances and decays, merchants must be consulted, ships provided, and a competent cargo of goods adventured, to make new voyages to foreign parts, to supply those losses; and when that is done, the casualties at sea are to be considered and those happen several ways, either by shipwreck, piracy, or fire. A master of a ship, and a man accounted both able, stout, and honest, having transported goods of several kinds, from *England* to a part of *Africa,* the River of *Gambia,* and had there exchanged his commodities for *negroes,* which was that he intended to make his voyage of, caused them all to be ship'd, and did not, as the manner is, shackle one to another, and make them sure, but having an opinion of their honesty and faithfulness to him, as they had promised; and he being a credulous man, and himself good natur'd and merciful, suffered them to go loose, and they being double the number of those in the ship, found their advantages, got weapons in their hands, and fell upon the sailors, knocking them on the heads, and cutting their throats so fast, as the master found they were all lost, out of any possibility of saving; and so went down into

53. *glisters* Clysters, enemas.   54. *assinigos* Little asses.

the hold, and blew all up with himself; and this was before they got out of the river. These, and several other ways there will happen, that extremely retard the work of sugar-making.

Now let us consider how many things there are to be thought on, that go to the actuating this great work, and how many cares to prevent the mischances, that are incident to the retarding, if not the frustrating of the whole work; and you will find them wise and provident men, that go on and prosper in a work, that depends upon so many contingents.

This I say, to stop those mens' mouths, that lie here at home, and expect great profit in their adventures, and never consider, through what difficulty, industry and pains it is acquired. And thus much I thought good to say, of the abilities of the planters.

The next thing is, of their natures and dispositions, which I found compliable in a high degree to all virtues, that those of the best sort of gentlemen call excellent; as, civilly in treating of strangers, with communicating to them any thing within the compass of their knowledge, that might be beneficial to them, in any undertaking amongst them, and assisting them in it, giving them harbour for themselves and servants. And if their intentions were to buy plantations, to make diligent enquiries for such as they desired, and to drive the bargain as near the wind for their advantages, as possibly they could, and to put themselves in some travels, in settling the business: Or, if that could not do them service, to recommend them to any friend they had, that lay more fit and convenient for their purpose. Loving, friendly, and hospitable one to another; and though they are of several persuasions, yet, their discretions ordered every thing so well, as there never were any fallings out between them: which to prevent, some of them of the better sort, made a law amongst themselves, that whosoever nam'd the word *Roundhead* or *Cavalier*,[55] should give to all those that heard him, a shot[56] and a turkey, to be eaten at his house that made the forfeiture; which sometimes was done purposely, that they might enjoy the company of one

55. *Roundhead or Cavalier* Beckles, *White Servitude and Black Slavery,* 22–23, points out that many of the Barbadian planters "had come to the colony as disgruntled Cavaliers and Roundheads trying to repair fortunes and make new ones. The factions brought with them very different political and religious views, hardened by war and intolerance, yet they were able to transcend these cleavages to achieve unity for the common exploitation of colonial resources. . . . The rise and development of this cohesive planter class was the central determinant of the nature of Barbadian servitude over the century."
56. *shot* Shoat, "a young weaned pig" (*OED*).

another; and sometimes this shot and this turkey would draw on a dozen dishes more, if company were accordingly. So frank, so loving, and so good natur'd were these gentlemen one to another; and to express their affections yet higher, they had particular names one to another, as, neighbour, friend, brother, sister. So that I perceived nothing wanting, that might make up a firm and lasting friendship amongst them; though after I came away, it was otherwise.

Sports and exercises they never us'd any, as bowling, shooting, hunting, or hawking; for indeed there are no places fit for the two first exercises, the country being so rocky, uneven and full of stumps of trees: and for the other two, they want game; for there are no kind of wild beasts in the island, nor any fowl fit to hawk at; besides the country is so woody, as there is no champian⁵⁷ to fly in; pheasants, partridges, heathpoults,⁵⁸ quails, or rayles,⁵⁹ never set foot upon this ground, unless they were brought there; and if so, they never liv'd: and for hawkes, I never saw but two, and those the merriest stirrers that ever I saw fly; the one of them was in an evening just at sun setting, which is the time the bats rise, and so are to a good height; and at a downcome,⁶⁰ this *Barbary* faulcon took one of them and carried it away.

Tame Beasts That Are Living on the Island

. . . .

Assinigoes.   Are here of exceeding great use in the island, carrying our sugar, down to the bridge, which by reason of the gullies, the horses cannot do: besides when the great rains fall, the ways are so deep, and full of roots, as when a horse puts in his leg between two roots, he can hardly pull it out again, having a great weight on his back; and if he fall, 'tis hard lifting him up. Whereas the assinigoes pick and choose their way, and sometimes choose out little ways in the wood; such as they know are fit for them to pass, which horses cannot do, because the ways are now too narrow for them, or if they were not, they would want much the wit of the assinigoes, to pick and choose their way. And if by chance the assinigoes fall, two *negroes* are able to help him up, and we seldom use more than two, for assistance to the Christian that has the charge of the carriages. One of these

57. *champian* "Expanse of level open country" (*OED*).
58. *heathpoults* Young heath birds.   59. *rayles* Rails, a common shooting bird.
60. *downcome* Swooping down.

assinigoes will carry 150 weight of sugar; some of the strongest 200 weight; our planters have been very desirous if it were possible to get mules there, for they would be of excellent use, in carrying their sugars, and working in the ingenio; but they had got none when I was there, but they were making trials, either to get some of those, or some large horse assinigoes, to breed with the mares of that country.

Hogs. We have here in abundance, but not wild or loose, for if they were they would do more harm than their bodies are worth; they are enclos'd, and every man knows his own: those that rear them to sell, do commonly sell them for a groat[61] a pound; weighing them alive; sometimes six pence if flesh be dear. There was a planter in the island, that came to his neighbour, and said to him, Neighbour I hear you have lately bought good store of servants, out of the last ship that came from *England,* and I hear withall, that you want provisions, I have great want of a woman servant; and would be glad to make an exchange; If you will let me have some of your woman's flesh, you shall have some of my hog's flesh; so the price was set a groat a pound for the hog's flesh, and six-pence for the woman's flesh. The scales were set up, and the planter had a maid that was extream fat, lazy, and good for nothing, her name was *Honor.* The man brought a great fat sow, and put it in one scale, and *Honor* was put in the other; but when he saw how much the maid outweighed his sow, he broke off the bargain, and would not go on: though such a case as this, may seldom happen, yet 'tis an ordinary thing there, to sell their servants to one another for the time they have to serve; and in exchange, receive any commodities that are in the island. I have said as much already of the largeness, weight and goodness of these hogs as is needful, and therefore I shall need no more.
. . . .

Of Lesser Animals and Insects

. . . .

One sort . . . of these harmful animals there are, which we call Chegoes;[62] and these are so little that you would hardly think them able to do any harm

61. *groat* A coin equal to four pence, no longer issued after 1662. The term also came to denote a very small sum of money.

62. *chegoes* More commonly known as chiggers or jiggers. *OED* quotes John Kersey, *Dictionarium Anglo-Brittannicum, or a General English Dictionary* (London, 1708): "*Chiego,* a small Creature that gets into the Feet of those that live in the Island of Barbadoes, and makes them very uneasie." However, the chigger is not confined to Barbados

at all, and yet these will do more mischief than the ants, and if they were as numerous as harmful, there were no enduring them. They are of a shape, not much unlike a louse, but no bigger than a mite that breeds in cheese, his colour blueish: an *Indian* has laid one of them on a sheet of white paper, and with my spectacles on I could hardly discern him; yet this very little enemy can and will do much mischief to mankind. This vermin will get through your stocken, and in a pore of your skin, in some part of your feet, commonly under the nail of your toes, and there make a habitation to lay his offspring, as big as a small tare, or the bag of a bee, which will cause you to go very lame, and put you to much smarting pain. The *Indian* women have the best skill to take them out, which they do by putting in a small pointed pin or needle, at the hole where he came in, and winding the point about the bag, loosen him from the flesh, and so take him out. He is of a blueish colour, and is seen through the skin, but the *negroes* whose skins are of that colour (or near it) are in ill case, for they cannot find where they are; by which means they are many of them very lame. Some of the chegoes are poisonous, and after they are taken out, the orifice in which they lay, will fester and rankle for a fortnight after they are gone. I have had ten taken out of my feet in a morning, by the unfortunate *Yarico*, an *Indian* woman.

Richard Steele, *The Spectator,* NO. 11

From *The Spectator,* no. 11 (13 March 1711).

Although Ligon furnishes the historical source, it was Sir Richard Steele (1672–1729) who conjured up the legend of Inkle and Yarico that so captivated the eighteenth-century imagination. Its publication in *The Spectator,* first as a single half-sheet periodical essay and then in volume form, ensured that the tale was widely disseminated and never out of print. Inkle and Yarico was the earliest extended short fiction included by Addison and Steele in *The Spectator* and easily the most celebrated. Whereas Steele frames the tale within a broader discursive argument concerning relations between the sexes, subsequent versions were almost invariably free-standing.

Steele ingeniously transformed the strands of Yarico's life as picked up from Ligon by making her with child by the young Englishman whose life she preserved rather than by a white servant on the plantation where she was later enslaved. But his most visible contribution to the tale was to christen his English traveler. The name Inkle, according to Price, *Inkle and Yarico Album,* is a "good English name . . . , or at least it would be a good English name if spelled with an H" (8). Steele may have chosen the name as a wry allusion to the young man's upbringing as a small tradesman, for *inkle* was a common haberdasher's term for "a kind of linen tape," sometimes of an inferior quality (*OED*). I am indebted to a graduate student, Andrea Verhoeven, for suggesting to me that "Steele invented the name Inkle as the character was an accountant ['a perfect master of numbers'] and would frequently be using ink." She cites an episode in *Black Skin, White Masks* in which Frantz Fanon recounts the experience of Mayotte Capécia, a woman of Martinique, who took an inkwell and emptied it over the head of a handsome white man to whom she was physically attracted, in order to make him black. Fanon comments that "she soon recognized the futility of such attempts. . . . So, since she could no longer try to blacken, to negrify the world, she was going to try in her own body and in her own mind, to bleach it" (45). In Ms. Verhoeven's radicalized interpretation, based on her reading of Fanon, "the choice of the name Inkle implies not only [his] occupation but also serves as a prediction, or even a desire for a sexual encounter with a woman of another racial background."

Price describes "the poignant story of Inkle and Yarico in *The Spectator* [as] one of the nearly flawless masterpieces of literature," though, he adds, "no succeeding rendition approached it in quality" (2). More recently, Mary Louise Pratt has commented on the "mythic status" of a story that "thematizes the breakdown of reciprocity by capitalist greed and highlights contradictions of the ideology of romantic love. No wonder it was unforgettable" (*Imperial Eyes,* 100).

The standard text of *The Spectator* is edited by Donald F. Bond (no. 11 appears in 1:47–51). The text printed here is taken from a copy of the 1711 folio in the Brotherton Library, University of Leeds. Some minor authorial emendations, introduced into the collected octavo edition of 1712 (and listed by Bond), have been silently incorporated.

Tuesday, March 13, 1711

Dat veniam corvis, vexat censura columbas. Juv.[1]

Arietta[2] is visited by all persons of both sexes, who have any pretence to wit and gallantry. She is in that time of life which is neither affected with the

---

1. *Dat . . . Juv.* Steele borrowed the epigraph from Juvenal, *Satires,* 2.1.63, translated in the commentary to a recent edition as "judgement acquits the ravens and condemns the doves" (Juvenal, *Satires, Book I,* ed. Braund, 138). Braund remarks that the proverbial contrast Juvenal employs is between male and female, "aggressor and victim, black and white . . . and between obscene and pure." However, ironic reversal in Inkle and Yarico presents the *black* woman as the innocent party.

As Braund points out (168), Juvenal's second satire has traditionally been interpreted as an attack on hypocritical homosexuals, but in fact "most of the material in the poem deals with the un-masculine sexuality of these men." Recollection of this may have prompted Steele to feminize Inkle's features.

2. *Arietta* Steele invented the name for this essay; she appears nowhere else in *The Spectator.*

follies of youth, or infirmities of age; and her conversation is so mixed with gaiety and prudence, that she is agreeable both to the young and the old. Her behaviour is very frank, without being in the least blameable; and as she is out of the tract of[3] any amorous or ambitious pursuits of her own, her visitants entertain her with accounts of themselves very freely, whether they concern their passions or their interests. I made her a visit this afternoon, having been formerly introduced to the honour of her acquaintance, by my friend *Will. Honeycomb,*[4] who has prevailed upon her to admit me sometimes into her assembly, as a civil, inoffensive man. I found her accompanied with one person only, a common-place talker, who, upon my entrance, rose, and after a very slight civility sat down again; then turning to *Arietta,* pursued his discourse, which I found was upon the old topic, of constancy in love. He went on with great facility in repeating what he talks every day of his life; and, with the ornaments of insignificant laughs and gestures, enforced his arguments by quotations out of plays and songs, which allude to the perjuries of the fair, and the general levity of women. Methought he strove to shine more than ordinarily in his talkative way, that he might insult my silence, and distinguish himself before a woman of *Arietta*'s taste and understanding. She had often an inclination to interrupt him, but could find no opportunity, 'till the larum[5] ceased of its self; which it did not 'till he had repeated and murdered the celebrated story of the *Ephesian* Matron.[6]

Arietta seemed to regard this piece of raillery as an outrage done to her sex, as indeed I have always observed that women, whether out of a nicer regard to their honour, or what other reason I cannot tell, are more sensibly touched with those general aspersions, which are cast upon their sex, than men are by what is said of theirs.

When she had a little recovered her self from the serious anger she was in, she replied in the following manner.

Sir, When I consider, how perfectly new all you have said on this subject is, and that the story you have given us is not quite two thousand years

3. *out of the tract of* Out of time for, too old for.
4. *Will. Honeycomb* Will Honeycomb, a former rake, is more than once employed in the fictive setting of *The Spectator* as an agent to introduce its shy narrator, Mr. Spectator, into the company of the fair sex.
5. *larum* Cacophony, hubbub.
6. Petronius's well-known story of the Ephesian matron is discussed in the introduction, pp. 10–11, and reproduced in appendix A.

The SPECTATOR.

Dat veniam corvis, vexat censura columbas. Juv.

Tuesday, March 13. 1711.

ARIETTA is visited by all Persons of both Sexes, who have any Pretence to Wit and Gallantry. She is in that time of Life which is neither affected with the Follies of Youth, or Infirmities of Age ; and her Conversation is so mixed with Gaiety and Prudence, that she is agreeable both to the Young and the Old. Her Behaviour is very frank, without being in the least blameable ; and as she is out of the Track of any amorous or ambitious Pursuits of her own, her Visitants entertain her with Accounts of themselves very freely, whether they concern their Passions or their Interests. I made her a Visit this Afternoon, having been formerly introduced to the Honour of her Acquaintance, by my Friend *Will. Honeycomb*, who has prevailed upon her to admit me sometimes into her Assembly, as a civil, inoffensive Man. I found her accompanied with one Person only, a Common-Place Talker, who, upon my Entrance, rose, and after a very slight Civility sat down again ; then turning to *Arietta*, pursued his Discourse, which I found was upon the old Topick, of Constancy in Love. He went on with great Facility in repeating what he talks every Day of his Life ; and, with the Ornaments of insignificant Laughs and Gestures, enforced his Arguments by Quotations out of Plays and Songs, which allude to the Perjuries of the Fair, and the general Levity of Women. Methought he strove to shine more than ordinarily in his Talkative Way, that he might insult my Silence, and distinguish himself before a Woman of *Arietta*'s Taste and Understanding. She had often an Inclination to interrupt him, but could find no Opportunity, 'till the Larum ceased of its self ; which it did not 'till he had repeated and murdered the celebrated Story of the *Ephesian* Matron.

Arietta seemed to regard this Piece of Raillery as an Outrage done to her Sex, as indeed I have always observed that Women, whether out of a nicer Regard to their Honour, or what other Reason I cannot tell, are more sensibly touched with those general Aspersions, which are cast upon their Sex, than Men are by what is said of theirs.

When she had a little recovered her self from the serious Anger she was in, she replied in the following manner.

Sir, When I consider, how perfectly new all you have said on this Subject is, and that the Story you have given us is not quite two thousand Years Old, I cannot but think it a Piece of Presumption to dispute with you : But your Quotations put me in Mind of the Fable of the Lion and the Man. The Man walking with that noble Animal, showed him, in the Ostentation of Human Superiority, a Sign of a Man killing a Lion. Upon which the Lion said very justly, *We Lions are none of us Painters, else we could show a hundred Men killed by Lions, for one Lion killed by a Man.* You Men are Writers, and can represent us Women as Unbecoming as you please in your Works, while we are unable to return the Injury. You have twice or thrice observed in your Discourse, that Hipocrisy is the very Foundation of our Education ; and that an Ability to dissemble our Affections, is a professed Part of our Breeding. These, and such other Reflections, are sprinkled up and down the Writings of all Ages, by Authors, who leave behind them Memorials of their Resentment against the Scorn of particular Women, in Invectives against the whole Sex. Such a Writer, I doubt not, was the celebrated *Petronius*, who invented the pleasant Aggravations of the Frailty of the *Ephesian* Lady ; but when we consider this Question between the Sexes, which has been either a Point of Dispute or Raillery ever since there were Men and Women, let us take Facts from plain People, and from such as have not either Ambition or Capacity to embellish their Narrations with any Beauties of Imagination. I was the other Day amusing my self with *Ligon*'s Account of *Barbadoes* ; and, in Answer to your well-wrought Tale, I will give you (as it dwells upon my Memory) out of that honest Traveller, in his fifty fifth Page, the History of *Inkle* and *Yarico*.

Mr. *Thomas Inkle* of *London*, aged 20 Years, embarked in the *Downs* on the good Ship called the

5. Joseph Addison and Richard Steele, *The Spectator*, no. 11 (13 March 1711), recto and verso of half sheet. (Courtesy of the Brotherton Collection, University of Leeds.)

the *Achilles*, bound for the *West-Indies*, on the 16th of *June* 1647, in order to improve his Fortune by Trade and Merchandize. Our Adventurer was the third Son of an eminent Citizen, who had taken particular Care to instill into his Mind an early Love of Gain, by making him a perfect Master of Numbers, and consequently giving him a quick View of Loss and Advantage, and preventing the natural Impulses of his Passions, by Prepossession towards his Interest. With a Mind thus turned, young *Inkle* had a Person every way agreeable, a ruddy Vigour in his Countenance, Strength in his Limbs, with Ringlets of fair Hair loosely flowing on his Shoulders. It happened, in the Course of the Voyage, that the *Achilles*, in some Distress, put into a Creek on the Main of *America*, in Search of Provisions: The Youth, who is the Hero of my Story, among others, went ashore on this Occasion. From their first Landing they were observed by a Party of *Indians*, who hid themselves in the Woods for that Purpose. The *English* unadvisedly marched a great distance from the Shore into the Country, and were intercepted by the Natives, who flew the greatest Number of them. Our Adventurer escaped among others, by flying into a Forest. Upon his coming into a remote and pathless Part of the Wood, he threw himself breathless on a little Hillock, when an *Indian* Maid rushed from a Thicket behind him: After the first Surprize, they appeared mutually agreeable to each other. If the *European* was highly Charmed with the Limbs, Features, and wild Graces of the Naked *American*; the *American* was no less taken with the Dress, Complexion and Shape of an *European*, covered from Head to Foot. The *Indian* grew immediately enamoured of him, and consequently sollicitous for his Preservation: She therefore conveyed him to a Cave, where she gave him a Delicious Repast of Fruits, and led him to a Stream to slake his Thirst. In the midst of these good Offices, she would sometimes play with his Hair, and delight in the Opposition of its Colour, to that of her Fingers: Then open his Bosome, then laugh at him for covering it. She was, it seems, a Person of Distinction, for she every day came to him in a different Dress, of the most beautiful Shells, Bugles and Bredes. She likewise brought him a great many Spoils, which her other Lovers had presented to her; so that his Cave was richly adorned with all the spotted Skins of Beasts, and most Party-coloured Feathers of Fowls, which that World afforded. To make his Confinement more tolerable, she would carry him in the Dusk of the Evening, or by the favour of Moon-light, to unfrequented Groves and Solitudes, and show him where to lye down in Safety, and sleep amidst the Falls of Waters, and Melody of Nightingales. Her Part was to watch and hold him in her Arms, for fear of her Country-men, and wake on Occasions to consult his Safety. In this manner did the Lovers pass away their Time, till they had learn'd a Language of their own, in which the Voyager communicated to his Mistress, how happy he should be to have her in his Country, where she should be Cloathed in such Silks as his Wastecoat was made of, and be carried in Houses drawn by Horses, without being exposed to Wind or Weather. All this he promised her the Enjoyment of, without such Fears and Alarms as they were there Tormented with. In this tender Correspondence these Lovers lived for several Months, when *Yarico*,

instructed by her Lover, discovered a Vessel on the Coast, to which she made Signals, and in the Night, with the utmost Joy and Satisfaction accompanied him to a Ships-Crew of his Country-Men, bound for *Barbadoes*. When a Vessel from the Main arrives in that Island, it seems the Planters come down to the Shoar, where there is an immediate Market of the *Indians* and other Slaves, as with us of Horses and Oxen.

To be short, Mr. *Thomas Inkle*, now coming into *English* Territories, began seriously to reflect upon his loss of Time, and to weigh with himself how many Days Interest of his Mony he had lost during his Stay with *Yarico*. This Thought made the Young Man very pensive, and careful what Account he should be able to give his Friends of his Voyage. Upon which Considerations, the prudent and frugal young Man sold *Yarico* to a *Barbadian* Merchant; notwithstanding that the poor Girl, to incline him to commiserate her Condition, told him that she was with Child by him: But he only made use of that Information, to rise in his Demands upon the Purchaser.

I was so touch'd with this Story, (which I think should be always a Counterpart to the *Ephesian* Matron) that I left the Room with Tears in my Eyes; which a Woman of *Arietta*'s good Sense, did, I am sure, take for greater Applause, than any Compliments I could make her.

ADVERTISEMENTS.

LONDON: Printed for *Sam. Buckley*, at the *Dolphin* in *Little Britain*; and Sold by *A. Baldwin* in *Warwick-Lane*; where Advertisements are taken in.

old, I cannot but think it a piece of presumption to dispute with you: But your quotations put me in mind of the Fable of the Lion and the Man.[7] The man walking with that noble animal, showed him, in the ostentation of human superiority, a sign of a man killing a lion. Upon which the lion said very justly, *We lions are none of us painters, else we could show a hundred men killed by lions, for one lion killed by a man.* You men are writers, and can represent us women as unbecoming as you please in your works, while we are unable to return the injury. You have twice or thrice observed in your discourse, that hypocrisy is the very foundation of our education; and that an ability to dissemble our affections, is a professed part of our breeding. These, and such other reflections, are sprinkled up and down the writings of all ages, by authors, who leave behind them memorials of their resentment against the scorn of particular women, in invectives against the whole sex. Such a writer, I doubt not, was the celebrated *Petronius,* who invented the pleasant aggravations of the frailty of the *Ephesian* lady; but when we consider this question between the sexes, which has been either a point of dispute or raillery ever since there were men and women, let us take facts from plain people, and from such as have not either ambition or capacity to embellish their narrations with any beauties of imagination. I was the other day amusing my self with *Ligon's* account of *Barbadoes;* and, in answer to your well-wrought tale, I will give you (as it dwells upon my memory) out of that honest traveller, in his fifty fifth page, the history of *Inkle* and *Yarico.*[8]

Mr. *Thomas Inkle* of *London,* aged 20 years, embarked in the *Downs* on the good ship called the *Achilles,* bound for the *West-Indies,* on the 16th of *June* 1647,[9] in order to improve his fortune by trade and merchandize. Our

7. *the Fable of the Lion and the Man* This appears in Sir Roger L'Estrange's edition of *Fables from Aesop,* no. 240, pp. 208–9, with the reflection, "The Fancies of . . . Painters . . . are No Evidences of Truth; . . . 'Tis much Easier for a *Man* to make an *Ass* of a *Lyon* upon a *Pedestal,* then [than] in a *Forrest.*" Donald Kay, *Short Fiction in The Spectator,* 56, comments that the fable "is successfully presented in a narrative context . . . to counteract the ideas of . . . [the] commonplace talker about the constancy of love. . . . Steele very smoothly works the fable into the conversation, and . . . condenses it economically into two sentences." In modern editions of Aesop, it appears as fable 219.

8. Steele may have been quoting from either the first (1657) or the second (1673) edition of Ligon, since Yarico's story appears on the same page (55) in both.

9. *on the good ship . . . June 1647* Ligon also embarked "on the good ship called the *Achilles*" (1673, 1), setting sail on 16 June 1647 (see selection 1, headnote). In borrowing the name, perhaps Steele intends to imply a contrast between ancient heroism and the latter-day antihero of Arietta's tale.

adventurer was the third son of an eminent citizen, who had taken particular care to instill into his mind an early love of gain, by making him a perfect master of numbers, and consequently giving him a quick view of loss
and advantage, and preventing the natural impulses of his passions, by prepossession towards his interests. With a mind thus turned, young *Inkle* had
a person every way agreeable, a ruddy vigour in his countenance, strength
in his limbs, with ringlets of fair hair loosely flowing on his shoulders. It
happened, in the course of the voyage, that the *Achilles,* in some distress,
put into a creek on the main of *America,* in search of provisions: The youth,
who is the hero of my story, among others, went ashore on this occasion.
From their first landing they were observed by a party of *Indians,* who hid
themselves in the woods for that purpose. The *English* unadvisedly marched
a great distance from the shore into the country, and were intercepted by
the natives, who slew the greatest number of them. Our adventurer escaped
among others, by flying into a forest. Upon his coming into a remote and
pathless part of the wood, he threw himself, tired and breathless, on a little hillock, when an *Indian* maid rushed from a thicket behind him: After
the first surprize, they appeared mutually agreeable to each other. If the
European was highly charmed with the limbs, features, and wild graces of
the naked *American;* the *American* was no less taken with the dress, complexion and shape of an *European,* covered from head to foot. The *Indian*
grew immediately enamoured of him, and consequently solicitous for his
preservation: She therefore conveyed him to a cave, where she gave him a
delicious repast of fruits, and led him to a stream to slake his thirst. In the
midst of these good offices, she would sometimes play with his hair, and
delight in the opposition of its colour, to that of her fingers: Then open his
bosom, then laugh at him for covering it. She was, it seems, a person of
distinction, for she every day came to him in a different dress, of the most
beautiful shells, bugles and bredes.[10] She likewise brought him a great
many spoils, which her other lovers had presented to her; so that his cave
was richly adorned with all the spotted skins of beasts, and most party-
coloured[11] feathers of fowls, which that world afforded. To make his confinement more tolerable, she would carry him in the dusk of the evening,
or by the favour of moon-light, to unfrequented groves and solitudes, and
show him where to lie down in safety, and sleep amidst the falls of waters,

10. *bugles and bredes* Glass beads and braiding.
11. *party-coloured* Variegated in color.

and melody of nightingales. Her part was to watch and hold him in her arms, for fear of her country-men, and wake him on occasions to consult his safety. In this manner did the lovers pass away their time, till they had learn'd a language of their own, in which the voyager communicated to his mistress, how happy he should be to have her in his country, where she should be clothed in such silks as his waistcoat was made of, and be carried in houses drawn by horses, without being exposed to wind or weather. All this he promised her the enjoyment of, without such fears and alarms as they were there tormented with. In this tender correspondence these lovers lived for several months, when *Yarico,* instructed by her lover, discovered a vessel off the coast, to which she made signals, and in the night, with the utmost joy and satisfaction accompanied him to a ship's-crew of his countrymen, bound for *Barbadoes.* When a vessel from the main arrives in that island, it seems the planters come down to the shore, where there is an immediate market of the *Indians* and other slaves as with us of horses and oxen.

To be short, Mr. *Thomas Inkle,* now coming into *English* territories, began seriously to reflect upon his loss of time, and to weigh with himself how many days interest of his money he had lost during his stay with *Yarico.* This thought made the young man very pensive, and careful what account he should be able to give his friends of his voyage. Upon which considerations, the prudent and frugal young man sold *Yarico* to a *Barbadian* merchant; notwithstanding that the poor girl, to incline him to commiserate her condition, told him that she was with child by him: But he only made use of that information, to rise in his demands upon the purchaser.

I was so touch'd with this story, (which I think should be always a counterpart to the *Ephesian* Matron) that I left the room with tears in my eyes; which a woman of *Arietta's* good sense did, I am sure, take for greater applause, than any compliments I could make her.

Frances Seymour, Countess of Hertford,

"The Story of Inkle and Yarico,

Taken out of the Eleventh *Spectator*"

"By a Lady." From *A New Miscellany: Being a Collection of
Pieces of Poetry from Bath, Tunbridge, Oxford, Epsom, and
Other Places, in the Year 1725* [London, 1726?], 32–37.

Verse renditions of Inkle and Yarico chiefly take two forms. The first employs third-person narration, allowing the poet to invest in and sometimes
amplify the traditional tale that stems from *The Spectator*. The other is personalized into the form of heroic epistle whereby Yarico is given rein to articulate the range of her emotions following her enslavement. Consciously
or otherwise, it is the distinction of Frances Seymour, Countess of Hertford (1699–1754), to have publicly initiated both forms. This poem and its
companion, "An Epistle from Yarico to Inkle, after He Had Sold Her for a
Slave" [3B], first appeared anonymously in *A New Miscellany . . . of Pieces
of Poetry* (sometimes referred to as the *Tunbridge Miscellany*), published in
1726, having previously circulated in manuscript. They were separately
reprinted with minor alterations in 1738 as the work of "The Right Hon.
the Countess of ****," and their authorship was ascertained only after two
centuries by her biographer, Helen Sard Hughes (*Gentle Hertford*, 419–20).

The Countess of Hertford belonged to an active literary coterie, including among her correspondents and friends the hymnologist Isaac Watts
and the poets Elizabeth Rowe and James Thomson. Thomson acknowl-
edged her patronage by dedicating his poem "Spring" to her in 1728 (it was
later collected into *The Seasons*). The preface to the *New Miscellany* helped
to initiate the view that her poetry was occasional by claiming that most of

its pieces were written by "Persons of Rank and Distinction" gathered at Bath and Tunbridge Wells "at that soft Season of the Year, which invites the Gay and the Wealthy to leave the busy Town, and pass their idle Time at those Places of Pleasure." To Watts she explained that she wrote "to amuse a leisure hour and to speak the sentiments" of her heart (Hughes, 420–22). According to Henry F. Steicher, it was Elizabeth Rowe who prompted Lady Hertford to contribute to *The New Miscellany* (*Elizabeth Rowe*, 61).

The poem has provoked some discussion. Price complains of its "prevailing vagueness" and "indefiniteness of setting" but recognizes that not identifying Inkle as an Englishman may have been deliberate: "A direct admission of his nationality would have been painful to the poetic countess and her readers" (*Inkle and Yarico Album*, 18). More recently, Moira Ferguson reiterates this idea and claims that, with its exotic setting, "the Countess's poem doubles as a miniature (mis)conduct book with a difference: it sculpts the dangers that lie in wait for unsuspecting women who take men at face value" (*Subject to Others*, 81). Moreover, she sees it as combining "aristocratic revulsion at go-getter mercantilist values with an implicit taboo on sexual conduct in early courtship" (85). Similarly, Norman Simms reads the poem as "an exemplary tale of male infidelity and colonial cruelty" that "gives to the story new priorities, balances, and patterns of development" ("A Silent Love Affair," 93–94). In particular, he comments on the unsaid and ironic elements, "the network of silences" within and beyond the poem, by which "the reader is made privy to the satisfaction Inkle feels at the price given for her" while, in her bondage, Yarico "is unable to know what his pleasing looks stand for" (99–100). Such canonical reassessments are a far cry from H. S. Hughes's ready depreciation of Lady Hertford's verse as "not great poetry" (*Gentle Hertford*, 422).

A youth there was, possess'd with every charm,
That might the coldest heart with passion warm;
His hair in waving ringlets careless flow'd,
His blooming cheeks with ruddy beauty glow'd;
Thro' all his person and attractive mein,[1]
Just symmetry and eloquence were seen:

---

1. *mein* Mien, countenance.

But niggard[2] Fortune had her aid with-held,
Lean poverty th' ill-fated youth compell'd
To distant climes to sail, in search of gain,
Which might his latter days in peace maintain.   10
By chance, or rather the decrees of heaven,
His vessel on a barb'rous coast was driven;
He, with a few unhappy stripplings more,
Ventur'd too far upon the fatal shore.
The cruel natives thirsted for their blood,
And issu'd furious from a neighbouring wood.
His friends all fell, by brutal rage o'er-power'd,
Their flesh the horrid *cannibals* devour'd;
Whilst he (alone) escap'd by speedy flight,
And, in a thicket, lay conceal'd from sight.   20
There he reflects on his companions fate,
His threat'ning danger, and abandon'd state:
As thus, in fruitless grief, he spent the day,
A negroe virgin chanc'd to pass that way;
He view'd her naked beauty with surprize,
Her well-proportion'd limbs, and sprightly eyes.
With his complexion, and gay dress amaz'd,
The artless nymph upon the stranger gaz'd;
Charm'd with his features and alluring grace,
His flowing locks and captivating face;   30
His safety now became her chiefest care,
A vaulted cave she knew, and hid him there:
The choicest fruits, the isle produc'd, she sought,
And kindly to allay his hunger brought;
And, when his thirst requir'd, in search of drink,
She led him to some chrystal fountain's brink.
Mutually charm'd, by various arts they strove,
T''inform each other of their mutual love;
A language soon they form'd which might express
Their pleasing cares and growing tenderness: 40
With tigers speckled skins she deck'd his bed,
O'er which the gayest plumes of birds she spread,

2. *niggard* Niggardly, ungenerous.

And every morning, with the nicest care,
Adorn'd her well-turn'd neck and shining hair,
With all the glittering shells and painted flowers,
That serve to deck the *Indian* virgin's bowers.
And when the sun descended in the sky,
And length'ning shades foretold the evening nigh,
Beneath some spreading palm's delightful shade,
Together sate the youth and lovely maid;   50
Or where some bubbling river gently crept,
She, in her arms secur'd him whilst he slept:
When the bright moon in midnight pomp was seen
And star-light glitter'd o'er the dewy green,
In some close arbour, or some fragrant grove,
He whisper'd vows of everlasting love;
And as upon the verdant turf he lay,
Oft he wou'd to th'attentive virgin say:
"Oh! cou'd I but, my *Yarico*, with thee,
Once more, my dear, my native country see,   60
In softest silks thy limbs shou'd be array'd,
Like that of which the clothes I wear are made;
What different ways my grateful soul wou'd find,
To indulge thy person, and divert thy mind!"
While she on the enticing accents hung,
Which smoothly fell from his perswasive tongue,
One evening, from a rock's impending side,
A *European* vessel she espy'd,
And made them signs to touch upon the shore,
Then to her lover the glad tidings bore;   70
Who, with his mistress to the ship descends,
And found the crew were country-men and friends.
Reflecting now upon the time he'd pass'd,
Deep melancholy all his thoughts o'ercast:
"Was it for this," (said he) "I cross'd the main,
Only a doting virgin's heart to gain?
Was this the treasure which I hop'd to find,
When first I dar'd the seas and faithless wind?
I needed not for such a prize to roam,
There are a thousand doting maids at home."   80

While thus his disappointed soul was toss'd,
The ship arriv'd on the *Barbadian*[3] coast;
Immediately the planters from the town
To trade for goods and negroe slaves came down;
And now his mind, by sordid interest sway'd,
Resolv'd to sell his faithful *Indian* maid;
Low at his feet for mercy she implor'd,
And thus, in moving strains, her fate deplor'd:[4]
"Oh! whither shall I turn to seek redress,
When thou'rt the cruel cause of my distress?   90
If the remembrance of our former love,
And all thy plighted vows want force to move,
Yet, for the helpless infant's sake I bear,
Listen, with pity, to my just despair.
Ah! let me not in slavery remain,
Doom'd all my life to drag a servile chain;
It cannot be.—Surely thy generous breast
An act so vile, so horrid, must detest.
But if thou hat'st me, rather let me meet
A gentler fate, and stab me at thy feet;   100
Then will I bless thee with my latest[5] breath,
And sink, contented, to the shades of death."

Not all she said cou'd his compliance move,
Forgetful of his vows, and promis'd love,
The weeping damsel from his knees he spurn'd,
And with her price[6] glad to the ships return'd.

Textual Variants

[Numbers refer to lines]

   Title. *Taken out of the eleventh Spectator* 1738: "A most moving Tale from the *Spectator*";
5. *and* 1738: "an";   8. *Lean* 1738: "And";   8. *th'ill-fated youth* 1738: "th'unhappy boy";

   3. *Barbadian* The 1738 text has "*Barbarian.*" Hulme, *Colonial Encounters,* 254, humorously credits the change to "the revenge of the unconscious."
   4. *deplor'd* The 1726 text reads "implor'd," a typographical repetition of the rhyming word from the previous line. I have supplied the 1738 reading here.
   5. *latest* Final, dying.
   6. *price* The bounty Inkle received for Yarico.

10. *his latter days in peace* 1738: "in ease his latter days";   11. *decrees* 1738: "decree";   21. *There* 1738: "Now";   23. *As* 1738: "Whilst";   25. *beauty* 1738: "beauties";   31. *chiefest* 1738: "tend'rest";   36. *some* 1738: "a";   42. *she* 1738: "were";   57. *And* 1738: "Then";   68. *espy'd* 1738: "descry'd";   77–78. Omitted from 1738;   81. *soul* 1738: "mind";   82. *Barbadian* 1738: "*Barbarian*";   87. *Low* 1738: "Soon";   88. *deplor'd* (1738) 1726: "implor'd";   95. *Ah!* 1738: "Oh";   97. *cannot be.—Surely* 1738: "cannot surely be!"   99. *hat'st* 1738: "hate";   101. *latest* 1738: "dying";   106. *glad* 1738: "pleas'd"

Frances Seymour, Countess of Hertford, "An Epistle from Yarico to Inkle, after He Had Sold Her for a Slave"

"By a Lady." From *A New Miscellany: Being a Collection of Pieces of Poetry from Bath, Tunbridge, Oxford, Epsom, and Other Places, in the Year 1725* [London, 1726?], 38–41.

Lady Hertford's short poem is the earliest known heroic epistle from Yarico to Inkle. This kind of dramatic monologue in epistolary form is written in the fashion of Ovid's *Heroides,* which were widely imitated in most of the major European languages during the seventeenth and eighteenth centuries. The most famous example in English is Alexander Pope's *Eloisa to Abelard* (1717), a poem that the Countess of Hertford greatly admired (Hughes, *Gentle Hertford,* 420).

The heroic epistle has been well described as "the preeminent form before the novel for ventriloquizing the female voice and representing women's inner lives" (Wechselsblatt, "Gender and Race in Yarico's Epistles," 202). It is probably because of the greater sensitivity of the "new" form of the novel in capturing women's inner thoughts and feelings that the Ovidian heroic epistle all but disappeared after the beginning of the nineteenth century. Though it is she who is accorded the first-person voice, the woman in a heroic epistle usually writes from the position of a lover or mistress who has been jilted and disempowered.

In one of the best recent analyses of the conventions of the heroic epistle, Linda S. Kauffman remarks that in such amorous discourse "the heroine always locates herself—spatially, temporally, emotionally—vis-à-vis the beloved. She draws attention to the bond (*foedus*) that links them, which she thinks should command loyalty (*fides*) from the lover to whom she proclaims her faithfulness (*fida*) and laments his infidelity, betrayal, or absence." Kauffman adds that "the heroine glorifies her tears, her heart, her tongue, her body as authentic registers of her emotions . . . Writing comes to signify her life's blood, illustrating her identification of her body with the text" (*Discourses of Desire*, 35, 37). Other useful accounts of the genre are Beer, "'Our Unnatural No-Voice,'" and Kates, "Chronicling the Heroic Epistle in England." Among the many examples of the use of heroic epistle to transmit Yarico's inner thoughts and feelings are selections 4, 6, 8, 10, 14, 15, and 16. For the employment of the Ovidian heroic epistle in Latin as an agency for casting the tale, see headnote to selection 11B.

If yet thou any memory retain
Of her thou'st doom'd in slav'ry to remain;
Oh! hear my sorrow,—'twill be some relief
To the dear author, to unfold my grief.
'Tis thy injustice, thy destructive scorn,
And not the chain I drag, for which I mourn:
That to my limbs (alone) does pain impart,
But thy ingratitude torments my heart.
Close in the deep recesses of my breast,
Thy lovely image still remains imprest,   10
And, spight of thy barbarity to me,
My faithful soul for ever doats on thee.
I well remember that unhappy day,
In which I gaz'd my liberty away;[1]
Charm'd with thy face, like polish'd iv'ry fair,
Thy beauteous features and inticing hair,
How did I tremble, lest thy bloom of life
Shou'd fall a prey to some barbarian's knife!
By love instructed first thy life to save,
I hid thee from them in a mossy cave,   20
And scarce durst venture out in search of food,

1. *gaz'd my liberty away* Wechselblatt comments that "by "gazing" on her future enslaver, the native woman . . . is . . . rendered the agent of her own appropriation" ("Gender and Race," 206).

Lest they (the while) shou'd revel in thy blood;
Yet by a sordid love of gain subdu'd,
You doom'd me to an endless servitude.
And when, in vain, thy stubborn heart to move,
By the remembrance of our loves, I strove,
I begg'd thee, for thy unborn infant's sake,
Compassion on my misery to take:
But you, o'er-power'd by cursed avarice,
For my condition, only rais'd my price.   30
When I beheld thee leave the fatal coast,
And every hope to move thy soul was lost,
How did I my neglected bosom tear,
With all the fury of a wild despair!
Then on the sand a stupid corpse I lay,
'Till (by my master's order) dragg'd away;
My sufferings were thy wretched infant's death,
Who, in one hour, receiv'd and lost his breath:
Yet still I must my hated life sustain,
Still linger on my anxious hours in pain.   40
For once I knew a hoary Christian priest,[2]
(His every act strict piety confess'd)
Who told me, that beyond the azure skies,
And silver moon, another region lies,
Where, after death, those souls[3] would surely go,
Who here unjustly were depress'd with woe,
If they petition'd the all-powerful god,
To smooth their passage, and direct their road;
And there in chrystal palaces, or bowers,
Adorn'd with greens and never-fading flowers,   50
Still wrapt in pleasure, which will know no end,
In songs and praises they their time shall spend.

---

2. *a hoary Christian priest* The figure is entirely Seymour's invention and exclusive to this poem. Ferguson sees him as a kind of secondary hero, a "worthy proponent of Christendom and foil to a godless Inkle" (*Subject to Others,* 82). However, the artlessness with which Yarico repeats the priest's precepts suggests that a more ironic or cynical interpretation would not be out of place here.

3. *souls* Sypher, *Guinea's Captive Kings,* 129, notes how relatively uncommon it was in the first half of the eighteenth century to endow a savage with a soul.

But those who (tir'd of life) themselves destroy,
He said, must never taste celestial joy,
But, underneath the earth, to pits retire,
Where they will burn in everlasting fire;
And, spight of all the ills which I endure,
I dare not venture such a dangerous cure:
He told me too (but oh! avert it, love,
And thou, great over-ruling power above)   60
That perjur'd men, wou'd to those pits be driven,
And ne'er must enter thro' the gate of heaven.
Think, if this sad conjecture shou'd be true,
Dear faithless youth (oh think!) what wilt thou do?

Textual Variants

[Numbers refer to lines]

Title. *sold* 1738: "left";   23. *love* 1738: "thirst";   24. *doom'd* 1738: "destined";   29. *cursed* 1738: "cruel";   50. *Adorn'd . . . flowers* 1738: "Deck'd with eternal greens and fragrant flowers";   51–52. 1738 reads: "In songs and praises they their lives should spend, / Entranc'd in pleasures which will never end."

4

William Pattison, "Yarico to Inkle:

An Epistle"

From *The Poetical Works of Mr. William Pattison, Late of Sidney College Cambridge* (London, 1728), 53–54.

This poem survives only as a fragment, first appearing in a posthumously published collection of the author's verse. William Pattison (1706–27) was the son of a small farmer in the south of England who, after showing considerable academic promise, was admitted as a student at Sidney-Sussex College, Cambridge. He left without a degree in 1726 and lived a brief and precarious existence as an impoverished poet in London, where he was given shelter by the bookseller Edmund Curll. His life was cut short by smallpox in July 1727 when his promised volume of poetry had already attracted a list of subscribers that included Alexander Pope. A memoir of the author, accompanying his *Poetical Works,* ends by remarking that "*One of the epistles* promised by Mr. *Pattison* . . . he left unfinished; but the Fragment of it, which he had begun, hereafter follows. It is that of *Yarico* to *Inkle.*" The fragment shows a close tonal familiarity with Ovid's heroic epistles (see headnote to selection 3B) yet assumes the reader knows the story of Inkle and Yarico. The celebrity of the tale after Steele introduced it made it attractive subject matter for both male and female writers. A succinct account of Pattison's life is found in *DNB*.

Dear, faithless man! if e'er that cruel breast
Love's pleasing toys, and soft delights, confest;
Distress like mine, may sure thy pity move,

For tender pity is the child of love!
But can compassion from thy bosom flow?
Source of my wrongs, and fountain of my woe!
Wilt thou, repentant, soften at my grief,
Melt at my tears, and lend a late relief!
What have I done? ah, how deserved thy hate?
Or was this vengeance treasur'd up by Fate?   10
Then will I mourn my fate's severe decree,
Nor charge a guilt so black, so base on thee;
For O! I know, ah no! I knew, thy mind
Soft as the *dove,* and as the *turtle* kind;[1]
How have I seen thy gentle bosom move,
And heave, contagious, to some *tale* of *love!*
How have I heard thee paint the *faithfull'st* pair,
Describe their bliss, and e'en their raptures share!
Then have thy lips, with sweet transition swore
Thy *love* more lasting, and thy *passion* more!   20

And what is *Truth,* if signs like these deceive!
Signs! that might win the wariest to believe.*

*[2]For a recital of this story, we must refer the reader to the *Spectator,* Vol. 1st. Numb. XI. That part of it which occasioned this Epistle was *Inkle's* selling *Yarico* for a slave, after she had proved with child by him, and been the means of his preservation from her salvage-countrymen.[3] The diction is perfectly *Ovidian,* and it is greatly to be lamented that we have no more of it.

Like this last work, was Fate's severe decree,
Just show'd our author's fruit, then fell'd the tree.

1. *the dove, and . . . the turtle kind* Traditionally, the phoenix and the turtledove were depicted as emblematic of enduring love, "the *faithfull'st* pair." Pattison may have intended an ironic echo of this famous legend by having Yarico praise Inkle for qualities more readily associated with the faithful turtledove. See Rowland, *Birds with Human Souls,* 46.
2. *footnote* Added by Curll or his editor.
3. *salvage-countrymen* Savage countrymen.

5

Anonymous, "The Story of Inkle and Yarico, from the Eleventh *Spectator*"

From the *London Magazine* 3 (May 1734): 257–58.

The self-referential opening to this anonymous poem ("an artless *dame* . . . / Unlearnt in schools, unblest with natal fire," 1–2) has led to the traditional assumption that its author was a woman (see Price, *Inkle and Yarico Album,* 9, and more recently, Ferguson, *Subject to Others,* 85–90). However, Wechselblatt, "Gender and Race," 201, has questioned this conclusion by arguing that "the invocation may suggest that a male author has taken up Steele's strategy of placing Yarico's story in the mouth of a woman." The narrative is related in the third person but, though pledging to unmask "the dire arts of faithless man" (4), cedes final moral judgment to the reader.

The poem closely follows the story line as established by Steele, but its framing has been transposed from its seventeenth-century source to a context that is simultaneously classical and pagan. In the depiction of the natives as cannibals, there are discernible echoes of Virgil's account of the cave of the Cyclops in the *Aeneid,* book 3. Within the poem, Inkle (called by his own name only in its title) is portrayed as both godlike in his image and of an effeminate attractiveness, finding favor in the eyes of Jove, who protects him from personal harm. As Ferguson notes (186), the added mythological elements introduce rather awkward homoerotic undertones. But whereas "all-pitying *Jove*" (32) succors Inkle, he shows no such compassion either toward his fellow sailors or to the tenderhearted Yarico, here "a negro virgin . . . [of] noble birth" (35, 38). Ironically, human pity, of the kind that Yarico has in abundance, is depicted as more than vulnerable.

Within the poem, it is a quality that is absent in the male-dominated immortal world and, as if by complicity, among the merchants of the slave trade.

Ye virgin train,[1] an artless *dame* inspire,
Unlearnt in schools, unblest with natal fire,[2]
To save this story from devouring fate,
And the dire arts of faithless man relate.
A youth I sing, in face and shape divine,
In whom both art and nature did combine
With heavenly skill to mingle ev'ry charm,
As gods of old did fair *Pandora*[3] form.
Stranger to virtue, this deceiver held
The box of mischiefs in his breast conceal'd;   10
His outward form each female heart enflam'd;
His inward beauty lurking avarice stain'd.
      Insatiate[4] love of gold, and hope of gain,
Encourag'd him to cut the yielding main;[5]
By winds, or waves, or the decrees of heaven,
His bark upon a barbarous coast was driven;
Possest by men who thirst for human blood,
Who live in caves, or thickets of the wood:

1. *Ye virgin train* The invocation addresses the Muses, virgin daughters of Jove and Mnemosyne. The figure is very common in the seventeenth and eighteenth centuries; see, for example, Henry Baker, "On the Death of Mrs. Halsey, Aged Nineteen" (in *Original Poems* [London, 1725], 1:17): "Mourn, O You Muses! mourn, You Virgin Train!" See also Dryden, *Palamon and Arcite* (1699), 3.1.244, and Pope, *Windsor Forest* (1713), line 160.

2. *unblest with natal fire* Lacking innate creative or poetic gifts.

3. *Pandora* In classical mythology the first woman, who, on opening Jove's gift of an elaborate box despite his prohibition, released all known evils into the world. Wechselblatt, "Gender and Race," 201, comments that the poem taps "an ancient tradition for representing woman as both the cause and the effect of her own victimization by men." By ironic inversion here, the "box of mischiefs" has become a male possession.

4. *Insatiate* Insatiable.

5. *cut the yielding main* Cross the seas; cf. Richard Glover, *Leonidas* (1737), 1.92–93: "the sliding prowe, / . . . parts the smooth and yielding main."

Untaught to plant (yet corn and fruits abound,
And fragrant flowers enamel[6] all the ground.)   20
Distrest, he landed on this fatal shore,
With some companions, which were soon no more;
The savage race their trembling flesh devour,
Off'ring oblations to th'infernal power.
Dreadfully suppliant, human limbs they tore,
(Accursed rites!) and quaft their streaming gore.[7]
Immortal *Jove* stoop'd from his azure sky,
Grieving a form so like his own shou'd die;[8]
On the fair youth *mercurial* speed bestow'd,
Swifter than thought he reach'd the shady wood.   30
   Beneath a nightly shade he panting lies,
Screen'd by all-pitying *Jove* from hostile eyes;
Yet gloomy sorrows and unmanly fears
Swell'd his sad breast which he bedew'd with tears:
When lo! a negro virgin chanc'd to rove
Thro' the thick mazes of the nodding grove,
Whose glitt'ring shells and elegant undress,
With various plumes, a noble birth confess.
With reverential fear, the well-shap'd maid
Thought him a god, and low obeisance paid.   40
His face like polish'd marble did appear;
His silken robe, and long-curl'd flaxen hair
Amaz'd the nymph; nor less her sparkling eyes,
And naked beauty, did the youth surprize.
Low at her feet, in suppliant posture laid,
With speaking eyes, he thus addrest the maid.
   "O let soft pity touch that lovely breast!
Succour a man, by various ills opprest:
Such finish'd grace does thro' your person shine,
Sure 'tis enliven'd by a soul divine."   50
   The tender negro look'd a kind reply

6. *enamel* Embellish.
7. *human limbs . . . streaming gore* Cf. Virgil, *Aeneid* (trans. John Dryden, 1697), 3.810–
11: "the dismal Flore / Was pav'd with mangled Limbs and putrid Gore."
8. *die* 1734: "dye."

Thro' pearls of pity, dropping from her eye;
With hands uplifted, did the gods implore,
That her relentless countrymen no more
Might stain their native land with human gore.
He seiz'd her hand, with tender passion prest,
While copious tears both love and fear confest.
The pitying maid view'd him with yielding eyes,
And from each bosom mutual sighs arise.

   His safety, now, became her only care,   60
A secret cave she knew, and hid him there;
Adorn'd it with the spoils of leopards slain,
Which other lovers ventur'd life to gain.
Through mazy thickets, and a pathless wood
She prest, advent'rous, with delicious food.
Daily her hand a rich repast did bring
Of ripen'd fruits, and waters from the spring:
But when declining, toward the close of day,
The crimson sun sets weary on the sea,
Strait to a shady grove, where fountains rise,   70
From woods defended, and inclement skies,
Where the wing'd warblers of the air conspire
From several boughs, to form a heavenly quire,
Adorn'd with fragrant flowers, and ever-green,
She leads the youth (delightful silvan scene!)
Where he, in peaceful slumbers, takes his rest,
Forgets his fears, and calms his tim'rous breast.

   In soft repose the beauteous lover lies,
While *Yarico* with care unseals her eyes;
With anxious fear the matchless maid attends,   80
Careful to save him from her barb'rous friends.

   The flowing curls which o'er his shoulders play'd
With artless beauty, pleas'd the negro maid;
She thought her fingers, when entangled there,
Like clouds uncircling *Berenice*'s[9] hair:

9. *Berenice* The wife of Ptolemy III Euergetes, who cut off her locks as a votive offering for the safe return of her husband. Her hair was stolen, however, and was believed to have been translated into a heavenly constellation. Once again Inkle's appearance is deliberately feminized.

The graceful youth confessing equal fire,
Did her just symmetry of shape admire.
  Oft would he say, "my *Yarico,* with thee
(My only bliss!) cou'd I my country see,
If ever I forget my vows of love,   90
Unblest, abandon'd, may I friendless rove.
To thee, alone, I owe the vital air;
My love and gratitude for ever share.
I'll gems provide, and silks of curious art,
With gifts expressive of my grateful heart:
Thou in a house by horses drawn shalt ride,
With me, thy faithful lover, by thy side:
The female train[10] shalt round with envy gaze,
Wonder, and silent sigh unwilling praise."
  Pleas'd with his words, desiring more to please,   100
She from a craggy cliff survey'd the seas;
A bark she spy'd, and did by signs implore,
That they would touch upon the sandy shore.
With joy she ran—"My love make haste away,
A vessel waits us, on the foaming sea."
Soon he the vessel's lofty side ascends,
And finds them to be countrymen, and friends.
With lovely *Yarico,* puts off to sea;
With equal joy they plough the watry way.
  When the fair youth, despairing, calls to mind   110
All hopes eluded of his wealth design'd;
Riches the seat of his affection seize,
And faithful *Yarico* no more can please.
Unhappy maid! to wasting sorrows born,
And fated evils undeserv'd to mourn.
  This youth was born too near the northern pole,[11]
Which chill'd each virtue in his frozen soul:
But near the sun, the nymph her birth confest,
Where ev'ry virtue glow'd within her breast,

  10. *The female train* Other women, womankind; cf. note 1.
  11. *born too near the northern pole* On theories that linked race and climate, see Aldridge,
"Feijoo and the Problem of Ethiopian Color"; also, more generally, Braude, "Sons of Noah."

Thus ore[12] lies in the earth, unfinish'd, cold;   120
But purg'd by fire, it brightens into gold.
   Propitious *Zephyrs*[13] fill their swelling sails;
They make *Barbadoes,* blest with prosp'rous gales.
The planters thick'ning[14] on the key[15] appear,
To purchase negroe slaves, if any there;
When the false youth, by cursed avarice sway'd,
Horrid to mention! sells his faithful maid.
   Amaz'd and trembling, silently she mourn'd,
While speaking tears her radiant eyes adorn'd.
Low at his feet, the lovely mourner lay;   130
Nor would to words her swelling heart give way.
She grasps his knees, in vain attempts to speak,
At length her words in moving accents break:
"O much lov'd youth, in tender pity spare
A helpless maid, my long-try'd faith revere.
From you this worst of human ills to prove,
Must break a heart that overflows with love.
Break not my heart, nor drive me to despair,
Lest you deface your lovely image there.
Ah! do not with consummate woe undo   140
A soul, that father, mother, country, left for you.
What sorrows must my tender parents mourn,
By me forsaken, never to return?
Transfer'd from them, to you my love I gave;
Unjust return! to sell me for a slave.
Oh call to mind the sacred oaths you've given,
Remember there are thunderbolts[16] in heaven.
But if the swelling sorrows in my breast
Your heart of adamant[17] can still resist,
Yet let the infant in my womb I bear,   150
The blessing taste of your paternal care."
   He thrust her from him with remorseless hand,
For her condition rais'd his first demand.

---

12. *ore* 1734: "oar."   13. *Zephyrs* Breezes.
14. *thick'ning* Crowding.   15. *key* Quay.
16. *thunderbolts* Jove's accustomed weapons.
17. *adamant* "A thing impenetrably hard" (*OED*).

Pleas'd with success he chearfully returns,
While hapless *Yarico* in bondage mourns.
The merchants all the prudent youth admire,
That could, so young, a trading soul acquire.

6

Anonymous, *Yarico to Inkle: An Epistle*

London: Printed for Lawton Gilliver, at *Homer's Head*
against St. *Dunstan's* Church in *Fleetstreet.* 1736.

The nimble fusion of pathos and private agony marks this as among the
finest of the sundry heroic epistles written from Yarico to Inkle. The narrative subtly unfolds the traditional tale to articulate the poignant finality
of Yarico's cruel enslavement. "Through her ineffectual appeal to her status
as the bearer of Inkle's child," remarks Wechselblatt, "Yarico reveals the mutual implication of domestic and colonial tyranny within the merging of
sensibility with primitivism" ("Gender and Race," 205).

The true authorship of the poem remains one of its more intriguing
puzzles. Its modern attribution, found in the *Eighteenth-Century Short-
Title Catalogue* and elsewhere, to the pen of Edward Moore (1712–57) is far
from secure. David Foxon describes it as "unconfirmed" while mistakenly
recording an early manuscript ascription in a copy of the 1736 first edition
now preserved in the J. H. Wrenn collection at the University of Texas at
Austin (*English Verse,* 2:478, M 434). Richard W. Oram, librarian at the
Harry Ransom Humanities Research Center at Austin, has kindly examined this copy for me, discovering that it has no annotations. Dr. Oram
writes to me that it was sold to Wrenn by T. J. Wise, who attributed the
poem to Moore but (as is common with Wise) without any accompanying
evidence. A further copy of the 1736 text offered for sale by the London
bookseller Percy Dobell contains a manuscript note on its title, "by Mr.
Edward Moore," but there is no indication whether this was a contemporary annotation (*Catalogue of Eighteenth Century Verse,* item 2705, p. 135). I
have not been able to ascertain the present whereabouts of the Dobell copy.

Yarico to Inkle: An Epistle was not included in the collected edition of
Moore's *Poems* (1756), and its attribution to him must now be regarded as

highly suspect. If it is indeed by him, it is an exceptionally accomplished early poem. Moore's subsequent career included authorship of *Fables for the Female Sex* (1744) and *The Gamester* (1753) and editorship of *The World* (1753), a collaborative series of moral essays in the style of *The Spectator.*

According to Price (*Inkle and Yarico Album*, 11–17), who seems to have been unaware of the ascription to Moore, the poem has been attributed, albeit erroneously, to the Rev. John Anketell (1750–?), curate of Donagh-endry parish, County Tyrone, Ireland, and also to Isaac Story of Massa-chusetts. It was reprinted with some minor variations and additions in the *Dublin Chronicle* (ten installments between 23 February and 19 March 1771) and separately reissued (Dublin, 1774) as the production of "a young gentleman of Trinity College." The same text was later included in An-ketell's *Poems on Several Subjects* (Dublin, 1793). In a circumstantial ac-count prefatory to the 1793 edition, Anketell avows that when he was a schoolboy "a relation of mine, long deceased, was so kind as to lend me the original poem of *Yarico to Inkle*, which he got from an intimate friend, the author of it, who had been dead many years before it came into my hands." Sadly if also disingenuously, Anketell makes no attempt to identify the "intimate friend." Ultimately he disclaims authorship of the poem, ac-knowledging that it would be "a kind of fraud" if he were to "pass as the author of it" (xxiii). That said, it was incorporated with Anketell's other poetic works in the 1793 edition and in a Boston reprint of 1795!

Far from having been its author, as was once widely believed in Amer-ica, Isaac Story (1774–1803) was the *printer* of the Marblehead (Salem) edi-tion of 1792. What is unusual about this text is that the final thirty-four lines have been replaced with the ending of the similarly named poem by Edward Jerningham, first published in 1766 [10]. As Price comments, the substitute ending, which employs "Jerningham's Yarico . . . a Nubian maiden of sometimes violent disposition, . . . fits but imperfectly" (14). No convincing reason has been advanced to explain the alteration, though the frequent reworking of this anonymous poem during the eighteenth cen-tury provides visible endorsement of the astonishing ductility of a tale that belonged more to the public domain than to a single authorial conscious-ness. The Marblehead text was reprinted at Boston in 1794.

The numerous textual variations within *Yarico to Inkle* present a biblio-graphical tangle too complex to be fully unraveled here. In addition to eleven discrete printed texts recorded by Price (156–57), several manuscript texts of the poem survive. Perhaps the most significant of these is McGill

MS 159, a nonauthorial verse compilation that includes several other poems. The laid paper of the manuscript has a watermark dated 1703. It was acquired in 1925 by McGill University, Montreal, also from the London bookseller Dobell. In a letter to me dated 19 February 1997, Richard Virr, curator of manuscripts at McGill, has advanced the attractive proposition that "this manuscript is a copy of the original manuscript which was textually edited and to which [the verse dedication] 'To *Miss* Arabella Saintloe' was added for publication in 1736."

Margaret Crum records at the Bodleian Library, Oxford, a manuscript text of "Verses to Miss Arabella Saintloe by the Author of an Epistle from Yarico to Inkle" (O 769; MS Eng. poet.e.40, fol. 127), incorrectly ascribing its authorship to Edward Jerningham. The Bodleian manuscript is part of a collection of verse, epitaphs, and riddles in the hand of Captain Gabriel Lepipre. A further manuscript of *Yarico to Inkle* (complete with the dedicatory verses) in the private collection of Dr. John Gilmore of the University of Warwick is ostensibly a copy made from the 1736 printed text.

In light of the McGill manuscript, I cannot be as categorical as Price in concluding "that the London edition of 1736 most accurately reproduces the text of the lost original" (14). Nevertheless, it is reprinted here as the best-known version and as the text to which all later editions of this poem owe a particular indebtedness. Selective departures taken from Anketell (1794) ("Ank.": available in *The Eighteenth Century* on microfilm, Reel 6815/11), and from the McGill manuscript ("McGill") are included in a list of textual variants at the end of the poem. Though it would make an interesting exercise, I have not attempted a complete collation.

Yarico to *Inkle.* An Epistle

Fate ne'er strikes deep, but when Unkindness joins.
——But there's a Fate in Kindness,
Still to be least return'd, where most 'tis given.[1]   *Dryden.*

---

1. *Fate ne'er strikes . . . 'tis given* The epigraph is taken from John Dryden's tragicomedy *Secret Love, or The Maiden-Queen* (1668), 4.2.92, 58–59, a play that disappeared from the stage after 1706 (see the California edition of *The Works of John Dryden,* 9:331). For the epigraph to the 1792 Marblehead edition, a passage from Virgil, *The Aeneid,* 1.539–40, has been substituted: "Quod genus hoc hominum? quæve hunc tam barbara morem / Permittit

To Miss *Arabella Saintloe*[2]

O *Saintloe,* brightest of the virgin train,
Approve my numbers, or I write in vain!
To you, fair patroness, these lines belong,[3]
Life of my hopes, and ruler of my song!
How shou'd the poet to the task be fir'd,
By you commanded, and by you inspir'd!
Soft as the melting accents of your tongue
Shou'd flow the language, and the sense as strong;
Smooth as your temper, easy as your air,
Keen as your wit, and as your judgment clear.

Too steep the hill for infant limbs to climb,
Superior labour to a muse like mine!
Yet still she keeps the dazling height in view,
And, faintly, copies what she learnt from you.

If o'er the plain-wrote tale the virgin's eye
Lets drop a tear, or lends a pitying sigh,
While tenderly she pleads the Negro's cause,[4]
And melts in soft compassion at her woes,

---

patria?" (What manner of men are these? What land is this /that allows them such barbarous ways?). Hulme, *Colonial Encounters,* 259, regards the employment of such poignant questions in this substitute epigraph as "carefully ambivalent, referring equally to Inkle's 'barbaric' action and to the English ship's inhospitable reception on the Caribbean coast." He also suggests that the epigraph invokes parallels between Inkle and Yarico and Virgil's story of Dido and Aeneas: "In both cases an amorous relationship develops between the traveller and an hospitable 'princess' of the country; in both cases their sexual union . . . herald[s] a period of bliss which is brought to an end when the traveller moves on, deserting the woman he had loved" (249).

2. *Miss Arabella Saintloe* The "fair patroness" of the invocation has so far eluded identification. However, the *Grub-Street Journal,* Thursday, 17 November 1737, records the marriage "last week, [of] Mr. Cranke, silkman, in the Poultry, to Miss St. Lo, an agreeable young lady, and 4000 l. [four thousand pounds] fortune" (see also *Gentleman's Magazine* 7 [November 1737]: 701). Also of the same family may be the Reverend Saint-Lo, canon of Wells, who subscribed to John Warren's *Sermons upon Several Subjects* (1739) and Captain John St Lo of the British Navy (*Gentleman's Magazine* 12 [July 1742]: 388).

3. *To you . . . these lines belong* In exploiting the form of heroic epistle (see headnote to selection 3B), the male poet uses the invocation to plead "the comparative inadequacy of his own muse . . . and his consequent need to appropriate the woman Saintloe's . . . by virtue of her gender and of his genre" (Wechselblatt, Gender and Race," 202–4).

4. *the Negro's cause* Yarico's translation from Native American to African has become inexorable (see introduction, p. 16).

You, *Saintloe,* shall her willing thanks receive,
Whose inspiration bad the story live.[5]

Yarico to Inkle

The Argument

The story of *Inkle* and *Yarico* is allow'd to be genuine; 'tis related first by Ligon, in his account of Barbadoes, from thence by the *Spectator,* and will as long as either lasts, be mention'd in competition with the blackest, most incredible piece of ingratitude, that history, or romance can furnish. The following epistle is suppos'd to be wrote by *Yarico* in the beginning of her slavery, just as *Inkle* was embarking for England, and contains a little history of her unprecedented ill usage, mix'd with entreaties and upbraidings, tenderness and reproaches.

From the sad place, where Sorrow ever reigns,
And hopeless wretches groan beneath their chains;
Where stern Oppression lifts her iron hand,
And restless Cruelty usurps command;
To sooth her soul, and ease her aking heart,
Permit a wretch her sufferings to impart:
To *Inkle* she complains, to him, who taught
Her hand in language to express her thought
Yet e'er your sails before the winds are spread,
A woman's sorrows with compassion read;   10
Her dying farewel from her pen receive,
And to her wrongs a tear in pity give.
    Fain wou'd I learn from whence your hate arose,
The cruel cause, and source of all my woes;
O tell me, why am I so wretched made?
For what unwilling crime am I betray'd?
Is it because I lov'd?—Unjust reward!
That love preserv'd you from the ills you fear'd;
If 'twas a fault, alas! I'm guilty still,
For still I love, and while I live I will;   20
No change of fortune, nor your cruel hate
Shall cure my passion, or its warmth abate.

___

5. [Verse invocation] Omitted from McGill and Anketell.

False as you are, how dare you trust anew
To winds and seas, as treacherous as you?
Think, will the gods you serve, if gods they are,
For crimes like your's, their punishments forbear?
If injur'd innocence their care be made,
Tho' I forgive, their certain vengeance dread.
What if your bark, by adverse tempests tost,
Shou'd on some barbarous shore like mine, be lost;   30
Think that you see your friends and you pursu'd
By savage people, greedy for your blood,
Who then wou'd snatch you from your pale dispair?
You'd find no *Yarico* to shield you there;
How would you wish you never had betray'd,
Or sold for trifling gain an helpless maid!
   O yet redeem me, while you've power to save,
And make me yours, if I must be a slave!
Your faithful slave, indeed, I'll ever prove,
And with continu'd care attend my love.   40
Think on the vows you have so often made,
How did you promise!—How have you betray'd!
Think, are these chains, these bitter woes her due,
Who left her country, and her friends for you!
And think, O think on the dear load I bear!
Must the poor babe a mother's sufferings share?
Shall the dear witness of our mutual flame
Be born to want, to misery, and shame?
"Whose tender care shall hush thy infant cry?
Or whose indulgent hand thy wants supply?   50
Behold the gift a father's love prepares!
Unceasing sorrow, and continu'd tears;
This is the portion destin'd to be thine,
Thou heir to all the wrongs that now are mine!"⁶
   O wou'd my pen in artful language tell
The sad variety of ills I feel;
Wou'd some kind power assist my thoughts to flow

---

6. The passage in quotation marks, lines 49–54, is supposedly addressed to the yet unborn child of their relationship.

Strong as my love, and piercing as my woe,
To paint the anguish of my aking heart,
My bitter sufferings, and severest smart,   60
Even you, barbarian! wou'd relieve my pain,
And pitying take me to your arms again.
    Remember, for 'tis sure you often must,
When the seas drove you on our fatal coast;
How did my cruel friends your life pursue!
And none of all who landed 'scap'd but you;
Pale with your fears, and breathless in the chace,
With wearied steps you ran from place to place,
Forlorn, distrest, you knew not where to go,
To shun the fury of the desp'rate foe: 70
Till chance, or rather some propitious god
Your feet conducted to a shady wood;
Screen'd from your hunter's eyes, but not your fears,
On the bare ground you lay o'erwhelm'd in tears;
Your speaking looks, and stifled groans confest
A wretch, with more than common ills opprest.
'Twas in that fatal shade, by fortune brought,
A shelter from the scorching heat I sought,
Or rather to indulge a secret tear,
Shed for your friends, whose cries had reach'd my ear.   80
There I beheld you, trembling as you lay,
And, e'er I knew it, look'd my soul away.
You saw me, and the sight encreas'd your fear,
You rose, and wou'd have fled—but knew not where!
Returning, at my feet your self you threw,
And did by earnest signs, for pity sue;
Fond of the charge, solicitous to save,
I rais'd and brought you to a secret cave;
To chear my love, delicious fruits I got,
And water from the chrystal fountain brought.   90
Pleas'd with my care, you held me to your breast,
And by expressive looks your thanks confest.
Such tender offices, unhop'd, dispel'd
Your gloomy fears, and your distraction heal'd;
The languid paleness from your visage fled,

And native bloom your glowing cheeks o'erspread.
Your eyes o'er all my naked beauties stray'd,
While mine your dress, and fairer face survey'd;
If you my well-proportion'd shape admir'd,
Your flowing locks my heaving bosom fir'd.   100
The tenderest things in words unknown you spoke,
But the soft meaning from your eyes I took;
No other language cou'd we use, or need,
For eyes beyond all eloquence persuade.
Enflam'd with love, with wanton joy you kist
My trembling lips, and panting to be blest,
You prest, and look'd, and strove—nor vainly strove,
For every power was softned into love,
Unskil'd in art, unable to deny,
Blushing, I yielded to the silent joy.   110
O happy hours of love! when all my care
Was but to please, and to preserve my dear;
Solicitous for nothing else, I knew
No thought, no wish for any thing but you.
Clasp'd in each other's arms conceal'd we lay,
And in soft pleasures wasted all the day;
But when the sun's discerning light withdrew,
And the mild evening's cooling breezes blew,
With cautious steps, thro' secret paths I led,
To some still grove, or unfrequented shade;   120
The murm'ring stream's enamell'd[7] bank we prest,
The murm'ring stream invited you to rest.
But careful of your safety, while you slept,
My waking eyes in constant watch I kept;[8]
My arm, incircled round your neck, was made
A guard, and tender pillow for your head.
Thus in soft slumbers stretch'd at ease you lay,
'Till op'ning morning summon'd us away;
In haste I cry'd, "Awake, awake my dear,

7. *enamell'd* "Beautified with various colours" (*OED*).
8. [Lines 74–124] Anketell omits these lines, linking the text with the following couplet: "By me alone was thy retreat perceiv'd, /And Oh! by love my soul was straight enslav'd!" The elision cuts out the most erotic portion of the poem.

The chirping birds approaching day declare;   130
See how the fainting stars foretel the morn,
Awake my dear, and to our cave return!"
    Whole months, secure in these retreats we past,
And each new hour came happier than the last;
Such was our love, so mutual was our flame,
Our hopes, and fears, and wishes were the same.
The various presents other lovers gave,
I brought to furnish, or adorn our cave;
With softest, parti-colour'd skins I made,
Perfum'd with sweetest flowers, a fragrant bed;   140
Had you a wish, that ever I deny'd,
Or was not with a willing care supply'd?
O what returns for such a waste of love!—
But still wou'd I intreat, and not reprove.
Yet let me mind you of what once you said,
While oaths confirm'd the promises you made.
"My *Yarico,* my love, my life," you cry'd,
"My dear preserver, and my choice's pride!
Thou kindest, softest cure of all my woe,
How shall I pay the gratitude I owe?   150
Thou power that mad'st me, hear me while I swear
Eternal truth, eternal love to her!
If thou vouchsaf'st me to behold once more
My dear, my long-lost friends, and native shore,
If ever I forget her tender care,
Do thou regardless hear my dying pray'r,
Drive me in bitterness of want to rove,
And shut me ever from the realms above!"
    Is he a god, whose curses you implor'd,
And shall his hand not grasp th'avenging sword?   160
Ne'er can you hope in sweet content to live,
Or know that comfort, you refus'd to give.
    Among the vices men abhor the most,
Ingratitude is sure of all accurst;
Can the just gods with pleasure look upon,
Or love the temper, so unlike their own?
Kind offices a kind requital claim,

He pays but half, who but returns the same;
He who gives first, a generous kindness shows,
The other, only pays a debt he owes.   170
But you, relentless to my cries and pray'rs,
Smile at my wrongs, and mock my falling tears.
Not one return of all the mighty debt,
But cruel rage, and persecuting hate;
This, this is all your nature can bestow,
And thus you *pay the gratitude you owe.*

   Time and my griefs this body shall decay,
This moving frame shall be but lifeless clay;
Then peaceful in the silent grave I'll rest,
Still this warm blood, and calm this glowing breast;   180
But the rememb'rance of my wrongs shall live,
Your treachery whole ages shall survive,
People, unborn, shall my sad tale relate
And curse your cruelty, and weep my fate.

   And if in distant years, some hapless maid
Shall be by faithless, barbarous man betray'd,
Condemn'd in sharpest misery to rove,
Unblest with hope, still curs'd with fatal love;
One to whom life, and liberty he owes,
From whose fond kindness every blessing flows,   190
Then shall the just comparison be made,
So trusted *Yarico,* and was betray'd.

   Think on that morn, when on the beach I stood,
And saw the bark[9] at anchor in the flood;
Strait to your cave with eager haste I ran,
"Behold my dear, a vessel on the main!
Away my love, nor longer let us live
Unknown to peace security can give!"
No more you needed. Pleasure in your eyes
Flash'd like a shooting blaze in evening skies;   200
Your eager arms around my neck you flung,
And on my lips in silent transport hung;
The mighty joy, too great to be exprest,

---

9. *bark* Vessel, ship.

Glow'd on your cheeks, and struggled in your breast.
"Adieu," you cry'd, "ye friendly shades adieu,"
(As in embraces to the shore we flew)
"And thou, my cave! thou ever kind retreat,
Scene of our pleasures, and my safety's seat,
Farewel! Ye cruel savages adieu!
Adieu to all, my *Yarico,* but you! 210
Thou, my preserver, shal't be ever near,
Reign in my soul, and every blessing share!"
　But why do I pursue th'ungrateful tale?
Why urge a cause, that never will prevail?
Why tell, when nearer to the ship we drew,
The waving colours you beheld, and knew?
"See, see my love, what heav'n relenting sends!
Behold my friends, my countrymen and friends!"
Then loud you cry'd, and wav'd your hands in air,
And strait we saw the hast'ning boat appear; 220
With lusty strokes we cut the yielding tide,
And joyful climb'd the lofty vessel's side.
　If from a life of long-continu'd fear,
From threat'ning cruelty, and anxious care,
From death, the greatest of all ills we dread,
To be in one propitious moment freed,
Be happiness that can addition know,
Your friend's embraces made it so to you.
　And now the ship unfurls her crackling sails,
Whose bending bosoms catch the rising gales, 230
Like distant clouds appears the less'ning shore,
'Till the faint prospect can be view'd no more.
"Adieu my country, and my friends adieu!
A lasting farewel here I take of you!"
Thus while I cry'd, as conscious of my fate,
Unusual sadness on my spirits sat,
My blood ran cold, my bosom heav'd with sighs,
And gushing sorrow trickled from my eyes.
But you with well-dissembled fondness came,
(Dissembled 'twas, and yet you look'd the same) 240
"O whence, my love, this change, that mournful look?"

You said, and mingled kisses as you spoke:
"What means my life? O tell me why you sigh?
Why steals the pearly moisture from thy eye?
Tell me, and let me cure the ills you feel,
Or share the anguish, that I cannot heal!"
Pleas'd with your words, suspecting no deceit,
Artless, I swallow'd the ensnaring bait;
Honest my self, I thought the world so too,
Nor fear'd deceit, for no deceit I knew;   250
No more I wept, my griefs were lull'd asleep,
'Till 'twas decreed I must for ever weep.

    Brisk blow the driving winds, the fleeting[10] ship
Cuts the thin air, and skims along the deep;
When on the deck a sudden shout we heard;
Barbadoe's welcome coast at last appear'd;
The busy sailors skip'd from place to place,
And smiling joy appear'd in every face.
But you sat silent, pensive and alone,
And meditated villany to come;   260
Then was the scheme of my undoing laid,
Then was the curs'd determination made.

    O say what mov'd you to the cruel deed!
Did it from hate, or thirst of gain proceed?
Urge nothing—for if love's not in our pow'r,
Is there from gratitude requir'd no more;
That's the strong tie, that shou'd for ever bind,
The surest charm to fix a generous mind.[11]

    10. *fleeting* Swift.
    11. [Lines 268–69] McGill inserts the following passage between these two lines:
What tho' the burning sun's discolouring rays,
Have shadow'd with a browner dye my face,
Yet was I thought most lovely to the sight,
The virgin's envy, and the youth's delight.
Nor was my birth unequal to my flame,
I from a race of sovereign princes came.
My love the noblest of the youthful train
With warm persuasion pleaded to obtain.
Alas! unheeded all their vows I heard,
Nor knew a tender wish 'till you appear'd,

Ye powers divine, who guide the world below,
Relieve, or teach me how to bear my woe!   270
Give me, O give me eloquence to move
His stubborn heart, and bring it back to love![12]
So shall my life be spent in grateful praise,
And lasting honours to your names I'll raise.
    And now I stood upon the long'd-for shore,
And fondly hop'd my hours of sorrow o'er;
You smil'd, and as you kindly prest my hand,
"Welcome," you cry'd, "my *Yarico,* to Land!
Thou kindest, dearest, tenderest, loveliest maid,
Now shall my promis'd gratitude be paid!"—   280
—O how unmanly is the flattering lie,
That chears, but to enhance our misery!
For that which aggravates our sorrows most,
Is to know happiness, and know it lost.
Such soothing words conceal'd the vile deceit,
And lull'd me unsuspecting of my fate.
But now no longer need the mask be on,
The means were over, for the end was won;
No more th'endearing look your falshood wears,
But all the monster in full light appears.   290
"Take her," you cry'd, "my right I here resign,
Her life and labours are by purchase thine!"
You ended, and the wretch, to whom you spoke
(Pride and ill-nature settled in his look)
Approach'd, and sternly seiz'd upon my hand,
And rudely hail'd me under his command.
    Such cruelty, what *savage* ever knew,

Subdu'd, I yielded up to your's alone,
Decreed the slave of love to be undone.
    The inserted passage also appears with minor differences in Anketell, leading Price
(*Inkle and Yarico Album,* 16) to conclude that these twelve lines must have been written by
him. If, as seems most probable, McGill MS 159 predates Anketell, the greater likelihood is
that they were part of the poem's original composition but omitted from the 1736 printed
text.
    12. [Lines 272–73] Anketell adds the following couplet between these lines: "Oh! make
him feel the horrors I endure, /And kindly fly my miseries to cure!"

Or, hearing, cou'd believe you meant it true?
Too true I found it, when with barbarous scoff,
And hate, unknown before, you shook me off;   300
Plung'd me o'erwhelm'd in every human ill,
Not to be spoke—And which I only feel.
   Can you forget, or did you ne'er regard
The sad distress, that in my soul appear'd?
How chill'd with horror, I cou'd scarce survive,
And mad, and blasted, stiffen'd yet alive?
How grov'ling at your feet, in wild dispair
I beat my bleeding breast, and tore my hair?
Then what did rage, and fear, and love not say
As madness prompted, and my pangs gave way?   310
"O save me, and this fatal doom reverse,
Which once endur'd, there is no further curse!
Or tell me why with vengeance you pursue
Her, who was life, and happiness to you?
Relentless can you stand to all I say?
Unchang'd? unmov'd?—O give compassion way!
Or kindly with some well-dissembled vow
Delude me still—it will be pious now!
But oh, I read my anguish in your look—
I can no longer—for my heart is broke.   320
Yet let my heaving breast, and streaming eyes
Speak for me, what my faultering tongue denies;
Recall the former image to your view
Of her that loves—that was belov'd by you;
That now o'erburden'd with a mother's cares,
The tender pledge of our endearments bears—
I feel the infant struggling in my womb,
As conscious of its misery to come:
O spare the guiltless babe—let nature move
Your heart to pity—tho' 'tis deaf to love!"   330
I cou'd no more—your cruel looks congeal'd
My flowing blood, and every vital[13] chill'd;
No more my bosom heav'd, my dying eyes

---

13. *vital* Bodily part, vital organ.

Were clos'd, and sense forsook me with my cries.
   O had it been for ever gone, indeed,
From what a world of woes had I been free'd!
But fate conspiring to protract my grief,
Unseal'd my eyes, and gave me back to life.
I found me, when my senses were restor'd,
In the curst house of him I call my lord.[14]   340
My bitter wrongs, in vain did I deplore,
For you, the source of all I saw no more.
   How shou'd I act in so severe distress?
Words cou'd not speak my anguish, nor redress:
But still to keep a glimm'ring hope alive,
(The last sad comfort wretches can receive)
I told my fatal story o'er with pain,
And su'd[15] for pity, but I su'd in vain!
Condemn'd to feel unutterable woes,
And all the wrongs that slav'ry can impose.   350
   Tho' deaf to justice, and love's softer claim,
O yet redeem me, in regard to fame!
For still the living story of my woe
Shall follow, and exclaim where'er you go;
Mankind will shun you, and the blasting tongue
Shall hoot the monster, as you pass along:
"Behold the wretch, whose breast to nature steel'd,
For kindness hated, for compassion kill'd!"
   Then (as you taught me) if there is to come
A day of general, just and awful doom,   360
If fit gradation be observ'd in pains,
O think, and tremble—what for you remains?
O what indeed!—unless you now incline
To shun the anguish by relieving mine;
So endless torments shall you change for peace,
And men, instead of cursing you, shall bless;
The gods in mercy will the deed regard,
And pay you with a penitent's reward.

14. *him I call my lord* Yarico is referring to her new owner or slavemaster.
15. *su'd* Sued.

Or if the state, you brought me to believe
Be but a story, fabled to deceive,   370
Yet sweet contentment never hope to own,
Or taste of soft repose—tho' stretch'd on down;
In vain for ease to business you'll repair,
My wrongs shall find you, and revenge me there.
   Forgive, thou still-lov'd author of my pain!—
My griefs are heavy, and I must complain.
O kill me—or some milder ill provide,
'Ere fate quite severs, and the seas divide.—
The thought distracts me—my strain'd eyes are dim,
And nature shivers at the dreadful theme.   380
—A thousand things my loaded heart wou'd say,
But Oh! my trembling hand will not obey;
Then let your fancy image my distress,
And yet—Oh yet, while you have power—redress!

Textual Variants

[Numbers refer to lines]

   1. *the* McGill, Ank.: "this";   1. *Sorrow* Ank.: "anguish";   8. *express* McGill: "impart";
21. *No* McGill: "The" Ank.: "Nor";   32. *for* McGill, Ank.: "of";   33. *pale* Ank.: "fell";
38. *must be* McGill: "must live" Ank.: "am doom'd";   52. *Unceasing* McGill: "Incessant";
52. *sorrow* Ank.: "trouble";   52. *and continu'd* McGill: "inexhausted";   52. *tears* Ank.:
"fears";   55. *would* McGill, Ank.: "could";   59. *paint* Ank.: "speak";   59. *aking* Ank.:
"bleeding";   60. *sufferings* Ank.: "pangs";   60. *severest* Ank.: "agonizing";   61. *Even . . .
pain* McGill, Ank.: "Hard as you are you'd mitigate my pain";   62. *And* McGill, Ank.: "Or";
65. *cruel* Ank.: "bloody";   74–124. See footnote 8;   82. *look'd* McGill: "gaz'd";   89. *my love*
McGill: "your mind";   105. *wanton* McGill: "eager";   112. *please* McGill: "save";   114. *No
thought, no wish* McGill: "Nor thought, nor wish'd";   126. *tender* McGill, Ank.: "easy";
133. *these retreats* Ank. "this recess";   143. *returns* McGill: "return";   169. *He who gives first*
McGill, Ank.: "Who gives at first";   169. *kindness* Ank.: "temper";   171. *relentless to* Ank.:
"regardless of";   183. *People, unborn* McGill, Ank.: "Men yet unborn";   183. *shall* Ank.:
"will";   183. *tale* Ank.: "lot";   191. *Then shall the just comparison be made* Ank.: "Then shall
draw the just comparison,";   192. *betray'd* Ank.: "undone";   200. *blaze* McGill, Ank.:
"light";   201. *you* Ank.: "were";   202. *And on my lips in silent transport hung* Ank: "In silent
transports on my lips you hung";   207. *thou ever* Ank.: "my ever";   208. *our pleasures* Ank.
"my happiness";   209. *Farewell! Ye cruel savages* McGill: "Farewell, and you, ye cruel men,"
Ank.: "Farewell! and ye, ye cruel men,";   211. *Thou* McGill, Ank.: "You";   211. *Shal't* 1736:
"Sha't";   McGill: "shall be";   214. *cause* McGill, Ank.: "suit";   215. *ship* Ank.: "shore";
219. *hands* McGill, Ank.: "hand";   221. *lusty* McGill, Ank.: "eager";   223. *fear* McGill,
Ank.: "care";   224. *threat'ning cruelty, and anxious care* McGill: "restless cruelty and restless

fear," Ank.: "threatn'ing cruelty, and restless fear";   227. *can addition* McGill: "can no addition";   238. *gushing* Ank.: "gulping";   239. *fondness* Ank. "sorrow";   243. *life* Ank. "dear"; 244. *thy* McGill, Ank.: "your";   250. *fear'd deceit* Ank.: "falsehood fear'd";   254. *cuts the thin air* McGill: "Beats the white wave" Ank.: "Buffs the white waves";   255. *we* McGill, Ank.: "is";   257. *busy* McGill: "chearful" Ank.: "cheerful";   260. *villany to come* McGill: "mischiefs yet to come" Ank.: "mischief yet undone";   267. *strong* Ank.: "grand"; 268. *generous* Ank.: "noble";   268–69. See footnote 11;   269. *guide* McGill, Ank.: "rule"; 272–73. See footnote 12;   273. *grateful* McGill, Ank.: "endless";   276. *fondly* Ank. "warmly"; 277. *kindly* Ank.: "fondly";   279. *loveliest* McGill, Ank.: "lovely";   282. *That chears* Ank.: "Which cheats";   285. *vile* Ank.: "black";   292. *Her life and labours are by purchase thine!* McGill, Ank.: "Your slave by purchase as she once was mine";   296. *hail'd* Ank.: "haul'd"; 301. *Plung'd me o'erwhelm'd* McGill: "Plunged me o'er" Ank.: "Then plung'd me o'er"; 302. *which* McGill, Ank.: "what";   309. *rage, and fear, and love* McGill: "fear, and rage, and love" Ank.: "rage, and love, and fear";   325. *That* McGill, Ank.: "Who";   328. *misery* Ank.: "wretchedness";   330. *deaf* McGill: "dead";   341. *deplore* McGill: "implore";   344. *speak* Ank.: "paint";   345. *But* McGill, Ank.: "Yet";   346. *receive* Ank.: "contrive";   354. *exclaim* Ank.: "acclaim";   363. *O what indeed!—unless you now incline* McGill, Ank.: "Unless sweet mercy shou'd your heart incline,";   372. *Or taste of soft repose—tho' stretch'd on down* McGill: "Remorse shall find you on the bed of down" Ank.: "Remorse shall find you on a bed of down";   374. *find* McGill, Ank.: "reach";   374. *revenge* Ank. "avenge";   379. *are* Ank.: "grow"

7

Stephen Duck, *Avaro and Amanda:*
A Poem in Four Canto's, Taken from "The
Spectator," VOL. I, NO. XI (Extracts)

From Stephen Duck, *Poems on Several
Occasions* (London, 1736).

Because of the changes in the names of the protagonists, Stephen Duck's poem in four cantos has not hitherto been distinguished as belonging to the Inkle and Yarico canon. However, the subtitle will make it obvious that it should be. It remains unclear why Duck decided to alter the names, though there are several later examples of the tale where this has also happened. The choice of "Avaro" for "Inkle" is to embody within his name the stigma of avarice (see note 2). To employ "Amanda" for "Yarico" is to convey the sense of one who both is loving (cf. French *amant*) and deserves to be loved (see also note 10). In its general outline, the poem follows the traditional story of Inkle and Yarico, though Duck pursues the ending to inflict a grisly punishment on Avaro.

Stephen Duck (1705–56), commonly known as "the thresher poet," came to exemplify for his age the supposition that poetic creativity might be viewed as innate. In light of his impoverished childhood in rural Wiltshire and early employment as a farm laborer, his surprising capacity to write nearly flawless verse was viewed as quite wonderful. As a self-taught poet, he turned with alacrity to any books he could afford, and among these were *Paradise Lost,* which he puzzled through with the aid of a dictionary, and also the volumes of *The Spectator.* Both informed *Avaro and Amanda:* Steele's essay from *Spectator,* number II, as the direct source of the tale itself, and Milton's great epic as a fund of poetic language and, in its portrayal of

Adam and Eve in Eden, as an inspiration for the idyllic coupling of the earthly lovers in canto 2.

Duck's most frequently discussed poem is *The Thresher's Labour* (1730), yet legitimate interest in this single work has had the unfortunate effect of obscuring much else that he wrote. *Avaro and Amanda* appeared in his *Poems on Several Occasions* (1736), a volume that was published by subscription and attracted a large readership. Before its publication he had already enjoyed royal patronage, receiving a pension from Queen Caroline and being appointed keeper of her private library at Richmond. Much later he took clerical orders, being appointed rector of Byfleet in Surrey. His life had a tragic end: struggling with depression, he drowned himself in a trout stream at Reading. Duck's powerful interiorizing of Avaro's "*conscious hell*" (642) in canto 4 reveals an early apprehension of the violence of suicide.

Stephen Duck's close familiarity with Inkle and Yarico may be read as indicative of the widespread permeation of the tale into almost every echelon of society. The tale's conjunction of civilization and primitivism may naturally have appealed to the poet, though in common with many others he seems unaware of the mismatch of indiscriminately piling on his heroine such casual racial signifiers as "*negro*" (line 8), "*Indian*" (157), and "*Moor*" (552). If the resulting poem veers too close to the didactic in its exposure of mercantile avarice, it is nonetheless a forceful indictment of slavery at a time when abolition was not yet part of the political agenda. The text presented here is taken from the 1736 edition of *Poems on Several Occasions*. I have made no attempt to collate it with later texts.

Canto I

What ills from want of education flow,
From avarice what cruel scenes of woe;
I mean to sing, except the tuneful maid[1]
Neglect my numbers, and refuse her aid.
Say, goddess, first, what made the youth explore
A foreign clime, and quit his native shore?
Say too, how on the barb'rous isle he came;
What mov'd the kindness of the *negro* dame?

1. *the tuneful maid* The muse of poetry.

What could provoke a faithless youth to sell
A friend, whose only crime was loving well?   10

   Now had *Avaro*[2] twenty winters pass'd,
His blooming features ev'ry beauty grac'd;
In silver rings, his loosely flowing hair
Hung o'er his shoulders, with a comely air;
Robust his limbs, and daring was his soul,
And vigour crown'd the well-proportion'd whole:
His graceful charms the ladies oft survey'd,
And oft their eyes an am'rous signal made;
But never could the tender passion move,
The stubborn youth was still averse to love;   20
Yet, tho' his breast was proof to *Cupid's* dart,
A more ignoble god enslav'd his heart.

   No mysteries of faith disturb'd his head;
For mysteries of faith he seldom read;
That moral law, which nature had imprest,
He blotted from the volume of his breast;
Yet in his mind his father's precepts bears,
Who often rung this lesson in his ears:
"Would you, my son, to happiness aspire,
Know, *gold* alone can happiness acquire;   30
He that hath gold, is pow'rful as a king,
Has valour, virtue, wisdom, ev'ry thing!
This to obtain, your utmost skill bestow;
And if you gain it, be not careful how:
If in the court, or camp, you take delight,
Then dare to flatter *there,* or *here* to fight:
Or, should the merchant's life your fancy please,
Be bold, and bravely venture on the seas;
Many by merchandize have gain'd renown,
And made the *Indies* wealth become their own."   40

   2. *Avaro* The name was also used by other poets as a figure of avarice, e.g., "Avaro . . . stor'd / With *Gold,* the God his *Soul* ador'd" (Edward Benlowes, *Theophila, or Loves Sacrifice* [1652], 10.228); "*Avaro,* by long use grown bold / In ev'ry ill which brings him gold" (Charles Churchill, *The Ghost* [1762], 2.456, in *Poetical Works,* ed. Douglas Grant [London, 1956], 92).

The youth imbib'd the precepts of his tongue,
Neglecting ev'ry law of right and wrong;
Taught by his sire to court destructive gain,
He burns to try his fortune on the Main.

While other youths, by wit or pleasure sway'd,
Frequent the play, the ball, or masquerade;
Avaro studious in his chamber stays,
Careless of balls, of masquerades, and plays;
There adds, subtracts, and, with unweary'd pain,
Learns all the rules of int'rest, loss and gain.   50

Next, from an old astronomer, he tries
To learn the planets' journey thro' the skies;
With *him,* at night, when heav'n serene appears,
He points the quadrant at the shining spheres;
The *Hyades,*[3] and frozen pole surveys,
Which guide the sailor o'er the distant seas;
Then maps and models of our globe prepares,
And carefully inspects both hemispheres;
From east to west he views the spacious round,
Pleas'd with the modern world *Columbus* found: 60
In hope elate,[4] the youth impatient stands,
And seems to grasp both *Indies* in his hands.
This sees the sire,[5] and hastily provides
A vessel, proof against the wind and tides.
The youth embarks, the soft propitious gales
Arise, and soon expand the swelling sails;
The ship glides swiftly o'er the liquid plain,[6]
And *Neptune* smiles, and courts him on the Main.

---

3. *The Hyades* "A group of stars near the Pleiades, in the head of the constellation Taurus" (*OED*). In popular astronomy, they were often associated with rainy weather.

4. *elate* Elated.

5. *the sire* Avaro's father.

6. *the liquid plain* The ocean. A not uncommon Augustan circumlocution; e.g., "While *British* Trees move on the liquid Plain, / And in their bellies the World's Treasure bear" (Samuel Cobb, *Pax Redux: A Pindarick Ode on the Return of His Majesty* [1697], 18.315–16); "Then glassy smooth lay all the liquid plain" (Homer, *Odyssey,* trans. Pope [1725–26], 5.501).

But see, how mortals are the sport of fate!
How oft unhappy, striving to be great!   70
Ere *Cynthia*[7] twice her monthly race had run,
An omen of the fatal storm begun:
The murm'ring wind arises by degrees,
And rocks the ship, and sweeps the curling seas;
Now louder, with impetuous force, it roars,
And shoves the swelling surges to the shores;
Till rapid rain, and flakes of bick'ring flame,
With dreadful thunder, vex th'ethereal frame.
Struck with surprize, the tim'rous merchant stands,
Nor knows what he forbids, or what commands: 80
Nor safely back, nor can he forwards go;
But trembling waits, and fears the fatal blow.

  Long time the sailors work against the wind,
With fruitless toil, to gain the port assign'd;
Till courage, hope, and all provisions fail'd,
And fear, despair, and want their souls assail'd.
Forc'd by the storm into a winding bay,
Their joyful eyes an *Indian* isle survey;
When straight they quit their ship, and gain the shore,
And for recruits[8] the savage land explore.   90

  Adjoining to the dreary beach, there stood
Wild shrubs and trees, that form'd a gloomy wood;
Where, close obscur'd, the crafty natives lay,
And watch'd the wand'ring crew, remote from sea:
Then forth they rush, and strait their bows prepare;
Too late the sailors see th'approaching war:
In vain the brave engage, or tim'rous fly;
The tim'rous, and the brave, promiscuous die;
The barb'rous fields are stain'd with purple gore,
And dreadful groanings echo to the shore.   100
Our youthful merchant 'scapes, and flies alone;
His fear impels, and safety prompts him on;

7. *Cynthia* The moon.   8. *recruits* Fresh supplies.

Thro' dusky woods he takes his trembling flight,
The dusky woods conceal him from their sight;
Till in the devious wilds, remote from foes,
Then, on the ground, he weeping vents his woes. . . .

[The canto concludes with Avaro cursing his hapless fate and ruing the fallacious charm of his father's advice.]

Canto II

All night in tears the pensive merchant lay,
And often wish'd, and fear'd the coming day;
Till, on the hills, the rising sun display'd
His golden beams, and chas'd away the shade:
Harmonious birds salute his chearful rays,
And hail the rosy morn with joyful lays;
While, stretch'd upon the ground, *Avaro* moans,
Answ'ring their tuneful songs with piercing groans.   150

Not distant far from where the youth was laid,
A purling stream, in pleasing murmurs, play'd;
And, by the margin of the crystal flood,
Two rows of trees in beauteous order stood;
Whose branches form'd a pendent arch above,
Diffusing gloomy verdure o'er the grove.
An *Indian* princess hither daily came,
Pleas'd with the grateful shade,[9] and cooling stream:
She now was walking to her lov'd retreat,
And heard the mourning youth lament his fate: 160
Fix'd in amaze, a-while she list'ning stood;
Then swift approach'd him, rushing thro' the wood.
Th'affrighted merchant rose with gazing eyes,
And tim'rous looks, that testify'd surprize:
Backward he starts; the dame, with equal fears,
Recedes as fast, and wonders what appears:

9. *grateful shade* Welcome shade; cf. "The verdant Arbour form'd a grateful Shade" (Duck, *The Shunammite* [1736], 217); "Where meeting Beeches weave a grateful Shade" (John Gay, *The Fan* [1714], 2.144, in *Poetry and Prose*, ed. Vinton A. Dearing, 2 vols. [Oxford, 1974], 1:70).

Yet, bolder grown, she soon advanc'd again,
Smit with the beauty of the godlike man:
His dress, and fair complexion, charm'd her sight;
Each glowing feature gave her new delight;   170
While love and pity both arose within,
And kindled in her soul a flame unseen.
With equal joy *Avaro* now survey'd
The native graces of the *negro* maid:
He view'd her arms, with various ribbands bound;
Her downy head, with painted feathers crown'd;
With bredes, and lucid shells, in circles strung,
Which shone refulgent, as they round her hung.

   As when, in splendid robes, a courtly maid
Begins the dance at ball or masquerade;   180
The pearls and di'monds shine with mingled light,
And glitt'ring pendants blaze against the sight.

   So shone the beauteous shells around her waist,
And sparkling gems, that deck'd her jetty breast;
All which *Avaro's* gazing eyes pursue,
Charm'd with her lovely shape, disclos'd to view:
Each limb appears in just proportion made,
With elegance thro' ev'ry part display'd:
And now his cares dissolve, new passions move;
And nature intimates, the change is *love.*   190

   Not far remote, a cooling grot was made,
In which the virgin often sought a shade:
Thick shrubs, and fruitful vines, around it grew;
And none, except herself, the mansion knew.
To this obscure *recess* the royal dame,
Rejoicing, with her lovely captive came:
Then, from the branches, with officious haste,
She plucks the fruits, which yield a sweet repast:
That done, she, with her bow, explores the wood;
Pierc'd with her shaft, the fowl resigns his blood.   200
Then back she hastens to her cool retreat,
And for *Avaro* dress'd the grateful meat:

To slake his thirst, she next directs his way,
Where crystal streams in wild meanders stray:
Nor lets him there, expos'd to foes, remain;
But to the cave conducts him safe again.

   So doats *Amanda*[10] on the merchant, while
She scorns the *lovers* of her *native isle:*
For all the heroes of her country strove,
With emulation, to attract her love;   210
And, when they could the painted fowls insnare,
Or pierce the savage beast in sylvan war,
The skins and feathers, trophies of their fame,
They gave for presents to the royal dame;
All which she to her lov'd *Avaro* brought,
And with them gaily deck'd his shining grot:
The spotted panther here she hung; and there,
With paws extended, frown'd the shaggy bear;
Here gaudy plumes appear, in lustre bright;
There shells and pearls diffuse a sparkling light.   220

   As when, to grace some royal prince's hall,
The skilful painter animates the wall;
Here warlike heroes frown in martial arms,
There a soft nymph displays her blushing charms;
A pleasing landscape next invites our eye,
And the room glows with sweet variety.

   Yet, still to give her lover more delight,
(Lest what he daily saw, should pall the sight)
When *Sol*[11] with purple cloath'd the western sky,
And shades extended shew'd the ev'ning nigh,   230
She to some verdant grove the youth convey'd,
Where nightingales harmonious music made:
Soft flow'rets were their couch; and, all around,

   10. *Amanda* The designation seems entirely inappropriate for a native woman, since the
now common name Amanda commenced as a literary invention in seventeenth-century
England (Withycombe, *The Oxford Dictionary of English Christian Names,* 18). Also see
headnote.
   11. *Sol* The sun; cf. "*Sol* thro' white Curtains shot a tim'rous Ray" (Pope, *The Rape of the
Lock* [1714], 1.13).

Diffusive sweets perfum'd the fragrant ground.
There oft she would his snowy bosom bare,
Oft round her fingers wind his silver hair;
Charm'd with the contrast, which their colours made,
More pleasing than the tulip's light and shade.
Nor was the youth insensible; but soon
Repaid her love, by shewing of his own: 240
Oft would his bosom heave with speaking sighs;
Oft would he gaze, and languish with his eyes:
Now on her panting breast his head repose,
To meet his head her panting breast arose;
While in her soul ecstatic raptures glow'd,
And her fond arms believ'd they clasp'd a god.

   So liv'd the happy pair, observ'd by none,
Till both had learnt a language of their own;
In which the youth, one ev'ning, in the shade,
Beguiles the harmless unsuspicious maid;   250
Leans on her breast, and, with a kiss, betrays;
Then vents his specious fraud in words like these:

   "Witness, ye gods, and all ye blest above,
(For ye can witness best, how well I love)
If e'er, among our blooming nymphs, I knew
Such pleasures, as my soul receives from you!
O dear *Amanda!* could I but, with thee,
Once more my happy native country see,
You should not there in lonely caves retreat,
Nor trace the burning sands with naked feet;   260
Your limbs, which now the sun and wind invade,
Should neatly be in softest silks array'd;
In gilded houses gaily should you ride,
By horses drawn, which prancing side by side,
Neigh, foam, and champ the bit with graceful pride;
Our time, in pomp and peace, should slide away,
And blooming pleasures crown the smiling day;
And, when the setting sun forsook the skies,
Approaching night should but increase our joys:
We would not on the chilling ground embrace,   270

Nor foes, as now, should interrupt our peace;
But both reposing on some easy bed,
Soft, as the fleecy down, that decks thy head,
The sportive god of love[12] should round us play,
While we, in raptures, pass'd the night away:
Then let us carefully, my dear, explore
The haven, where I first approach'd the shore.
Perhaps we shall some floating ship survey,
Safe to conduct us o'er the watry way:
Nor let the foaming waves your steps retard;   280
I'll guard you o'er, and be a faithful guard."

   How oft, alas! is innocence betray'd,
When love invites, and flatterers persuade?
How could the dame, a stranger to deceit,
Imagine such a heav'nly form a cheat?
She paus'd, she sigh'd; then, with a pensive look,
Half loth, and half consenting, thus she spoke:

   "*Once* has *Avaro* scap'd the raging Main:
Why would you tempt the fickle seas again?
To seek new dangers, when in safety here,   290
Would but provoke the deities you fear—
Sometimes, I own, we've been surpriz'd by foes,
Whose nightly walks have wak'd you from repose:
Yet still I guard your sacred life secure,
And always will—What can *Amanda* more?"

   Thus said, she clasp'd him in her loving arms,
Embrac'd his neck, and doated on his charms:
And now both shew their passions in their look,
And now connubial *Hymen*[13] both invoke;
In sportive joys they clos'd the genial day,   300
While *Philomela*[14] sung the nuptial lay;
Till soon the youth reclin'd upon her breast,
And golden slumbers seal'd their eyes to rest.

---

12. *The sportive god of love* Cupid.   13. *Hymen* The Roman god of marriage.
14. *Philomela* The nightingale.

[In canto 3, Amanda recounts to Avaro a troubling dream in which she imagined being abandoned to slavery. The lovers are interrupted by some hunters whose intrusion persuades Amanda of the necessity of escape from their present situation.]

Canto IV

Farewel, bright goddess of th'*Idalian* grove![15]   480
Farewel, ye sportive deities of *love!*
No longer I your pleasing joys rehearse;
A rougher theme demands my pensive verse;
A scene of woes remains to be display'd,
Indulgent love with slavery repaid:
Ingratitude, and broken vows, and lies,
The mighty ills, that spring from avarice,
Provoke my lays: Your aid, ye muses, bring;
Assist my tragic numbers, while I sing.
Say, what ensu'd, when, on the briny deep,   490
The watchful dame beheld a floating ship?
She call'd, and beckon'd to it from the shore;
Then to the youth the grateful tidings bore;
And said, "I something see, like wingèd trees,
(Strange to behold!) fly swiftly o'er the seas;
Their bulky roots upon the billows float:
Say, is not this the ship, you long have sought?
Or I mistake, or, by the gods command,
This comes to bear us to your native land:
Then hasten, see the partner of your heart,   500
With you, her guide, is ready to depart;
My father, mother, friends, I bid adieu,
Friends, father, mother, not so dear as *you.*"

To whom the youth, with smiling brow, reply'd:
"O thou true pattern of a faithful bride!

---

15. *bright . . . Idalian grove!* Venus, the goddess of love. A shrine devoted to her worship existed in ancient times at Idalium in Cyprus and surfaced as a common trope in eighteenth-century poetry (e.g., "Th'Arcadian Pastures and th'Idalian Grove," George Granville, "In Praise of Mira," 1.24, in *The Genuine Works in Verse and Prose,* 3 vols. [London, 1736], 1:45).

Who dar'st thy father, mother, friends resign;
And risque thy own dear life, to rescue mine!—
If I forget the debt I owe to *thee,*
May all the gods forget their care of *me!*
In more wild deserts let me rove again;   510
Nor find a friend, like *thee,* to ease my pain!
There let the vultures, wolves, and tigers tear
This body, *thou* hast kindly nourish'd here!"

So saying, to the beach he straight descends;
And, by the flag, discerns the crew his friends:
And now his heart exults within his breast;
His loving mate an equal joy confest;
She, with him, gladly ventures on the main,
Unthinking of her future toil and pain.

So, to the plough, the heifer, yet unbroke,   520
Walks chearful on, nor dreads th'impending yoke;
Till, in the fields, urg'd with the piercing goad,
She groans, and writhes, reluctant with her load.

The *British* bark was to *Barbados* bound:
Th'expected shore the sailors quickly found;
Where, safe from danger, now the perjur'd youth,
False to his former vows of sacred truth,
Reflecting, counts the int'rest he had lost,
While fate detain'd him on the *Indian* coast:
The frugal thoughts suppress his am'rous flame,   530
And prompt him to betray the faithful dame.
Yet scarce he can the cursed fact pursue;
But hesitates at what he fain would do:
For, tho' his av'rice moves him to the ill,
His gratitude within him struggles still;
And, 'twixt two passions, neither guides his will.

As when two scales, which equal loads suspend,
Sway to and fro; alternate both descend,
Till undeclining[16] each aloft abides,
Nor this, nor that, the doubtful weight decides.   540

16. *undeclining* No longer declining.

So stood the doubtful youth a-while; nor wou'd
Forsake the evil, nor pursue the good;
Till, as the sailors in the haven stay,
To purchase slaves, the planters croud the key:[17]
One asks, for what the *negro* may be sold;
Then bids a price, and shews the tempting gold:
Which when *Avaro* views with greedy eyes,
He soon resolves to gain th'alluring prize;
Nor oaths, nor gratitude, can longer bind;
Her fate he thus determines in his mind: 550

"Suppose I should conduct this *Indian* o'er;
And thus, instead of gold, import a *Moor*—
Would not my sire, with stern contracted brows,
Condemn my choice, and curse my nuptial vows?
Was it for this I learn'd the merchant's art?
Only to gain a doating *negro*'s heart!
Was it for this the raging seas I crost?
No; gold induc'd me to the *Indian* coast;
And gold is offer'd for this simple dame;
Shall I refuse it, or renounce my flame?—   560
Let am'rous fools their tiresome joys renew,
And doat on *love*, while *int'rest* I pursue."
He added not; for now, intent on gold,
And dead to all remorse, the *dame* he sold.

Amanda stood confounded with surprize,
And silently reproach'd him with her eyes:
She often tried to speak; but when she try'd,
Her heart swell'd full, her voice its aid deny'd;
And, when she made her fault'ring tongue obey,
These words, commix'd with sighs, found out their way.   570

"Who can the mystic ways of fate explain?
Am I awake, or do I dream again?
Is *this* the sad reward of all my care?
Was it for this I chear'd thee in despair?
The gods above (if any gods there be)

17. *key* Quay.

Witness what I have done to succour thee!
Yet, if my *kindness* can't thy pity move,
Pity the *fruits* of our unhappy *love:*
O let the infant, in my pregnant womb,
Excite thee to revoke my threaten'd doom;   580
Think how the future slave, in climes remote,
Shall curse the treach'rous sire, that him begot."

   So spake the mourning dame, but spake in vain;
Th'obdurate youth insults her with disdain;
Not all her *kindness* could his pity move,
Nor yet the *fruits* of their unhappy *love.*
But, as the flames, which soften wax, display
The same warm force to harden sordid clay;
That motive, which would melt another heart,
More harden'd his, and made him act a double villain's part.   590
He, for the child, demands a larger sum;
And sells it, while an embryo in the womb.

   And now he sternly takes her by the hand,
Then drags her on, reluctant, to the land;
While, as she walks, her dismal fate she moans,
The rocks around her echo to her groans:
"O base, ungrateful youth!" she loudly cries;
O base, ungrateful youth!" the shore replies:[18]
"And canst thou, cruel, perjur'd villain! leave
Thy tender infant too, an abject slave,
To toil, and groan, and bleed beneath the *rod?*
Fool that I was, to think thou wert a god!
Sure from some savage tyger art thou sprung—
No: tygers feed, and fawn upon their young:
But thou despisest all paternal cares,
The fate of infants, and their mother's pray'rs."

   In vain she does her wretched state deplore;
Pleas'd with the gold, he gladly quits the shore;
The ruffling winds dilate the sails, the ship

18. Cf. Pope, *The Rape of the Lock* (1714), 4.95–96: "O wretched Maid! she spread her Hands, and cry'd, / (While *Hampton*'s Ecchos, wretched Maid! reply'd)."

Divides the waves, and skims along the deep.   610
Three days the bellying canvas gently swells,
Clear shines the sun, and friendly blow the gales;
Then frowning clouds invest the vaulted sky,
And hollow winds proclaim a tempest nigh:
Fierce *Boreas*[19] loudly o'er the ocean roars,
Smoke the white waves, and sound the adverse shores;
While, to increase the horrors of the main,
Descends a deluge of impetuous rain.
The giddy ship on circling eddies rides,
Toss'd, and retoss'd, the sport of winds and tides.   620
Redoubled peals of roaring thunder roll,
And flames, conflicting, flash from pole to pole,
While guilty thoughts distract *Avaro*'s soul.
Of life despairing, tho' afraid to die,
One fatal effort yet he means to try:
While all the busy crew, with panting breath,
Were lab'ring to repel the liquid death;[20]
Avaro from the stern the boat divides,[21]
And yields up to the fury of the tides:
Toss'd on the boist'rous wave, the vessel flies,   630
Now sinking low, now mounting to the skies;
Till soon the storm decreas'd, and, by degrees,
Hush'd were the winds, and calm the ruffled seas;
The sailors safely steer their course again,
And leave *Avaro* floating on the main;
Who landed quickly on a lonely isle,
Where human feet ne'er print the baleful soil;
A dreary wilderness was all appear'd,
And howling wolves the only sound he heard;
A thousand deaths he views before his eyes,   640
A thousand guilt-created fiends arise;
A *conscious hell* within his bosom burns,
And racks his tortur'd soul, while thus he mourns:

19. *Boreas* The north wind.   20. *the liquid death* Drowning.

21. *divides* Separates himself. Duck may have had in mind here the story of Jonah, a bearer of ill luck, who was cast into the sea by the sailors. Avaro's fate, however, is quite different from that of his Old Testament forebear.

"Curs'd be the precepts of my selfish sire,
Who bad me after fatal gold aspire!
Curs'd be myself, and doubly curs'd, who sold
A faithful friend, to gain that fatal gold!—
O! could these gloomy woods my sin conceal,
Or in my bosom quench this fiery *hell;*
Here would I pine my wretched life away,   650
Or to the hungry savage fall a prey—
But can the gloomy woods conceal my sin,
Or cooling shadows quench the *hell* within?
No; like some spirit banish'd heav'n, I find
Terrors in ev'ry place, to rack my mind;
Tormenting conscious plagues increase my care,
And guilty thoughts indulge my just despair—
O! where shall I that piercing eye evade,
That scans the depths of hell's tremendous shade?"

So saying, straight he gave a hideous glare,   660
With rolling eyes, that witness'd strong despair:
Then drew his pointed weapon from the sheath,
Confus'dly wild, and all his thoughts on death;
To pierce his trembling heart he thrice essay'd,
And thrice his coward arm deny'd its aid:
Meanwhile a howling wolf, with hunger prest,
Leap'd on the wretch, and seiz'd him by the breast;
Tore out his heart, and lick'd the purple flood;
For earth refus'd to drink the *villain's* blood.

8

John Winstanley, "Yarico's Epistle to Inkle: A Poem, Occasioned by Reading *Spectator*, VOL. I, NO. II"

From *Poems Written Occasionally by the Late John Winstanley*, 2 vols. (Dublin, 1751), 2:8–16.

Lawrence Marsden Price's peremptory dismissal of this poem as "perhaps deservedly forgotten" was prompted most by a reservation that it is "less pictorial than its predecessors and is reflective rather than narrative" (*Inkle and Yarico Album,* 19). Certainly Winstanley's poem assumes that the reader is already familiar with the outline of the traditional story, to which almost no direct reference is made. In addition, this is a poem that does not engage, except obliquely, the problem of slavery or designate any particular geographical or racial setting to the tale. (Yarico's reference to herself as "fair as the *rose*" [120] is a figurative allusion to her beauty rather than to her complexion.) Winstanley introduces slight but significant modifications to the story by attributing Inkle's release from the "swarthy crowd / In quest of prey" (88–89) to Yarico's personal intervention and, most tellingly, by imagining her as now a maternal figure suckling the baby boy that is the offspring of their union. The strength of the poem is in its resonantly elegiac strain, its lyrical articulation of the finality of Yarico's situation. Winstanley's poem is an interior monologue that, at its best, poignantly exploits the form of heroic epistle as a means of simultaneously expressing contradictory emotions of natural love, aggrieved innocence, and utter loss. Its reflective and elegiac elements anticipate poetic renditions of the tale from rather later in the century.

Almost nothing is known about John Winstanley (1678?–1750). A first volume of his *Poems Written Occasionally* was published in Dublin in 1742, and the second volume, edited by his son George, appeared posthumously, again in Dublin, in 1751. Among those who subscribed to the first volume were Jonathan Swift, Alexander Pope, and Edward Moore (see headnote to selection 6). The title pages of the volumes describe Winstanley as a fellow of Trinity College, Dublin, though his name has not been located in the list of graduates. Most commentators consider that he was an Irishman, and several of his poems have recently found their way into Deane, *Field Day Anthology of Irish Writing*, vol. 1. See *DNB;* O'Donoghue, *Poets of Ireland*, 487.

Here let a *captive* fetch a panting groan,
Dissolv'd in flowing tears till now unknown;
And swan-like enter with a mournful strain,[1]
A *sea* of toil, a *world* of boundless pain.
Still is there left me freedom to deplore,
To kiss and grasp my now abandon'd shore,
Nor hope to taste its short-liv'd pleasures more;
Still have I freedom to expose thy shame,
Perfidious man, and curse the hated name.

Ye conscious breezes that around me play,   10
Bear the soft breathings of my soul away;
My sighs in whispers to his breast impart,
And tend to pity his relentless heart.

Sooner cou'd *zephirs*[2] tear the stately oak,
Or falling *waters* cleave the flinty rock,
Than such a message pierce his stubborn mind,
And teach an o'ergrown ruffian to be kind:
Whom neither tears nor plighted vows cou'd move,

---

1. *swan-like . . . mournful strain* The swan was supposed to utter sound only just before dying (cf. swan song).
2. *zephirs* Breezes, winds.

Nor sacred ties of long-continu'd love.
Furies[3] conspir'd to constitute his frame,   20
Confirm'd in guilt, and obstinate in shame.

   Beneath what boding *planet* was I born?
What odious *star* o'er-rul'd that fatal *morn?*
And curs'd my entrance on this stage of life,
Big with the dire presages of my grief.
Did e'er such loads of sorrow sink a breast,
With so much *love* and *innocence* possess'd?
Why don't th'immortal *gods* (if *gods* there are)
Make so much *love* and *innocence* their care,
Those two grand *virtues* that our lives controul,   30
And sweeten ev'ry passion of the soul?

   Ah! wheresoe'er I turn my weeping eyes,
Waves peep o'er *waves*, o'er *billows billows* rise
The lengthen'd prospect terminates in air,
A dreadful gulph of sorrow and despair.
There must I lie, that ocean must entomb
My lifeless carcass in its chrystal womb;
Where none can point me out beneath the wave,
Or write the mournful story on my grave.

   It grieves me to recal the golden days,   40
When crown'd with gems and never-fading bays,[4]
In awful majesty I cou'd advance,
And 'midst a crowd of lovers lead the dance.
None was so gay, so brisk, so sprightly seen
To trip in gambols o'er the verdant green.
Alas! too soon our vernal flow'rs decay,
Too soon that *phantom, Pleasure,* steals away:
Our limpid stream of *bliss* glides on too fast,
And ends a frightful *cataract* at last.

3. *Furies* Avenging deities.
4. *never-fading bays* Traditionally, a crown of bay leaves could symbolize virginity. The withering of the bay tree was seen as an omen of death.

How oft did I my ignorance bemoan?   50
How labour hard to make my accents known?
How with my tears and deep-fetch'd sighs complain,
To breathe th'endearments of my soul in vain?
When yet in words unknown they were convey'd,
And motion seemingly sincere repay'd.
Passion, express'd in words untaught can't move,
'Tis sweet to be intelligible in love.

    Oh, had I ne'er believ'd thy flatt'ring eyes!
Too fond to love, too loving to be wise.
Oft' have I led thee to the purling floods,   60
To silent groves and unfrequented woods;
Where birds in consort ply'd their warbling throats,
And *Philomelas*[5] tun'd their softest notes.
Oft have I laid thee in the jess'mine[6] bow'r,
And cull'd to garnish thee from ev'ry flow'r:[7]
Bad thee no more for distant regions weep,
And sooth'd the sorrows of thy heart asleep;
Check'd ev'ry sullen thought with tender care,
Compos'd the waving ringlets of thy hair:
View'd each transporting feature of thy face,   70
And innocently smil'd on ev'ry grace.
Oft on my knee thy drooping head sustain'd,
And in thy then soft bosom dipt my hand,
Thy faithless bosom! but alas, cou'd ne'er
Discern ingratitude sit brooding there;
Ingratitude, that damps and cankers all,
And spreads a venom o'er the tainted soul;
That, tyrant-like, in its full force display'd,
Requites with injuries the guiltless maid;
At sight of which each mark of love's forgot,   80
And thousand favours dwindle into nought.

    Now weeping my dejected fate I mourn,
Now with regret and indignation burn,

5. *Philomelas* Nightingales.   6. *jessmine* Jasmine.
7. *cull'd . . . flower* Picked different flowers with which to adorn you.

When lonely pensive I recal to mind,
As on a mossy bank you lay reclin'd;
In all the pomp of blooming roses drest,
Nor half so gay the *monarch* of the *west:*
When, on a sudden, lo, a swarthy crowd
In quest of prey came rustling thro' the wood;
I interpos'd, and with loud cries implor'd   90
The eager crew to spare my sleeping lord:
Beauty in tears their rav'nous breasts cou'd move,
'Tis brave to pity the soft pangs of love.
What have not I, unhappy creature, done
To save a life so fatal to my own?

  So have I seen beneath a verdant shade
The glorious *silk-worm* innocently lay'd,
Still toil and labour to his own decay,
And spin until he spun his life away.

  Ye *stars,* inferior ministers of light,   100
That cheer the gloomy shade of silent night,
Have seen me bear the circling chain of woes,
And sacrifice my own to his repose;
When sleep (to wretched me design'd in vain)
Had spread its balmy wings o'er ev'ry plain;
And in deep silence hush'd each dewy grove,
Whilst anxious I was kept awake by love.

  O *Liberty,* thy *god-like form* I find
Still haunt my heart, still springing in my mind;
Solac'd by thy serene, engaging eyes,   110
The gaudy pomp of *empire* I'd despise;
At plumy crests and speckl'd robes I'd frown,
Nor condescend so low as to a *crown.*
How blest was I beneath his gentle sway,
My *grotto* smil'd, and all around was gay.
Thou gav'st a beauty to each budding flow'r,
And *paradise* was lodg'd in ev'ry bow'r.
Then in the height of bliss, from shade to shade,
Thro' scenes of pleasing solitude I stray'd;

Fair as the *rose,* and sprightly as the *hind,*   120
And as the *linnet*[8] free and unconfin'd:
While rival youths each morn my arbour grac'd,
With glitt'ring shells in beauteous order plac'd:
Peace shone divinely bright thro' ev'ry grove,
And all around was *liberty* and *love.*

    Fain[9] would I stifle each convulsive sigh,
Fain let thy name within my bosom die;
Fain from my breast thy loathsome image tear,
But ah too lasting is the *pledge* I bear;
Pledge, did I say? sad *pledge!* nay let it be   130
Torn from my womb whate'er remains of thee.
But, hark! the *child,* to gen'rous pity wrought,
Affrighted, startles at th'enormous thought;
Bids me the tumult of my mind controul,
And, conscious, dictates patience to my soul;
Tells me in whispers he'll my bliss restore,
Renounce the father, and be his no more.
O thou dear *partner* of my grief, I'll find
In thee a *child,* a *husband* and a *friend.*
While yet, *sweet babe,* to my fond bosom prest,   140
Thou like a *pearl* hang'st pendant on my breast,
Thy soul with early courage I'll inspire,
To brave the insults of a treach'rous *sire;*
In spite of scorn and cruelties we'll live,
And lost in sympathy forget to grieve.

    Farewel, ye purling *streams* and silent *dales,*
Ye flow'ry *meads* and ever-blooming *vales;*
By you, false man, from their embraces torn,
My ravish'd joy and transient bliss I mourn.

    Such sorrows rack the wand'ring *linnet's* breast   150
When exil'd she bemoans her rifl'd nest;

---

    8. *linnet* According to Ad de Vries, *Dictionary of Symbols and Imagery,* 300, the linnet was traditionally supposed to symbolize both courtship and motherly love.
    9. *Fain* Willingly, rather.

Oft' she looks back, and wings around the wood,
Where once erect her mossy fabrick stood.

    But oh! in vain these loud unpity'd cries,
In vain the tears fall streaming from my eyes.
I'll call propitious *heav'n* to my defence,
And calmly triumph in my *innocence:*
Nor trust again that monstrous creature, *man,*
Or in my bosom hug the direful bane;
But boldly venture with th'insulting crew,   160
And bid the world, with all its joys, *adieu.*

9

Salomon Gessner, "Continuation of the Story of Inkle and Yarico"

First published in 1756. From *The Works of Solomon Gessner, Translated from the German,* 2 vols. (Liverpool, 1802), 2:230–38.

Several writers attempted to pursue the story of Inkle and Yarico beyond its conventional ending. Gessner's once admired sequel was first published in English in a wretched translation of 1771 (appearing in the *Weekly Magazine, or Edinburgh Amusement* 14:197–200). It is taken here from a more reliable text present in a collected edition of the author's works. Salomon Gessner of Zurich (1733–88), author and artist, was one of the few German-speaking writers before Goethe and Schiller to become well known in England and America. His *Der Tod Abels* (*The Death of Abel*), 1758, enjoyed a huge circulation, its English translation going through at least eighteen editions between 1761 and 1782. It was widely praised in its day for its pathos and perceived moral propriety.

Gessner's continuation of the tale was originally conceived as a second part to a rather turgid narrative poem, *Inkel und Yariko,* by his fellow Swiss, Johann Jakob Bodmer, which had been based on the story as told by Steele. Both Bodmer's poem and Gessner's rhythmic prose sequel were first published in Zurich in 1756. Gessner's version was not included with his collected works until after his death, though during his lifetime it was separately translated and published in France and Holland as well as in England.

In his effort to capture the full pathos of the situation, Gessner creates what John Hibberd has described as "a sentimental, melodramatic tribute in poetic prose to the power of remorse and the innate goodness of man." In its "happy ending" that brings Inkle and Yarico together, the piece anticipates Colman's comic opera. But for all its moral optimism in displaying

the triumph of virtue over depravity, its ridiculously oversentimental effu-
sions make for an Inkle who is far less credible as a man of feeling than he
was as a cad. It is hardly less easy not to squirm at the gendering of Yarico
as a homespun and self-effacing handmaid. Hibberd is right to conclude
that here a "potentially moving story is not exploited to the full, and the
psychology is rudimentary" (*Salomon Gessner,* 23–25). Except by her tearful
embrace, Inkle's final question to Yarico ("How canst thou so love one who
has treated thee with such inhuman ingratitude?") remains unanswered. In
its shortcomings, Gessner's Inkle and Yarico provides a fine example of the
cult of sensibility at its least controlled and its most contagiously lachrymose.

[The first part of the story has been omitted, as too familiar to the English
reader to require repetition here.]¹

The unfortunate Yarico was thus sold as a slave to the governor of the
island, by her cruel and unworthy lover. No sooner had her new protector
heard her melancholy history, than summoning an officer of justice, he
sent him to arrest Inkle. "This wretch," said he, "shall pass five years in
slavery, as a slight² punishment for his inhuman ingratitude."

   Inkle stood in the mean time, musing on the shore: "what have I done!"
said he, "to secure a wretched gain. I have sold the woman who so tenderly
loved me; who preserved my life." He threw the gold with horror from
him; then musing again, he said: "but wherefore do I torment myself?—
The deed in truth was cruel, but—it is done—I have sold her to a worthy
master.—I feel it, Oh! I feel it—many an uneasy hour will the recollection
of this deed give me—but it is done." So saying, he again attempted to take
up the purse. A cold chill crept through his blood. "Give me not to another! Oh! give me not to another," continued he, weeping. "These were
the last words that her trembling lips pronounced to me: I will not hesitate
to follow thee as thy slave; thou shalt see me willingly submit to the hard-
est labour thou canst impose, so I may still be near thee; still enjoy the sight
of thee. Oh! let me be thy slave, I and the unfortunate fruit of thy love."—

   1. *[The first . . . here]* This is the translator's note.
   2. *slight* Lenient, small.

Here he turned pale, and the dews of terror and remorse stood on his brow: he started, and trembled, as one, who in the very attempt to injure innocence, hears the thunder burst over his head.

Thus he stood when the messengers of the governor approached him. "Wretch," said they, "as a punishment for thy inhuman crime, the governor condemns thee to labor five years as his slave. Quick, strip thyself of those garments, and assume the habit of thy new condition." Inkle undressed himself, and while he put on the apparel of a slave, tears flowed down his cheeks. "Too mild a punishment indeed," said he, "for my crime, I am happy in being thus punished: perhaps the remembrance of my guilt may by this be made less insupportable." They led him now to hard labor among the common slaves; and wretched as he was, he yet felt easier while he thus suffered for his transgression.

In the mean time, Yarico, who still wept the infidelity of her lover, was treated with the greatest kindness by the governor; and after a few days was sent, loaded with presents, on board a vessel, which was to convey her again to her native shore. In silent melancholy she stood upon the deck, and watched with tearful eyes the lessening shore receding from her view, one of her companions approaching her, said, "Why mournest thou, thou dark brown maiden? Ought'st thou not rather to rejoice in returning to thy native country, in departing from a land where thou wert sold to slavery?"

"I ought indeed to rejoice," returned the dark brown maid, "but I have left the shore where dwells my faithless lover: I have left it without shedding one parting tear upon his bosom. Oh that I could but have folded him in one last embrace! and I had done so, but that the cruel one denied it me! where is he, tell me, where is my love?"—"The governor of the island," answered her companion, "has condemned him to five years of slavery as a slight punishment for his crime. I saw him myself employed in hard labour among the slaves"—"Unfortunate Inkle!" exclaimed Yarico, "hadst thou never beheld me, thou hadst not now been suffering for a crime that originated in me. Tell me, my friend! tell me, how did he support his punishment? What did he? what said he, when thou saw'st him among the slaves?"

"When I saw him, he was employed in cultivating the ground, and was bending down over his work; but suddenly he raised himself, and contemplating with tearful eyes his slave's apparel, and the hatchet in his hand, 'Ye are worthy of me, ye wretched weeds,'[3] he said, 'and thou hatchet art more

3. *weeds* Garments, clothes.

precious to my hand than a royal sceptre. If one ray of comfort remains to gladden my life, it is that which I experience from thus suffering the punishment of my crime. Oh Yarico! my beloved!—Wretch that I am, wherefore do I pollute with my lips, the name of a maiden whom I have treated with such base ingratitude!' While he thus spoke, the other slaves had paused from their labour to attend to him, and stood in silent attention, leaning on their spades.

'Friends!,' cried he to them—'but no! I am not worthy to call myself the friend of man; despise me; abhor me;—I am a disgrace to human nature; nothing is human of me but the form; even of that I am unworthy. Hear, and abhor me:—A beautiful maiden saved my life upon a foreign shore; she nursed me tenderly, and tenderly loved me. I promised to take her with me to the place of my birth, where she should enjoy in my arms the reward of her love and benevolence. Delighted, and full of tender affection, she accompanied me to the vessel. We landed first on this shore, and here—listen and shudder at my hateful ingratitude, I sold her as a slave, and sold with her the unborn fruit of our love. Oh! how she wept! how she wrung her hands!—Despise me—shun me, I am not worthy the society of man: ye birds! sing not for me as I labour, fly from the place where I am, as ye would shun a wilderness in which some wretched object of corruption moulders.'"

Yarico heard, and wept: she rang⁴ her hands, and sighed, and lamented to the receding shore. "Oh Inkle! my beloved! dost thou weep thy infidelity? Alas! what more is wanting to insure my perfect forgiveness. Wretched that I am, every instant I am departing farther from thee. Alas! shall I never see thee more—never behold the dear offspring of our love smile in thine arms, and lisp to thee the name of father? Ah! could I but be near thee! could I but share thy misery, and wipe from thy loved brow the damps of anguish and despair!"—Thus she lamented, till the last shores of the island disappeared; and one wide and boundless expanse of water surrounded her; soon her native shores advanced, as if from the clouds, to meet her sight.

In the mean time, Inkle laboured among the slaves: the painful remembrance of his crime was deeply impressed on his contracted brow; and his recollection of the tenderness and fidelity of the dark brown maid, had revived and increased his former affection for her. "Where art thou my Yarico! Ah! lost to me for ever, thou, and my child: never will it call me

4. *rang* Wrung.

father, unless after thou hast related to it my cruelty and ingratitude, it repeats my name and shudders!"

A whole year did Inkle suffer: at length, as by moonlight, he wept under the shade of a solitary tree, the overseer of the slaves approached him, and commanded him to follow him. He led him to the governor's garden. "—Inkle," said the governor, "thy severe penitence has not passed unrewarded by heaven: a person who arrived to-day on the island, has purchased thy freedom." Inkle heard, and stood unmoved; no gleam of joy sparkled in his eyes, or glanced across his pallid face. "Dost thou not rejoice in thy liberty," said the governor? "My lord," replied Inkle (fixing his eyes bedewed with tears upon the ground) "how can I rejoice? can I hope pardon from heaven, while the sighs of my beloved, the tears of my child—wretch that I am, do I venture to pronounce those names that must for ever condemn me! How can I taste of pleasure while I am despicable to myself? where can I be happy? where, Oh! where can I find rest. Oh! my lord, permit me to suffer the punishment of my crime: allow me to remain your slave."

As he thus spoke, a female rushed from behind the neighbouring trees. It was Yarico. She was dressed in the gayest ornaments of variegated shells and feathers; a garland of flowers encircled her head, and in her arms she held a beautiful infant. "Oh Inkle!," she exclaimed, sobbing, as she threw herself upon his bosom, "deny me not! it is I who have ransomed thee; receive thy faithful wife, thy lovely infant!" Inkle threw himself at her feet and embraced her knees: his violent emotion deprived him of the power of articulating. "My Yarico! my beloved," at length he said, "dost thou not start in horror from me? can it be thou who hast ransomed me? Oh! how canst thou so love one who has treated thee with such inhuman ingratitude!"—"Oh Inkle! my beloved, arise," said Yarico. "Let me no longer languish to embrace thee; deprive thy child no longer of thy paternal kiss."

Edward Jerningham,

Yarico to Inkle: An Epistle

From the first edition (London, 1766).

Now a forgotten figure, in his own day Edward Jerningham (1727–1812) had an unenviable reputation as a self-promoting dabbler in poetry. The third son of a landed family from Norfolk, he was educated as a Catholic at the English College at Douai and later in Paris. He appears to have nurtured a high opinion of his own literary talent, though this was not usually shared by those with whom he came in contact. Fanny Burney dismissed him as "all daintification in manner, speech, and dress," and in similar sardonic timbre, Horace Walpole frequently referred to him as "the Charming Man." When he sent a copy of one of his poems to Edmund Burke, the latter responded in mock hyperbole: "You have caught new fire by approaching . . . so near to the sun of our poetical system. How long will the astronomers calculate the time before you can cool? The painters have warmed their imaginations at the same reservoir of heat and light. You reflect new rays on them." Unable to catch the sarcasm, Jerningham proudly showed Burke's letter to Walpole, who confided to Mary Berry his regret that the would-be poet "should be so flattered, when in truth he has no genius; there is no novelty, no plan, . . . in his poetry, though many of his lines are pretty." Among others to whom Jerningham sent copies of his verse was Thomas Jefferson, then in Paris, who responded politely but then disposed of the volume. See *DNB; Horace Walpole's Correspondence,* ed. Wilmarth Lewis, 11:211; *Papers of Thomas Jefferson,* ed. Julian P. Boyd, 15:96–97, 143. The only full-length study is Bettany, *Edward Jerningham and His Friends).*

Yarico to Inkle: An Epistle was first published in 1766 as a quarto volume, priced at one shilling. Between 1767 and 1806, the poem appeared in at least eight separate London editions of the author's poems (all published during his lifetime), as well as in reprints in Philadelphia (1790) and Dublin (1789) and a translation into German (Giessen, 1778). In addition, the final section was transposed to form the ending in some versions of the similarly named poem sometimes attributed to Edward Moore (see selection 6 headnote).

Early impressions of the poem generally belie Jerningham's equivocal reputation as a versifier who could not be taken too seriously. The *Gentleman's Magazine* (36 [1766]: 143) remarks on its expressing "the situation and sentiments of *Yarico* with great force and beauty," while the *Critical Review* (21 [1766]: 154) augments this by adding that "we never observed the lady talk so much in character before. Her page contains the genuine language of distress, and breathes every sentiment of varied woe." Only the *Monthly Review* (34 [1766]: 324) complains that "the epistle . . . has not answered our expectations. . . . Yarico . . . complains in too trite, if not too feeble a manner."

Modern criticism has been sparse. Price describes the poem as "perfervid" (*Inkle and Yarico Album,* 136), while Carolyn Kates, in her study of the heroic epistle in England, praises Jerningham for the way he "effectively captures the frenzied state of the betrayed heroine as Ovid did" ("Chronicling the Heroic Epistle," 212). Finally, Wechselblatt comments interestingly on the textual reversal that takes place within the poem from "Yarico as . . . protector of Inkle, to Inkle as conqueror of the native woman" ("Gender and Race," 207).

In capturing the range of emotions and the fervor of Yarico's despair, Jerningham shows a poetical imagination highly attuned to the genre of heroic epistle (see headnote to selection 3B). His skill is as a close, sometimes slavish, imitator of a well-established form, creating a poem that often seems too highly crafted for modern taste. Jerningham is a literary magpie whose poetry is overwrought with allusive echoes of other poets (see references in the footnotes).

In outline, the *Epistle* adheres to the traditional tale but with some unusual departures in its details. The most significant is the Africanizing of Yarico from Indian maid to a woolly-haired Nubian princess "with blood illustrious circling thro' these veins" (159) whose parents have been put to the sword by merciless Christian invaders. As an Englishman ("Albion's son," 13) and a Christian, Inkle displays a shallow indifference that makes him appear particularly callous alongside Yarico's passionate sensitivity. That she never directly names him suggests the distance between them. Within the monologue, Yarico expresses contradictory desires to return home or to take her own life, perhaps intended to reflect her emotional bewilderment and sense of betrayal and loss. Jerningham appears blind to the racial and social ambiguities inscribed within a text that upholds European ideas of hierarchy though "utter'd from a sable breast" (68).

The text reproduced here is taken from the first edition of 1766. No attempt has been made to collate it with later printings.

With falsehood lurking in thy sordid breast,
And perj'ry's seal upon thy heart imprest,
Dar'st thou, Oh Christian, brave the sounding waves,[1]
The treach'rous whirlwinds, and wide-yawning graves?
Regardless of my woes securely go,
Nor curse-fraught accents from these lips shall flow;
My fondest wish shall catch thy flying sail,
Attend thy course, and urge the fav'ring gale:
May ev'ry bliss thy God confers be thine,
And all thy share of woe compris'd in mine.   10

One humble boon is all I now implore,
Allow these feet to print their kindred[2] shore:
Give me, Oh Albion's[3] son, again to roam
For thee deserted my delightful home:
To view the groves that deck my native scene,
The limpid stream, that graceful glides between:
Retrieve the fame I spurn'd at love's decree,
Ascend the throne which I forsook for thee:
Approach the bow'r—(why starts th'unbidden tear?)
Where once thy *Yarico* to thee was dear.   20

---

1. *the sounding waves* Cf. Virgil, *Aeneid* (trans. John Dryden, 1697), II.843–44: "Above the sounding waves . . . / . . . he stemmed the stormy tide."
2. *kindred* Native, familial.   3. *Albion's* England's.

The scenes the hand of time has thrown behind
Return impetuous to my busy mind:[4]
"What hostile vessel quits the roaring tide
To harbour here its tempest-beaten side?
Behold the beach receives the ship-wreck'd crew:
Oh mark their strange attire and pallid hue!
Are these the Christians, restless sons of pride,
By av'rice nurtur'd, to deceit allied?
Who tread with cunning step the maze of art,
And mask with placid looks a canker'd heart?   30
Yet note, superior to the num'rous throng,
(Ev'n as the citron[5] humbler plants among)
That youth!—Lo! Beauty on his graceful brow
With nameless charms bids ev'ry feature glow.
Ah! leave, fair stranger, this unsocial ground,
Where danger broods, and fury stalks around:
Behold thy foes advance—my steps pursue
To where I'll screen thee from their fatal view:
He comes, he comes! th'ambrosial feast[6] prepare,
The fig, the palm-juice,[7] nor th'Anâna[8] spare: 40
In spacious canisters[9] nor fail to bring
The scented foliage of the blushing spring:
Ye graceful handmaids, dress the roseate bow'r,[10]
And hail with music this auspicious hour;
Ah no! forbear—be ev'ry lyre unstrung,[11]

---

4. *Return . . . mind.* In the ensuing passage (lines 23–62) flagged by quotation marks, Yarico's imagination moves backward in time to recollect the moment of Inkle's first landing on her native shores.

5. *citron* Lemon tree.

6. *ambrosial feast* A celestial feast; cf. Homer, *Iliad* (trans. Pope [1720]), 20.281: "The Grace and Glory of th'Ambrosial Feast." In Greek mythology, ambrosia was the fabled food or sometimes drink of the gods.

7. *palm-juice* Coconut milk.   8. *Anâna* Pineapple.

9. *canisters* Wicker baskets for fruit.

10. *roseate bow'r* Bower of roses; cf. William Collins, "Ode to Mercy" (1746), 25: "To thee we build a roseate bower."

11. *be . . . unstrung* The reference to the lyre indicates that Jerningham has totally abandoned an American Indian context for his version of the tale.

More pleasing music warbles from his tongue;
Yet, utter not to me the lover's vow,
All, all is thine that friendship can bestow:
Our laws, my station,[12] check the guilty flame,
Why was I born, ye powers, a Nubian dame?[13]   50
Yet see around at love's enchanting call,
Stern laws submit, and vain distinctions fall:
And mortals then enjoy life's transient day,
When smit with passion they indulge the sway:
Yes! crown'd with bliss we'll roam the conscious[14] grove,
And drink long draughts of unexhausted love:
Nor joys alone, thy dangers too I'll share,
With thee the menace of the waves I'll dare:
In vain—for smiles his brow deep frowns involve,
The sacred ties of gratitude dissolve,   60
See Faith distracted rends her comely hair,
His fading vows while tainted zephyrs[15] bear!"

   Oh thou,[16] before whose seraph-guarded throne
The Christians bow and other gods disown,
If wrapt in darkness thou deny'st thy ray,
And shroud'st from Nubia[17] thy celestial day!
Indulge this fervent pray'r to thee address'd,
Indulge, tho' utter'd from a sable breast:
May gath'ring storms eclipse the cheerful skies,
And mad'ning furies from thy hell arise: 70
With glaring torches meet his impious brow,
And drag him howling to the gulf below!
Ah no!—May heav'n's bright messengers descend,
Obey his call, his every wish attend!

   12. *station* Position, status.
   13. *a Nubian dame* Yarico has been translated into a native of northeast Africa. The ancient kingdom of Nubia stretched along the Nile in the area now occupied by southern Egypt and northern Sudan.
   14. *conscious* As if alive with human thoughts or feelings. *OED* cites Sir John Denham's *Cooper's Hill* (1643), 277, "Thence to the Coverts, and the conscious Groves."
   15. *zephyrs* Winds.   16. *thou* The Christian God.
   17. *Nubia* Seemingly the allusion is to Yarico herself rather than to her country.

Still o'er his form their hov'ring wings display!
If he be blest, these pangs admit allay:[18]
Me still her mark let angry fortune deem,
So thou may'st walk beneath her cloudless beam.
Yet oft to my wrapt ear didst thou repeat,
That I suffic'd to frame thy bliss compleat: 80
For love's pure flame I took thy transient fires:
We fondly credit what the heart desires.
I hop'd, alas! to breathe thy native air,
And vie in splendor with the British fair:
Ascend the speedy car[19] enchas'd with gold,
With robes of silk this pearl-deck'd form infold:
Bid on this jetty[20] hand the diamond glow,
And chosen rubies sparkle from my brow.
Deluded sex! the dupes of man decreed,
We, splendid victims, at his altar bleed.   90
The grateful accents of thy candy'd[21] tongue,
Where artful flatt'ry too persuasive hung,
Like flow'rs adorn'd the path to my disgrace,
And bade destruction wear a smiling face.
Yet form'd by nature in her choicest mould,
While on thy cheek her blushing charms[22] unfold,
Who could oppose to thee stern virtue's shield?
What tender virgin would not wish to yield?
But pleasure on the wings of time was born,
And I expos'd a prey to grinning scorn[23]   100
Of low-born traders—mark the hand of Fate!
Is *Yarico* reduc'd to grace the state,
Whose impious parents, an advent'rous band,
Imbrued with guiltless blood my native land:

---

18. *allay* Abatement, alleviation.   19. *car* Carriage.
20. *jetty* Jet-black.
21. *candy'd* Candied, flattering; cf. Shakespeare, *Hamlet*, 3.2.65, "Let the candied tongue lick absurd pomp."
22. *her blushing charms* Cf. Stephen Duck, *Avaro and Amanda* ([7], line 224): "There a soft nymph displays her blushing charms."
23. *grinning scorn* Cf. John Oldham, "A Satyr, in Imitation of the Third of Juvenal" (1684, line 235: "exposing men to grinning scorn."

Ev'n snatch'd my father from his regal seat,
And stretch'd him breathless at their hostile feet?
Ill-fated prince! The Christians sought thy shore,
Unsheath'd the sword, and mercy was no more.[24]

But thou, fair stranger, cam'st with gentler mind
To shun the perils of the wrecking wind.   110
Amidst thy foes thy safety still I plann'd,
And reach'd for galling[25] chains the myrtle band:
Nor then unconscious of the secret fire
Each heart voluptuous throbb'd with soft desire:
Ah pleasing youth, kind object of my care,
Companion, friend, and ev'ry name that's dear!
Say, from thy mind canst thou so soon remove
The records pencil'd by the hand of love?
How as we wanton'd on the flow'ry ground
The loose-rob'd pleasures danc'd unblam'd around: 120
Till to the sight the growing burden prov'd,
How thou o'ercamst—and how, alas! I lov'd!
Too fatal proof! since thou, with av'rice fraught,
Didst basely urge (ah, shun the wounding thought!)
That tender circumstance—reveal it not,
Lest torn with rage I curse my fated lot:
Lest startled reason abdicate her reign,
And madness revel in this heated brain:
That tender circumstance—inhuman part—
I will not weep, tho' serpents gnaw this heart: 130
Frail, frail resolve! while gushing from mine eye
The pearly drops these boastful words belie.
Alas! can Sorrow in this bosom sleep,
Where strikes Ingratitude her talons deep?
When he I still adore, to nature dead,
For roses plant with thorns the nuptial bed?
Bids from the widow'd couch kind peace remove,
And cold indiff'rence blast the bow'r of love?

24. [Lines 102–8]. *Is Yarico . . . no more.* The annihilation of Yarico's parents by the Christian invaders is entirely Jerningham's own contrivance.
25. *galling* "Making sore by chaffing or rubbing" (*OED*).

What time his guardian pow'r[26] I most requir'd,
Against my fame and happiness conspir'd!   140
And (do I live to breathe the barb'rous tale?)
His faithful *Yarico* expos'd to sale!
Yes, basely urg'd (regardless of my pray'rs,
Ev'n while I bath'd his venal hand with tears)
What most for pity call'd—I can no more—
My future child—to swell his impious store:
All, all mankind for this will rise thy foe,
But I, alas! alone endure the woe:
Alone endure the fest'ring hand of care,
The bleeding soul, and swoonings of despair.   150
Was it for this I left my native plain,
And dar'd the tempest brooding on the main?
For this[27] unlock'd (seduc'd by Christian art)
The chaste affections of my virgin heart?
Within this bosom fan'd the constant flame,
And fondly languish'd for a mother's name?
Lo! every hope is poison'd in its bloom,
And horrors watch around this guilty womb.

  With blood illustrious circling thro' these veins,
Which ne'er was chequer'd with plebeian stains,   160
Thro' ancestry's long line ennobled springs,
From fame-crown'd warriors and exalted kings:
Must I the shafts of infamy sustain?
To slav'ry's purposes my infant train?
To catch the glances of his haughty lord?[28]
Attend obedient at the festive board?[29]
From hands unscepter'd take the scornful blow?
Uproot the thoughts of glory as they grow?

  26. *his guardian pow'r* Cf. Homer, *Iliad* (trans. Pope [1720], 24.304): "Your sole Defence,
your guardian Pow'r is gone!"
  27. *Was it for this. . . . For this* Lines 151–53 echo Belinda's cries after the loss of her lock
of hair in Pope's *The Rape of the Lock* (1714), 4.97–102. Cf. Duck, *Avaro and Amanda* [7],
lines 555–58 and 574.
  28. *his haughty lord* Presumably the slaveowner.
  29. *board* Table.

Let this pervade at length thy heart of steel;
Yet, yet return, nor blush, oh man, to feel: 170
Ah! guide thy steps from yon expecting fleet,
Thine injur'd *Yarico* relenting meet:
Bid her recline woe-stricken on thy breast,
And hush her raging sorrows into rest:
Ah! let the youth that sent the cruel dart,
Extract the point envenom'd[30] from her heart:
The peace he banish'd from this mind recall,
And bid the tears he prompted cease to fall.
Then while the stream of life is giv'n to flow,
And sable hue o'erspread this youthful brow;   180
Or curl untaught by art this woolly hair,
So long, so long to me shalt thou be dear.

Say, lovely youth, flow all my words in vain,
Like seeds that strew the rude ungrateful plain?[31]
Say, shall I ne'er regain thy wonted[32] grace?
Ne'er stretch these arms to catch the wish'd embrace?
Enough—with new-awak'd resentment fraught
Assist me, heav'n! to tear him from my thought;
No longer vainly suppliant will I bow,
And give to love what I to hatred owe;   190
Forgetful of the race from whence I came,
With woe acquainted, but unknown to shame.
Hence, vile Dejection, with thy plaintive pray'r,
Thy bended knee, and still descending tear:
Rejoin, rejoin the pale-complexion'd train—
The conflict's past—and I'm myself again.

Thou parent sun! if e'er with pious lay[33]
I usher'd in thy world-reviving ray!
Or as thy fainter beams illum'd the west,
With grateful voice I hymn'd thee to thy rest!   200

30. *envenom'd* Poisoned.
31. *ungrateful plain* Cf. Dryden, *Georgics,* 2.427: "The wild olive shoots, and shades the ungrateful plain."
32. *wonted* Accustomed, usual.   33. *lay* Song.

Beheld with wond'ring eye thy radiant seat,
Or sought thy sacred dome with unclad feet!
If near to thy bright altars as I drew,
My votive lamb, thy holy flamen,[34] slew!
Forgive! That I, irrev'rent of thy name,
Dar'd for thy foe indulge th'unhallow'd flame:
Ev'n on a Christian lavish'd my esteem,
And scorn'd the sable children of thy beam.
This poniard[35] by my daring hand imprest
Shall drink the ruddy drops that warm my breast: 210
Nor I alone, by this immortal deed
From slav'ry's laws my infant shall be freed.
And thou, whose ear is deaf to pity's call,
Behold at length thy destin'd victim fall;
Behold thy once-lov'd Nubian stain'd with gore,
Unwept, extended on the crimson floor:
These temples clouded with the shades of death,
These lips unconscious of the ling'ring breath:
These eyes uprais'd (ere[36] closed by fate's decree)
To catch expiring one faint glimpse of thee.   220
Ah! then thy *Yarico* forbear to dread,
My fault'ring voice no longer will upbraid,
Demand due vengeance of the pow'rs above,
Or, more offensive still, implore thy love.

34. *flamen* Priest.   35. *poniard* Dagger.
36. *ere* Sooner, rather.

Anonymous, "Epistle from Yarico to Inkle"

From *The Lady's Magazine* 13 (1782): 664.

This and the following short poem were first located by Benjamin Bissell, *American Indian in English Literature of the Eighteenth Century,* 198–99. They are good examples of how the story could be condensed into a succinct lyrical form, employing the mode of verse epistle. Both poems show a studied naïveté in their articulation of Yarico's emotions and assume that the reader knows the story. Their full pathos depends on our awareness of the heartlessness of her enslavement. Price describes this poem as "in reality a song rather than a letter . . . and . . . suitable for singing" (*Inkle and Yarico Album,* 33–35). It is composed in a traditional ballad stanza, though without accompanying music. Its author has yet to be identified.

I

Far from ungrateful Inkle's flight
   I pass the lonely hours;
No more I wander with delight,
   In those sequester'd bowers.

II

Thy image haunts my pensive breast
   That heaves full oft a sigh;
Ne'er will this bosom be at rest
   Till Yarico shall die.

III

Then farewell Inkle, faithless swain,
    Thy loss I'll still deplore;
And of thy broken vows complain,
    Till Yarico's no more.

10

[Peter Pindar], "Yarico to Inkle"

From the *Scots Magazine* 55 (May 1793): 242.

First appearing in the *Scots Magazine,* this anonymously published poem was soon after reprinted in the *Gentleman's Magazine* (63 [June 1793]: 560), where it was accompanied by a verse translation into Latin by Lord Deerhurst (1758–1831), later seventh earl of Coventry. The poem and its translation, titled "Yarico ad Inklum," also appeared in *The Times* (no. 2705, 10 June 1793). The practice of rendering Inkle and Yarico into Latin, whether as translation or original invention, may not have been common, though I have identified at least one earlier example. A heroic epistle by the Dutch poet Jacobus Henricus Hoeufft, titled "Iaricus, Puellae Americanae, ad Ynclum, Anglum, Epistola," was published in his *Pericula Poëtica* (n.p., 1783), 32–37. It is a minor but amusing irony, reflecting the mythical status Inkle and Yarico had acquired by the late eighteenth century, that the story was deemed worthy to be reworked in Latin employing a classical form invented by Ovid (see headnote to selection 3B). The omission of Deerhurst's translation from the present selection is not intended as a comment on its quality.

The attribution of "Yarico to Inkle" to Peter Pindar may seem a little fortuitous, depending as it does on a collation of bibliographical details gleaned from its early printings. Accompanying the poem in *The Times* is the caption, "By the Author of the Gipsy Ballad." (The "Gipsy Ballad" had appeared anonymously in the newspaper on 7 June.) However, in both the *Scots Magazine* and the *Gentleman's Magazine,* the same poem, "A Gypsey Ballad," with the author named as Peter Pindar, is printed adjacent to "Yarico to Inkle." "Peter Pindar" was the pseudonym adopted by John Wolcot (1738–1819), best recalled as a prolific and sometimes scabrous verse satirist. "Yarico to Inkle" is a far cry from the loose conversational idiom of much of his writing, though his *Pindariana* (1795) does contain sentimental love poetry of a similar style. The poem was set to music by Friedrich Heinrich Himmel (1765–1814), musician to the King of Prussia, and published in London, c. 1805 (copy in Bodleian Library, Oxford).

When night spreads her shadows around,
  I will watch with delight on thy rest;
I will soften thy bed on the ground,
  And thy cheek shall be lodg'd on my breast.

Love heeds not the storm nor the rain;
  On *me* let their fury descend,
This bosom shall never complain
  While it shelters the life of a friend.

O tell me what tears thee away?
  To a *fair one,* ah! wouldst thou depart?   10
Alas! to thy Yarico say
  What maiden will love like this heart?

Though resolv'd not my sorrows to hear;
  Though resolv'd from a mourner to fly;
The ocean shall bear thee a tear,
  And the winds shall convey thee a sigh!

12

George Colman the Younger, *Inkle and Yarico: An Opera, in Three Acts*

First staged and published in 1787.

George Colman's comic opera was far from being the first play based on the tale of Inkle and Yarico. Two decades earlier, Sebastian-Roch Nicolas Chamfort's comedy *La jeune Indienne* (1764) had proved a tremendous hit on the French stage; but though translated into German, Danish, Italian, Spanish, and Dutch, it was never rendered into English or performed in the British Isles. Despite some superficial similarities between the two, it is highly unlikely that Colman had read or seen Chamfort's play before writing his own (see Chamfort, *La jeune Indienne,* ed. Chinard, 30–31). Earlier still and probably the first attempt at dramatizing the story is *Incle and Yarico* (1742), a tragedy in three acts usually ascribed to a Mrs. Weddell. This portentous and turgid drama was intended for performance at the Theatre Royal in Covent Garden but was wisely rejected by the theater managers. A synopsis of its plot may be found in Price, *Inkle and Yarico Album,* 35–43.

Colman's *Inkle and Yarico,* with songs set to music by the composer Samuel Arnold (1740–1802), was unquestionably the most popular English comic opera of the late eighteenth century, and with the exception of Sheridan's *School for Scandal* (1777), the most widely performed new play on the London stage during the last quarter of the century. Some idea of its extraordinary success can be gleaned from the fact that, after its triumph at the Little Theatre in the Haymarket, where it was first staged on 4 August 1787, it was put on during the ensuing season at Covent Garden, with a fresh cast and to equal acclaim. At the time, it was almost unprecedented for a new play to be transferred from one London theater to another in this way (Hogan, *London Stage,* 910). When Elizabeth Billington took the part of Yarico at Covent Garden (first performance 26 January 1789), new songs were added and a "Negro Dance" was incorporated so that, even when running simultaneously, the two productions would have been recognizably distinct. In the London theater, between 1787 and 1800, *Inkle and Yarico* was staged a total of 164 times.

Outside London it developed into a favorite touring piece and was revived with great frequency up and down the country and abroad for the next fifty years. At Dublin, where it was first put on at the Smock Alley Theatre in December 1787, "a very crowded and brilliant audience . . . enjoy[ed] their evening's entertainment without . . . having their ears wounded by indelicacies, more savage than the war-hoop of the Indians whom the piece presented" (Walsh, *Opera in Dublin,* 273–74). With the opening of a new theater (the present Georgian Theatre) at Richmond in the North Riding of Yorkshire in 1788, Colman's musical comedy, still a novelty, was the natural choice for its first production (Rosenfeld, *Georgian Theatre,* 13). Elsewhere, Alfred Lowenberg records performances of the play in Kingston, Jamaica (1788), New York (1789), Philadelphia (1790), Calcutta (1791), and Boston (1794). He notes that it was even being revived at New York as late as 22 April 1844 (*Annals of Opera,* 446). With the advent of the Victorian era, however, it gradually dropped out of the repertory.

Although Colman wrote the play and was the librettist for its songs, a large part of its broader appeal was due to Samuel Arnold's fine ear for an expressive tune. The music to *Inkle and Yarico* has been dismissed as "unambitious" (Fiske, *English Theatre Music,* 478), and in one sense it was. Many of the songs are simply reworkings of well-known popular airs. The beautiful love duet beginning "O say, simple maid," shared by Inkle and Yarico in the first act, followed Colman's libretto but recycled the musical score of another air made popular two years before by Mrs. Stephen Kemble, the actress who first came to play the part of Yarico (see note 30). Music scholars have contended that several songs are adapted from operatic arias by Giovanni Paisiello (1740–1816) and others. If the songs were, in the words of a contemporary review, "mostly compiled" (*Town and Country Magazine* 19 (1787): 386), that took nothing away from the éclat with which they were received. Even the sternest of critics succumbed to the charm of Mrs. Kemble as Yarico, whose "sweet and pathetic tones and . . . exquisite plaintiveness . . . brought tears into the eyes of the whole audience" (*General Magazine* 1 [1787]: 161).

Theatrical records show that, in common with other musical entertainments of its age, different songs were randomly employed for different performances. When a company from Drury Lane en route to Edinburgh halted briefly at Harrogate to perform the piece in 1806, an unspecified number of additional songs were assigned to the actor who played Inkle (Rosenfeld, *Georgian Theatre*, 41–42). The actor-manager, Tate Wilkinson, alludes with some displeasure to a performance of *Inkle and Yarico* at Liverpool in 1793 in which the play was acted without songs (*Wandering Patentee*, 2:191). The enormous success of the work owed not a little to the considerable license with which it was constantly being refashioned. In that sense it accords strikingly with the no less adaptable tale it tells. A vocal score to the opera, printed within a month of its first performance, contains Arnold's music to sixteen of the songs (facsimile by Belwin Mills [Melville, N.Y., 1977]). Two additional songs, "Simplicity, Thou Fav'rite Child" and "What Citadel So Proud Can Say," composed by Arnold for John Henry Johnstone, who first played Inkle at Covent Garden, were published separately in 1788.

No authorial manuscript of the play is known to be extant. However, the copy (prepared by a careful amanuensis) for submission to John Larpent, the examiner of plays, survives in the Huntington Library (MacMillan, *Catalogue of the Larpent Plays*, no. LA 782). It represents the fullest text of Colman's libretto and includes a fragment of the original ending (see introduction, p. 25). Accompanying the manuscript is a letter to Larpent, signed by Colman, dated from the "Theatre Royal Haymarket, July 25th 1787," in which he writes that "the following Opera, is, with the Permission of the Right Honourable the Lord Chamberlain designed for Representation at this Theatre." Also included is a verse prologue, dated 1789, that does not appear to have been printed. The manuscript has a catch or trio ("Straight thro' the Woodlands Lies Our Way"), to be sung at the end of the opening scene by Inkle, Medium, and Trudge, which does not seem to have come through to the opening night.

ESTC lists eleven separately published editions of the play before 1800. Of these, four are London imprints ("Printed for G. C. J. and J. Robinson Pater-Noster-Row"), dating from 1787 (three issues), 1788, 1789, and 1792. There are four Dublin imprints, all between 1787 and 1789, a Glasgow edition of 1796, and two American editions (Philadelphia, 1792, and Boston,

1794). According to the title page of the London edition of 1787, the text it prints is "as performed at the *Theatre-Royal* in the Hay-Market, on Saturday, August 11th, 1787," which was the play's fourth performance. Colman's twentieth-century biographer tells us that though first-night critics were on the whole highly complimentary, several complained about the dramatist's excessive use of punning and wordplay. As a consequence, Colman immediately excised many passages that he considered verbose or redundant to the plot (Bagster-Collins, *George Colman the Younger,* 35–36). The 1787 edition reflects this by printing Colman's excisions within the text but enclosing them throughout within double quotation marks. Two songs, "Christians Are So Good They Say," to be sung by Trudge in act 2, scene 1, and, in the following scene, Sir Christopher Curry's "O Give Me Your Plain Dealing Fellows" (neither present in the Larpent manuscript) are set off in this way and do not appear in the vocal score. The surgery, though not radical, significantly sharpens the play.

In the early nineteenth century, Mrs. Elizabeth Inchbald negotiated with Colman the right to publish *Inkle and Yarico* as volume 20 of her multivolume edition of *The British Theatre.* The title page proclaims that her edition was "printed . . . from the prompt book," and it reads very much as an acting text of the opera. The text omits almost all those passages that Colman had excised and, if indeed marked up for printing from a theatrical promptbook, probably best represents the play as it came to be performed. Colman's sensitivity about some of Mrs. Inchbald's prefatory remarks led to an acrimonious exchange of letters, in which she rather ambivalently professed "the admiration I have for Inkle and Yarico . . . yet that very admiration warned me against unqualified praise, as the mere substitute for ridicule. . . . Had I exposed any faults but such as you could easily argue away . . . you would have been too much offended (Peake, *Memoirs of the Colman Family,* 316–21). The *National Union Catalogue* lists numerous other nineteenth-century texts of the play.

I have followed here the practice adopted elsewhere in this anthology of representing texts through those versions that had the widest currency. The text printed below is based on Mrs. Inchbald's promptbook or acting edition. However, Colman's prologue of 1789 (which throws interesting light on the play) has been rescued from the Larpent papers. Also, those songs that appear in the 1787 vocal score but were either omitted or truncated by Mrs. Inchbald have been restored. Whether they were dropped by Colman or added later by Samuel Arnold, I have made no attempt to incorporate those songs not present in the vocal score. Several silent corrections have been made after comparing Mrs. Inchbald's text with the Larpent manuscript and the 1787 first edition.

A much fuller contextual discussion of the play will be found in the introduction, pp. 18–27. Eighteenth-century critics of *Inkle and Yarico* concurred in praising it for its strong plot and for the importance of its subject matter, though a recurrent judgment was that it risked being let down by a "dialogue [that] . . . too often degenerates into pun" (*Town and Country Magazine* 19 [1787]: 376). Its topicality as an antislavery play was widely recognized at a time when abolition was such a burning issue. "This piece," reports an opening night reviewer in *The Times*, "is managed with much judgment, and abounds with many noble and liberal sentiments. These had a very striking effect on the audience, who received them with the most hearty approbation, and . . . with general applause" (Monday, 6 August 1787). "The subject is well handled," claims J. W. Lake writing a full forty years later, "and was happily chosen at the time to stimulate the already awakening sympathy of the British public, in behalf of the untutored, fettered, friendless blacks" (*Dramatic Works of George Colman the Younger*, 1:xi). Few if any seemed troubled that Colman and Arnold had largely ignored the real atrocities of the slave trade in favor of sentimentalizing the story. The lighthearted manner of the opera was at once its charm and its weakness. Following the abolition in 1833 of slaveholding throughout the British colonies, it is little wonder the play seems to have lost its currency.

After disappearing from the stage for approximately 150 years, *Inkle and Yarico* has very recently been "rediscovered," enjoying two remarkable revivals during the spring of 1997. The more spectacular of these was presented on the grounds of Holder House, a former sugar plantation, as part of the Barbados Opera Festival. Arnold's music was reorchestrated to incorporate a Caribbean steel band, exotic dancers, and a brilliant carnival that included fire eaters and stiltsmen. *Inkle and Yarico* was described by an enthusiastic reviewer in the *Financial Times* (29–30 March 1997) as "a gem waiting to be exploited further." No less significant was the production mounted the following month in England at the Cambridge Festival Theatre (25–26 April). This was a highly successful attempt to replicate what the director described in the program notes as the "strongly historical and even slightly pantomimic feel for the piece, . . . to express a skewed world against which love and understanding can, eventually, flourish." Without claiming absolute authenticity, the production endeavored to balance the play's "appalling attitudes and offensive lines" within a structure that affirms that "love and good sense can triumph over bigotry." It is a similar ambiguous sense of *Inkle and Yarico* as an antislavery dialectic that is also innately racist that fuels much of the present debate about the play and about racial awareness both in the era from which it emerged and, of course, in our own.

Inkle and Yarico; An Opera, in Three Acts

PERSONS REPRESENTED

Haymarket

Inkle	Mr. Bannister, jun.
Sir Christopher Curry	Mr. Parsons
Medium	Mr. Baddeley
Campley	Mr. Davies
Trudge	Mr. Edwin
Mate	Mr. Meadows
Yarico	Mrs. Kemble
Narcissa	Mrs. Bannister
Wowski	Miss George
Patty	Mrs. Forster

Covent Garden

Inkle	Mr. Johnstone
Sir Christopher Curry	Mr. Quick
Campley	Mr. Davies
Medium	Mr. Wewitzer
Trudge	Mr. Edwin
Mate	Mr. Darley
Yarico	Mrs. Billington
Narcissa	Mrs. Mountain
Wowski	Mrs. Martyr
Patty	Mrs. Rock

Prologue[1]

Again we venture, cheer'd by summer skies,
To bring in plain array and usual guise,
Scenes you have oft view'd here with gracious eyes.
No airs of foreign opera we borrow,
But Yarico resumes her genuine sorrow;
And, as the scene commands in various places,
Our ladies lay by rouge, and *black* their faces.
   Yet, you'll behold tonight—nor think it strange!
Before the piece concludes some little change.
A change not made to damp the glow of youth,
But "To set passion on the side of truth."
Here first, not following the stale narration,
In Inkle's heart was wrought a reformation.
But how shou'd he, all guilt, for pardon plead?
How prove his penitence sincere indeed?
Unwise to aggravate offences past, ⎫
Struggling on others his own shame to cast, ⎬
And even a father's reverend name to blast. ⎭
Here then, yet not in spleen or anger done,
An anxious parent's hand corrects a son.
Nature, with culture not quite unrefin'd,
And growing years matur'd his youthful mind,
While you well pleas'd, to hail a muse-struck child,
Upon his earliest efforts partial smil'd.
Ah! think not then that arrogant and vain,
We boast to add new graces to the scene;
Or now, with pedant chymistry[2] design,
The sterling ore of genius to refine;
No! we but claim the charter of the stage,
'Gainst vice and folly constant war to wage;
To teach young poets the first rule of art,

---

   1. *Prologue* This appears at the head of the Larpent manuscript with the title "Prologue to Inkle and Yarico. 1789." It seems to have been written (probably by Colman himself) in response to the phenomenal success of the opera.
   2. *pedant chymistry* Alchemy.

To charm the fancy, and improve the heart.
Awhile with patience yet attention bend!
Your sentence a brief hour or two suspend!
Then judge impartially our little cause
We dread your censure! but ask no applause.

Inkle and Yarico

Scene,—First on the Main of America: Afterwards in Barbadoes.[3]

ACT THE FIRST

SCENE I

An American Forest.

Medium   [*Without.*] Hilli ho! ho!

Trudge   [*Without.*] Hip! hollo! ho!—Hip!—

Enter Medium and Trudge

Med.   Pshaw! it's only wasting time and breath. Bawling won't persuade him to budge a bit faster, and, whatever weight it may have in *some* places, bawling, it seems, don't go for argument here. Plague on't! we are now in the wilds of America.

Trudge.   Hip, hillio—ho—hi!—

Med.   Hold your tongue, you blockhead, or—

Trudge.   Lord! sir, if my master makes no more haste, we shall all be put to sword by the knives of the natives. I'm told they take off heads like hats, and hang 'em on pegs, in their parlours. Mercy on us! My head aches with the very thoughts of it. Hollo! Mr. Inkle! master; hollo!

Med.   [*Stops his mouth.*] Head aches! Zounds, so does mine, with your

3. *Scene . . . Barbadoes* The scenes for the opening production at the Theatre Royal, Haymarket, were painted by Michael Angelo Rooker, its principal scene painter. Patrick Conner, *Michael Angelo Rooker*, 134, states that "at the auction of Rooker's possessions held in the month after his death, over a hundred of his stage designs were disposed of, and yet no more than a handful can be traced today." The present whereabouts of any of his designs for *Inkle and Yarico* are unknown.

The importance accorded to scene painting can be attested from another source, the playbill announcing a new production in Charleston, South Carolina, on 8 April 1793, which includes: "In the course of the opera, the following scenes will be presented: An American Forest painted by Mons. Odin [Audin]; Yarico's cave, hung with the skins of wild beasts, painted by Mr. Schultz; a scene of Rocks by Mons. Odin; a sea with a ship in full sail, by Mr. Schultz; the Town of Barbadoes with a calm sea and a Ship at anchor, by Mr. Schultz" (Willis, *Charleston Stage in the Eighteenth Century,* 168–69).

confounded bawling. It's enough to bring all the natives about us; and we shall be stripped and plundered in a minute.

Trudge. Aye; stripping is the first thing that would happen to us; for they seem to be woefully off for a wardrobe. I myself saw three, at a distance, with less clothes than I have, when I get out of bed: all dancing about in black buff; just like Adam in mourning.[4]

Med. This is to have to do with a schemer! a fellow who risks his life, for a chance of advancing his interest.—Always advantage in view! Trying, here, to make discoveries, that may promote his profit in England. Another Botany Bay scheme,[5] mayhap. Nothing else could induce him to quit our foraging party, from the ship; when he knows every inhabitant here is not only as black as a pepper-corn, but as hot into the bargain—and *I,* like a fool, to follow him! and then to let him loiter behind.—Why, nephew!—Why, Inkle.—[*Calling.*]

Trudge. Why, Inkle—Well! only to see the difference of men! he'd have thought it very hard, now, if I had let him call so often after me. Ah! I wish he was calling after me now, in the old jog-trot[6] way, again. What a fool was I to leave London for foreign parts!—That ever I should leave Threadneedle-street,[7] to thread an American forest, where a man's as soon lost as a needle in a bottle of hay![8]

4. *dancing about in black buff . . . in mourning* Dancing naked as if Adam had been attired in black mourning clothes. In European iconography, Adam is traditionally represented as a white man. The intricacy of the biblical simile is apparent if we recall that, before the Fall, Adam (the first man) was "naked . . . , and . . . not ashamed," whereas after eating of the forbidden fruit he hid from God in sorrow or mourning at his nakedness (Gen. 2:25, 3:10). Colman's image contrasts naked innocence and postlapsarian shame.

5. *Botany Bay scheme* As a means of replacing British colonies recently lost in America and of establishing a new penal settlement, a first batch of convicts was transported from England to Botany Bay in New South Wales in 1787. It was to land in January 1788, so that the expedition would have been still at sea when *Inkle and Yarico* was first performed. Subsequently the shores of Australia were claimed as British territory.

6. *jog-trot* Easygoing, unhurried.

7. *Threadneedle-street* A street in the City at the heart of London's financial district. *Brewer's Dictionary of Phrase and Fable,* 900, claims that "the name may have arisen from the sign of an inn, *The Three Needles* (though none of that name is recorded in the neighbourhood), or from some connexion with the Needlemakers' Company, whose arms are 'three needles in fesse argent.'" The Bank of England, which stands there, is often referred to as the Old Lady of Threadneedle Street.

8. *as a needle . . . hay!* A proverbial expression, more commonly now "a needle in a haystack." *Bottle* is a now obsolete word for "bundle." Colman introduces the simile to sustain Trudge's pun on *thread* and *needle.*

Med.   Patience, Trudge! Patience! If we once recover the ship—

Trudge.   Lord, sir, I shall never recover what I have lost in coming abroad. When my master and I were in London, I had such a mortal snug birth of it! Why, I was *factotum.*[9]

Med.   Factotum to a young merchant is no such sinecure, neither.

Trudge.   But then the honour of it. Think of that, sir; to be clerk as well as *own man.* Only consider. You find very few city clerks made out of a man, now-a-days. To be king of the counting-house, as well as lord of the bed-chamber. Ah! if I had him but now in the little dressing-room behind the office; tying his hair, with a bit of red tape,[10] as usual.

Med.   Yes, or writing an invoice in lampblack, and shining his shoes with an ink-bottle, *as usual,* you blundering blockhead!

Trudge.   Oh, if I was but brushing the accounts or casting up the coats! mercy on us! what's that?

Med.   That! What?

Trudge.   Didn't you hear a noise?

Med.   Y—es—but—hush! Oh, heavens be praised! here he is at last.

Enter Inkle.

Now, nephew!

Inkle.   So, Mr. Medium.

Med.   Zounds, one would think, by your confounded composure, that you were walking in St. James's Park,[11] instead of an American forest: and that all the beasts were nothing but good company. The hollow trees, here, sentry boxes, and the lions in 'em, soldiers; the jackalls, courtiers; the crocodiles, fine women; and the baboons, beaus. What the plague made you loiter so long?

Inkle.   Reflection.

Med.   So I should think; reflection generally comes lagging behind. What, scheming, I suppose; never quiet. At it again, eh? What a happy trader is your father, to have so prudent a son for a partner! Why, you are the carefullest Co.[12] in the whole city. Never losing sight of the main

9. *factotum* Jack of all trades; servant.

10. *a bit of red tape* In allusion to the name Inkle, "a kind of linen tape" (*OED*).

11. *St. James's Park* The park in Westminster favored for its fine walks and vistas. A portion of the park was enclosed to contain deer and other animals in the wild. In Charles II's time it provided the setting for William Wycherley's play *Love in a Wood, or St. James's Park* (1671) and for Rochester's poem "A Ramble in St. James's Park" (1680).

12. *Co.* Company.

chance; and that's the reason, perhaps, you lost sight of us, here, on the main of America.

Inkle.   Right, Mr. Medium. Arithmetic, I own, has been the means of our parting at present.

Trudge.   Ha! A sum in division, I reckon. [*Aside.*]

Med.   And pray, if I may be so bold, what mighty scheme has just tempted you to employ your head, when you ought to make use of your heels?

Inkle.   My heels! Here's pretty doctrine! Do you think I travel merely for motion? What, would you have a man of business come abroad, scamper extravagantly here and there and every where, then return home, and have nothing to tell, but that he has *been* here and there and every where? 'Sdeath,[13] sir, would you have me travel like a lord?

Med.   No, the Lord forbid!

Inkle.   Travelling, uncle, was always intended for improvement; and improvement is an advantage; and advantage is profit, and profit is gain. Which in the travelling translation of a trader, means, that you should gain every advantage of improving your profit. I have been comparing the land, here, with that of our own country.

Med.   And you find it like a good deal of the land of our own country— cursedly encumbered with black legs,[14] I take it.

Inkle.   And calculating how much it might be made to produce by the acre.

Med.   You were?

Inkle.   Yes; I was proceeding algebraically upon the subject.

Med.   Indeed!

Inkle.   And just about extracting the square root.

Med.   Hum!

Inkle.   I was thinking too, if so many natives could be caught, how much they might fetch at the West Indian markets.

Med.   Now let me ask you a question, or two, young cannibal catcher, if you please.

Inkle.   Well.

Med.   Ar'n't we bound for Barbadoes; partly to trade, but chiefly to carry home the daughter of the governor, Sir Christopher Curry, who has till now been under your father's care, in Threadneedle-street for polite English education?

13. *'Sdeath* A common diminutive of the oath "*God's death.*"
14. *black legs* Swindlers.

Inkle.   Granted.

Med.   And isn't it determined, between the old folks, that you are to marry Narcissa, as soon as we get there?

Inkle.   A fixed thing.

Med.   Then what the devil do you do here, hunting old hairy negroes, when you ought to be obliging a fine girl in the ship? Algebra, too! You'll have other things to think of when you are married, I promise you. A plodding fellow's head, in the hands of a young wife, like a boy's slate, after school, soon gets all its arithmetic wiped off: and then it appears in its true simple state: dark, empty, and bound in wood, Master Inkle.

Inkle. Not in a match of this kind. Why, it's a table of interest from beginning to end, old Medium.

Med.   Well, well, this is no time to talk. Who knows but, instead of sailing to a wedding, we may get cut up, here, for a wedding dinner: tossed up for a dingy duke, perhaps, or stewed down for a black baronet, or ate raw by an inky commoner?

Inkle. Why sure you aren't afraid?

Med.   Who, I afraid? Ha! ha! ha! No, not I! What the deuce should I be afraid of? Thank Heaven I have a clear conscience, and need not be afraid of any thing. A scoundrel might not be quite so easy on such an occasion; but it's the part of an honest man not to behave like a scoundrel: I never behaved like a scoundrel—for which reason I am an honest man, you know. But come—I hate to boast of my good qualities.

Inkle. Slow and sure, my good, virtuous Mr. Medium! Our companions can be but half a mile before us: and, if we do but double their steps, we shall overtake 'em at one mile's end, by all the powers of arithmetic.

Med. Oh curse your arithmetic!

[Exeunt.]

SCENE II

Another part of the Forest.—A ship at anchor in the
bay at a small distance.—Mouth of a cave.

Enter Sailors and Mate, as returning from foraging.

Mate.   Come, come, bear a hand, my lads. Tho' the bay is just under our bowsprits, it will take a damned deal of tripping to come at it—there's hardly any steering clear of the rocks here. But do we muster all hands? All right, think ye?

1st Sail.   All to a man—besides yourself, and a monkey—the three land

lubbers, that edged away in the morning, goes for nothing, you know—
they're all dead, may-hap, by this.

Mate. Dead! you be—Why they're friends of the captain; and if not
brought safe aboard to-night, you may all chance to have a salt eel for
your supper—that's all—Moreover the young plodding spark, he with
the grave, foul weather face, there, is to man the tight little frigate, Miss
Narcissa—what d'ye call her? that is bound with us for Barbadoes. Rot
'em for not keeping under weigh, I say! But come, let's see if a song will
bring 'em too. Let's have a full chorus to the good merchant ship, the
Achilles,[15] that's wrote by our captain.

Song

> *The Achilles, though christen'd, good ship, 'tis surmis'd,*
> *From that old man of war, great Achilles, so priz'd,*
> *Was he, like our vessel, pray fairly baptiz'd?*
>   *Ti tol lol, &c.*

> *Poets sung that Achilles—if, now, they've an itch*
> *To sing this, future ages may know which is which;*
> *And that one rode in Greece—and the other in pitch.*
>   *Ti tol lol, &c.*

> *What tho' but a merchant ship—sure our supplies:*
> *Now your men of war's gain in a lottery lies,*
> *And how blank they all look, when they can't get a prize!*[16]
>   *Ti tol lol, &c.*

> *What are all their fine names? when no rhino's*[17] *behind,*
> *The Intrepid, and Lion, look sheepish you'll find;*

15. *the Achilles . . . our captain.* John Adolphus, *Memoirs of John Bannister,* 1:165, writes:
"The name of the ship is curiously retained in this story in all its shapes: in the Achilles Mr.
Ligon departed from England; the same name is given by Steele to the vessel which leaves
Inkle on shore; and Mr. Colman has not only preserved it, but made it the basis of a quib-
bling song, sung by the mate and crew."

16. *lottery . . . prize!* State lotteries had been introduced in 1778 and were notorious as a
cause of widespread bankruptcy and ruin. M. Dorothy George, *London Life in the Eighteenth Century,* 316, remarks that "there was a mania among all classes for lottery insurances,
by which any person could insure any number for any amount against coming up blank."
The last state lottery until modern times was held in 1826.

17. *rhino* Common eighteenth-century slang for money, often "ready rhino." The origin

Whilst, alas! the poor Æolus can't raise the wind!
Ti tol lol, &c.

Then the Thunderer's dumb; out of tune the Orpheus;
The Ceres has nothing at all to produce:
And the Eagle[18] *I warrant you, looks like a goose,*
Ti tol lol, &c.

1st Sail.   Avast! look ahead there. Here they come, chased by a fleet of black devils.

Midsh.   And the devil a *fire* have I to give them. We han't a grain of powder left. What must we do lads?

2nd Sail.   Do? Sheer off to be sure.

Midsh.   [*Reluctantly.*] Well, if I must, I must. [*Going to the other side, and holloing to Inkle, &c.*] Yoho, lubbers! Crowd all the sail you can, d'ye mind me!

[*Exeunt sailors.*]

Enter Medium, running across the stage,
as pursued by the Blacks.

Med.   Nephew! Trudge! run—scamper! Scour—fly! Zounds, what harm did I ever do to be hunted to death by a pack of bloodhounds? Why nephew! Oh, confound your long sums in arithmetic! I'll take care of myself; and if we must have any arithmetic, dot and carry one for my money.

[*Runs off.*]

Enter Inkle and Trudge, hastily.

Trudge.   Oh! that ever I was born, to leave pen, ink, and powder for this!

Inkle.   Trudge, how far are the sailors before us?

Trudge.   I'll run and see, sir, directly.

Inkle.   Blockhead, come here. The savages are close upon us; we shall scarce be able to recover our party. Get behind this tuft of trees with me; they'll pass us, and we may then recover[19] our ship with safety.

Trudge.   [*Going behind.*] Oh! Threadneedle-street, Thread—

---

of the term is uncertain, though Brewer, *Dictionary of Phrase and Fable,* 654, links it to the phrase "to pay through the nose," pointing out that *rhinos* is Greek for nose.

18. *The Intrepid . . . the Eagle* Fictitious names of British ships.

19. *recover* Return to.

Inkle. Peace.

Trudge. [*Hiding.*]—Needle-street. [*They hide behind trees. Natives cross. After a long pause, Inkle looks from the trees.*]

Inkle. Trudge.

Trudge. Sir. [*In a whisper.*]

Inkle. Are they all gone by?

Trudge. Won't you look and see?

Inkle. [*Looking round.*] So all is safe at last. [*Coming forward.*] Nothing like policy in these cases; but you'd have run on, like a booby![20] A tree, I fancy, you'll find, in future, the best resource in a hot pursuit.

Trudge. Oh, charming! It's a retreat for a king, sir: Mr. Medium, however, has not got up in it; your uncle, sir, *has run on like a booby;* and has got up with our party by this time, I take it; who are now most likely at the shore. But what are we to do next, sir?

Inkle. Reconnoitre a little, and then proceed.

Trudge. Then pray, sir, proceed to reconnoitre; for the sooner the better.

Inkle. Then look out, d'ye hear, and tell me if you discover any danger.

Trudge. Y—Ye—s—Yes.

Inkle. Well, is the coast clear?

Trudge. Eh! Oh lord!—Clear! [*Rubbing his eyes.*] Oh dear! oh dear! the coast will soon be clear enough now, I promise you—The ship is under sail, sir!

Inkle. Confusion! my property carried off in the vessel.

Trudge. All, all, sir, except me.

Inkle. They may report me dead, perhaps, and dispose of my property at the next island. [*The vessel appears under sail.*]

Trudge. Ah! there they go. [*A gun fired.*]—That will be the last report we shall ever hear from 'em I'm afraid.—That's as much as to say, Good bye to ye. And here we are left—two fine, full-grown babes in the wood!

Inkle. What an ill-timed accident! Just too, when my speedy union with Narcissa, at Barbadoes, would so much advance my interests.—Ah, my Narcissa, I never shall forget thy last adieu.—Something must be hit upon, and speedily; but what resource? [*Thinking.*]

Trudge. The old one—a tree, sir.—'Tis all we have for it now. What

20. *booby* Blockhead, nincompoop.

would I give, now, to be perched upon a high stool, with our brown desk squeezed into the pit of my stomach—scribbling away an old parchment!—But all my red ink will be spilt by an old black pin of a negro.

Song[21]

[Last Valentine's Day][22]

> *A voyage over seas had not enter'd my head,*
> *Had I known but on which side to butter my bread,*[23]
> *Heigho! sure I—for hunger must die!*
> *I've sail'd like a booby; come here in a squall,*
> *Where, alas! there's no bread to be butter'd at all!*
> > *Oho! I'm a terrible booby!*
> > *Oh, what a sad booby am I!*
>
> *In London, what gay chop-house*[24] *signs in the street!*
> *But the only sign here is of nothing to eat.*
> *Heigho! that I—for hunger should die!*
> *My mutton's all lost; I'm a poor starving elf!*
> *And for all the world like a lost mutton myself.*
> > *Oho! I shall die a lost mutton!*[25]
> > *Oh! what a lost mutton am I!*
>
> *For a neat slice of beef, I could roar like a bull;*[26]
> *And my stomach's so empty, my heart is quite full.*
> *Heigho! that I—for hunger should die!*
> *But, grave without meat, I must here meet my grave,*

21. Colman's libretto for Trudge's song consists of a string of commonplace proverbial phrases. The songs assigned to English lower-class characters such as Trudge and Patty are invariably of this kind.

22. *Last Valentine's Day* The tune employed here appears to be borrowed from a hunting song, "Black Sloven" (the name of a favorite horse), which begins "Last Valentine's Day when bright Phoebus shone clear" and ends with the refrain "Ta-le-o Ta-le-o Ta-le-o." A version of the song was published in *Universal Magazine* 48 (February 1771): 95–96.

23. *which side . . . my bread* Proverbial; see *ODEP*), 81: "His bread is buttered on both sides."

24. *chop-house* "A mean house of entertainment where provision ready dressed is sold" (Johnson, *Dictionary*, 1755); an eating house specializing in muttonchops and beefsteaks.

25. *a lost mutton* Cf. *Two Gentlemen of Verona*, 1.1.93, "I, a lost mutton, gave your letter to her."

26. *roar like a bull* Proverbial; see *ODEP*, 680.

For my bacon, I fancy, I never shall save.
Oho! I shall ne'er save my bacon![27]
I can't save my bacon, not I!

Trudge. Hum! I was thinking—I was thinking, sir—if so many natives could be caught, how much they might fetch at the West India markets!

Inkle. Scoundrel! is this a time to jest?

Trudge. No, faith, sir! Hunger is too sharp to be jested with. As for me, I shall starve for want of food. Now you may meet a luckier fate: you are able to extract the square root, sir; and that's the very best provision you can find here to live upon. But I! [*Noise at a distance.*] Mercy on us! here they come again.

Inkle. Confusion! Deserted on one side, and pressed on the other, which way shall I turn?—This cavern may prove a safe retreat to us for the present. I'll enter, cost what it will.

Trudge. Oh Lord! no, don't, don't—We shall pay too dear for our lodging, depend on't.

Inkle. This is no time for debating. You are at the mouth of it: lead the way, Trudge.

Trudge. What! go in before your honour! I know my place better, I assure you—[*Aside.*] I might walk into more mouths than one, perhaps.

Inkle. Coward! then follow me. [*Noise again.*]

Trudge. I must, sir; I must! Ah, Trudge, Trudge! what a damned hole are you getting into!

[*Exeunt into a Cavern.*]

SCENE III

A cave, decorated with skins of wild beasts, feathers, &c.
In the middle of the scene, a rude kind of curtain, by way of
door to an inner apartment.

Enter Inkle and Trudge, as from the mouth of the cavern.

Inkle. So far, at least, we have proceeded with safety. Ha! no bad specimen of savage elegance. These ornaments would be worth something in England.—We have little to fear here, I hope: this cave rather bears the pleasing face of a profitable adventure.

Trudge. Very likely, sir! But for a pleasing face, it has the cursed'st ugly

27. *save my bacon* Proverbial; see *ODEP,* 700.

mouth I ever saw in my life. Now do, sir, make off as fast as you can. If we once get clear of the natives' houses, we have little to fear from the lions and leopards: for by the appearance of their parlours, they seem to have killed all the wild beast in the country. Now pray, do, my good master, take my advice, and run away.

Inkle.   Rascal! Talk again of going out, and I'll flea[28] you alive.

Trudge.   That's just what I expect for coming in.—All that enter here appear to have had their skins stript over their ears; and ours will be kept for curiosities—We shall stand here, stuffed, for a couple of white wonders.

Inkle.   This curtain seems to lead to another apartment: I'll draw it.

Trudge.   No, no, no, don't; don't. We may be called to account for disturbing the company: you may get a curtain-lecture,[29] perhaps, sir.

Inkle.   Peace, booby, and stand on your guard.

Trudge.   Oh! what will become of us! Some grim, seven-foot fellow ready to scalp us.

Inkle.   By heaven! a woman!

      [*As the curtain draws, Yarico and Wowski discovered asleep.*]

Trudge.   A woman! [*Aside.*]—[*Loud.*] But let him come on; I'm ready— dam'me, I don't fear facing the devil himself—Faith it is a woman—fast asleep too.

Inkle.   And beautiful as an angel!

Trudge.   And egad! there seems to be a nice, little plump bit in the corner; only she's an angel of rather a darker sort.

Inkle.   Hush! keep back—she wakes. [*Yarico comes forward—Inkle and Trudge retire to opposite sides of the scene.*]

Song—Yarico

When the chace of day is done.
And the shaggy lion's skin,
Which for us, our warriors win,
Decks our cells at set of sun;
Worn with toil, with sleep opprest,
I press my mossy bed, and sink to rest.

---

28. *flea* Flay.

29. *curtain-lecture* "A reproof given by a wife to a husband in bed" (Johnson, *Dictionary,* 1755).

Then, once more, I see our train,
With all our chase renew'd again:
Once more 'tis day,
Once more our prey
Gnashes his angry teeth, and foams in vain.
Again, in sullen haste, he flies,
Ta'en in the toil, again he lies,
Again he roars—and, in my slumbers, dies.

[*Inkle and Trudge come forward.*]

Inkle.   Our language!

Trudge.   Zounds, she has thrown me into a cold sweat.

Yar.   Hark! I heard a noise! Wowski, awake! whence can it proceed? [*She awakes Wowski, and they both come forward—Yarico towards Inkle; Wowski towards Trudge.*]

Yar.   Ah! what form is this?—are you a man?

Inkle.   True flesh and blood, my charming heathen, I promise you.

Yar.   What harmony in his voice! What a shape! How fair his skin too— [*Gazing.*]

Trudge.   This must be a lady of quality, by her staring.

Yar.   Say, stranger, whence come you?

Inkle.   From a far distant island; driven on this coast by distress, and deserted by my companions.

Yar.   And do you know the danger that surrounds you here? Our woods are filled with beasts of prey—my countrymen too—(yet, I think they couldn't find the heart)—might kill you.—It would be a pity if you fell in their way—I think I should weep if you came to any harm.

Trudge.   O ho! It's time, I see, to begin making interest with the chamber maid. [*Takes Wowski apart.*]

Inkle.   How wild and beautiful! sure there is magic in her shape, and she has rivetted me to the place. But where shall I look for safety? let me fly and avoid my death.

Yar.   Oh! no—don't depart.—But I will try to preserve you; and if you are killed, Yarico must die too! Yet, 'tis I alone can save you; your death is certain, without my assistance; and, indeed, indeed you shall not want it.

Inkle.   My kind Yarico! what means, then, must be used for my safety?

Yar.   My cave must conceal you: none enter it, since my father was slain in battle. I will bring you food by day, then lead you to our unfrequented groves by moonlight, to listen to the nightingale. If you should sleep, I'll watch you, and awake you when there's danger.

Inkle. Generous maid! Then, to you will I owe my life; and whilst it lasts, nothing shall part us.

Yar. And shan't it, shan't it indeed?

Inkle. No, my Yarico! For when an opportunity offers to return to my country, you shall be my companion.

Yar. What! cross the seas!

Inkle. Yes, Help me to discover a vessel, and you shall enjoy wonders. You shall be decked in silks, my brave maid, and have a house drawn with horses to carry you.

Yar. Nay, do not laugh at me—but is it so?

Inkle. It is indeed!

Yar. Oh wonder! I wish my countrywomen could see me—But won't your warriors kill us?

Inkle. No, our only danger on land is here.

Yar. Then let us retire further into the cave. Come—your safety is in my keeping.

Inkle. I follow you—Yet, can you run some risk in following me?

DUET

[O Say, Bonny Lass][30]

Inkle. *O say, simple maid, have you form'd any notion*
  Of all the rude dangers in crossing the ocean?
  When winds whistle shrilly, ah! won't they remind you,
  To sigh with regret, for the grot left behind you?

30. *O Say, Bonny Lass* Colman and Arnold were far from averse to recycling popular melodies. "O Say, Bonny Lass" is listed in *Catalogue of Printed Music in the British Library,* 43:77, as "A favorite new Scotch song and duett" (ca. 1780), with arrangements for guitar and for two guitars. The *Catalogue* also records that a favorite rendition of the tune was sung by Miss Satchell and Mr. Mahon at Covent Garden in 1785. By 1787 Elizabeth Satchell had become Mrs. Stephen Kemble, and it was she who first made famous the part of Yarico. For Robert Burns's ex tempore piece "On Seeing M[rs.] Kemble in Yarico—," see introduction, p. 33.

Fiske, *English Theatre Music,* 479, comments that "this lovely tune ... has been described as a Scotch reel, though it does not look Scotch and cannot be a reel. . . . *Inkle and Yarico* made it famous, and in the following decade Haydn arranged it with appreciative care for [the Scottish folk song collector] George Thomson."

Yar.   *Ah! no, I could follow, and sail the world over,*
         Nor think of my grot, when I look at my lover;
         The winds, which blow round us, your arms for my pillow,
         Will lull us to sleep, whilst we're rock'd by each billow.

Inkle.   *Then, say, lovely lass, what if haply espying*
           A rich gallant vessel with gay colours flying?

Yar.   *I'll journey, with thee, love, to where the land narrows,*
         And sling all my cares at my back with my arrows.

Both.   *O say then my true love, we never will sunder,*
          Nor shrink from the tempest, nor dread the big thunder:
          Whilst constant, we'll laugh at all changes of weather,
          And journey all over the world both together.

[*Exeunt; as retiring further into the cave.*]

Manent Trudge and Wowski.

Trudge.   Why, you speak English as well as I, my little Wowski.

Wow.   Iss.

Trudge.   Iss! and you learnt it from a strange man, that tumbled from a big boat, many moons ago, you say?

Wows.   Iss—Teach me—teach good many.

Trudge.   Then, what the devil made them so surprized at seeing us! was he like me? [*Wowski shakes her head.*] Not so smart a body, mayhap. Was his face, now, round and comely, and—eh! [*Stroking his chin.*] Was it like mine?

Wows.   Like dead leaf—brown and shrivel.

Trudge.   Oh, oh, an old shipwrecked sailor, I warrant. With white and grey hair, eh, my pretty beauty spot?

Wows.   Iss; all white. When night come, he put it in pocket.

Trudge.   Oh! wore a wig. But the old boy taught you something more than English, I believe.

Wows.   Iss.

Trudge.   The devil he did! What was it?

Wows.   Teach me put dry grass, red hot, in hollow white stick.

Trudge.   Aye, what was that for?

Wows.   Put in my mouth—go poff, poff!

Trudge.   Zounds! did he teach you to smoke?

6. "Oh Say Simple Maid Have You Formed Any Notion" ("a favorite Ballad, Sung by M^r. Banister, & Mr^s. Kemble, in the Opera of *Inkle & Yarico,* Composed by Doctor Arnold"). Engraved sheet, ca. 1788. (Courtesy of the Brotherton Collection, University of Leeds.)

Wows.   Iss.

Trudge.   And what became of him at last? What did your countrymen do for the poor fellow?

Wows.   Eat him one day—Our chief kill him.

Trudge.   Mercy on us! what damned stomachs, to swallow a tough old tar! Ah, poor Trudge! your killing comes next.

Wows.   No, no—not you—no—[*Running to him anxiously.*]

Trudge.   No? why what shall I do, if I get in their paws?

Wows.   I fight for you!

Trudge.   Will you? Ecod she's a brave good-natured wench? she'll be worth a hundred of your English wives.—Whenever they fight on their husband's account, it's *with* him instead of *for* him, I fancy. But how the plague am I to live here?

Wows.   I feed you—bring you kid.

Song—Wowski

[One Day, I Heard Mary Say.][31]

> *White man, never go away—*
> *Tell me why need you?*
> *Stay, with your Wowski, stay:*
> *Wowski will feed you.*
> *Cold moons are now coming in;*
> *Ah, don't go grieve me!*
> *I'll wrap you in leopard's skin:*
> *White man, don't leave me.*
>
> *And when all the sky is blue,*
> *Sun makes warm weather,*
> *I'll catch you a cockatoo,*
> *Dress you in feather.*
> *When cold comes, or when 'tis hot,*
> *Ah, don't go grieve me!*
> *Poor Wowski will be forgot—*
> *White man, don't leave me!*

31. *One Day . . . Mary Say Catalogue of Printed Music in the British Library,* 43:292, identifies the tune as a lyric with words by R. Crawford, of which it records at least one printing from the 1740s. The opening line to the song is "One day I heard Mary say, *I'll never leave thee.*" The burden of Wowski's song closely parallels this.

Trudge.   Zounds! leopard's skin for winter wear and feathers for a summer's suit! Ha, ha! I shall look like a walking hammer-cloth,[32] at Christ-
mas, and an upright shuttlecock, in the dog days.[33] And for all this, if
my master and I find our way to England, you shall be part of our travelling equipage; and, when I get there, I'll give you a couple of snug
rooms, on a first floor, and visit you every evening, as soon as I come
from the counting-house. Do you like it?

Wows.   Iss.

Trudge.   Damme, what a flashy fellow I shall seem in the city! I'll get her
a *white* boy to bring up the tea-kettle.[34] Then I'll teach you to write and
dress hair.

Wows.   You great man in your country?

Trudge.   Oh yes, a very great man. I'm head clerk of the counting-house,
and first valet-de-chambre of the dressing-room. I pounce[35] parchments,
powder hair, black shoes, ink paper, shave beards, and mend pens. But
hold! I had forgot one material point—you aren't married, I hope?

Wows.   No: you be my chum-chum!

Trudge.   So I will. It's best, however, to be sure of her being single; for
Indian husbands are not quite so complaisant as English ones, and the
vulgar dogs might think of looking a little after their spouses. But you
have had a lover or two in your time; eh, Wowski?

Wows.   Oh, iss—great many—I tell you.

Duet[36]

Wows.   *Wampum, Swampum, Yanko, Lanko, Nanko, Pownatowski,[37]*
Black men—plenty—twenty—fight for me,
White man, woo you true?

32. *hammer-cloth* Cloth covering the driver's seat in a carriage.

33. *the dog days* "The hottest and most unwholesome period of the year" (*OED*), so
called because of the appearance of the Dog Star, Sirius.

34. *a white boy . . . tea-kettle* As illustrated most famously in William Hogarth's *A Harlot's Progress* (1732), plate 2, it was fashionable in eighteenth-century England to employ
black boys as servants at the tea table. For a perceptive commentary on this and its relation
to the slave trade, see Dabydeen, *Hogarth's Blacks*, 114.

35. *pounce* Prepare parchment for writing, usually by applying to the surface a fine powder made of pulverized cuttleshell.

36. *Duet* The Larpent manuscript gives the source of this tune as the "*Indian Dance in
Robinson Crusoe.*" A pantomime afterpiece, *Robinson Crusoe, or Harlequin Friday,* devised
by R. B. Sheridan, with music by Thomas Linley, was first performed at Drury Lane on 29
January 1781. It was regularly revived during the early 1780s.

37. *Pownatowski* An anonymous reviewer of the play in the *Critical Review* 64 (1787):

Trudge. Who?

Wows. You.

Trudge. Yes, pretty little Wowski!

Wows. Then I leave all, and follow thee.

Trudge. Oh then turn about, my little tawny tight one!
   Don't you like me?

Wows. Iss, you're like the snow!
   If you slight one—

Trudge. Never, not for any white one;
   You are beautiful as any sloe.

Wows. Wars, jars, scars, can't expose ye,
   In our grot—

Trudge. So snug and cosy!

Wows. Flowers, neatly
   Pick'd, shall sweetly
   Make your bed.

Trudge. Coying, toying,
   With a rosy
   Posy,
   When I'm dozy,
   Bear-skin nightcaps too shall warm my head.

Both Bear-skin nightcaps, &c. &c.

ACT THE SECOND

SCENE I

*The Quay at Barbadoes, with an Inn upon it. People employed
in unlading vessels, carrying bales of goods, &c.*

Enter several planters.

1st Plant. I saw her this morning, gentlemen, you may depend on't. My telescope never fails me. I popp'd upon her as I was taking a peep from my balcony. A brave tight ship, I tell you, bearing down directly for Barbadoes here.

2nd Plant. Ods, my life! rare news! We have not had a vessel arrive in our harbour these six weeks.

227, is perhaps the first to remark on the oddity of giving Wowski, "an American girl, . . . a Polish name, and . . . , in one of the songs, . . . a Polish lover." Similarly, the *Monthly Review*, 77 (1787): 389, considers that "the Polish denominations of *Wowski*, and *Pownatowski*, are . . . very flagrant mistakes."

3rd Plant. And the last brought only Madam Narcissa, our Governor's daughter, from England; with a parcel of lazy, idle, white folks about her. Such cargoes will never do for our trade, neighbour.

2nd Plant. No, no; we want slaves. A terrible dearth of 'em in Barbadoes, lately! But your dingy passengers for my money. Give me a vessel like a collier, where all the lading tumbles out as black as my hat. [*To 1st Planter.*] But are you sure, now, you aren't mistaken?

1st Plant. Mistaken! 'sbud,[38] do you doubt my glass? I can discover a gull by it six leagues off: I could see every thing as plain as if I was on board.

2nd Plant. Indeed! and what were her colours?

1st Plant. Um! why English—or Dutch—or French—I don't exactly remember.

2nd Plant. What were the sailors aboard?

1st Plant. Eh! why they were English too—or Dutch—or French—I can't perfectly recollect.

2nd Plant. Your glass, neighbour, is a little like a glass too much: it makes you forget every thing you ought to remember. [*Cry without,* "A sail, a sail!"]

1st Plant. Egad, but I'm right though. Now, gentlemen!

All. Aye, aye; the devil take the hindmost.[39]

[*Exeunt hastily.*]

Enter Narcissa and Patty.

Song[40] [—Narcissa]

Freshly now the breeze is blowing,
As yon ship at anchor rides;
Sullen waves, incessant flowing,
Rudely dash against the sides.

38. *'sbud* A mild oath or interjection, probably a corruption of "God's blood." Similar exclamations, such as 'Sblood, Odsbobs (God's body), 'Sbobs, and Od, are sprinkled through the play.

39. *devil . . . hindmost* Proverbial; see *ODEP,* 183–84.

40. *Song* This short song does not appear in the Larpent manuscript and may have been composed by Arnold in the final days before the first production. The vocal score provides it with an alternative opening line, "Fresh and strong the breeze is blowing" (the title by which the aria was best known) and gives it as sung in "mezza voce" by Mrs. Bannister, Colman's original Narcissa. As Roger Fiske remarks, the song "has an accompaniment intended to suggest waves" (*English Theatre Music,* 479). *The Catalogue of Printed Music in the British Library* lists further arrangements of this quite popular song by William Shields, ca. 1805, and A. H. Enright, ca. 1817.

> *So my heart, its course impeded,*
> *Beats in my perturbed breast;*
> *Doubts, like waves by waves succeeded,*
> *Rise, and still deny it rest.*

Patty. Well, ma'am, as I was saying—

Nar. Well, say no more of what you were saying—Sure, Patty, you forget where you are; a little caution will be necessary now, I think.

Patty. Lord, madam, how is it possible to help talking? We are in Barbadoes here, to be sure—but then, ma'am, one may let out a little in a private morning's walk by ourselves.

Nar. Nay, it's the same thing with you in doors.

Patty. I never blab, ma'am, never, as I hope for a gown.

Nar. And your never blabbing, as you call it, depends chiefly on that hope, I believe.

Patty. I have told the story of our voyage, indeed, to old Guzzle,[41] the butler.

Nar. And thus you lead him to imagine I am but little inclined to the match.

Patty. Lord, ma'am, how could that be? Why I never said a word about Captain Campley.

Nar. Hush! hush! for heaven's sake.

Patty. Aye! there it is now. But if our voyage from England was so pleasant, it wasn't owing to Mr. Inkle, I'm certain. He didn't play the fiddle in our cabin, and dance on the deck, and come languishing with a glass of warm water in his hand, when we were sea-sick. Ah, ma'am, that water warm'd your heart, I'm confident. Mr. Inkle! No, no; Captain Cam—

Nar. There is no end to this! Remember, Patty, keep your secrecy, or you entirely lose my favour.

Patty. Never fear me, ma'am. But if somebody I know is not acquainted with the Governor, there's such a thing as dancing at balls, and squeezing hands when you lead up, and squeezing them again when you cast down. I'm as close as a patch-box.[42] Mum's the word, ma'am, I promise you.

---

41. *Guzzle* Colman may have recalled that the character of the innkeeper in Henry Fielding's *Don Quixote in England,* first performed at the Haymarket Theatre in 1734, was similarly named.

42. *patch-box* "A box for holding patches for the face" (*OED*).

Song[43]

This maxim let ev'ry one hear,
 Proclaim'd from the north to the south,
Whatever comes in at your ear,
 Should never run out at your mouth.[44]
We servants, like servants of state,
 Should listen to all, and be dumb;
Let others harangue and debate,
 We look wise—shake our heads—and are mum.

The judge, in dull dignity drest,
 In silence hears barristers preach,
And then, to prove silence is best,[45]
 He'll get up, and give 'em a speech.
By saying but little, the maid
 Will keep her swain under her thumb;[46]
And the lover that's true to his trade
 Is certain to kiss, and cry mum.

[*Exit.*]

Nar How awkward is my present situation! Promised to one, who, perhaps, may never again be heard of; and who, I am sure, if he ever appears
to claim me, will do it merely on the score of interest—pressed too by
another, who has already, I fear, too much interest in my heart—what
can I do? What plan can I follow?

Enter Campley.

Camp. Follow my advice, Narcissa, by all means. Enlist with me under
the best banners in the world. General Hymen[47] for my money! little
Cupid's his drummer: he has been beating a round rub-a-dub on our
hearts, and we have only to obey the word of command, fall into the
ranks of matrimony, and march through life together.

43. *Song* Patty's song is the first of several that was omitted in Mrs. Inchbald's promptbook version of the play. It is present in the Larpent manuscript, the 1787 text, and the vocal
score. As with several other songs written by Colman (e.g., Trudge's "*A Voyage over Seas,*"
1.2), it is made up of a linked series of proverbial commonplaces.

44. *This maxim . . . at your mouth.* A less succinct permutation of "Hear and see and say
nothing" (*ODEP,* 362).

45. *silence is best* Cf. "Silence is the best ornament of a woman" (*ODEP,* 733).

46. *under her thumb* Proverbial; *ODEP,* 820.

47. *Hymen* The Roman god of marriage.

Nar. Then consider our situation.

Camp. That has been duly considered. In short, the case stands exactly thus—your intended spouse is all for money; I am all for love. He is a rich rogue; I am rather a poor honest fellow. He would pocket your fortune; I will take you without a fortune in your pocket.

Nar. Oh! I am sensible of the favour, most gallant Captain Campley; and my father, no doubt, will be very much obliged to you.

Camp. Aye, there's the devil of it! Sir Christopher Curry's confounded good character knocks me up at once. Yet I am not acquainted with him neither; not known to him even by sight; being here only as a private gentleman, on a visit to my old relation, out of regimentals, and so forth; and not introduced to the Governor, as other officers of the place. But then, the report of his hospitality—his odd, blunt, whimsical friendship—his whole behaviour—

Nar. All stare you in the face; eh, Campley?

Camp. They do, till they put me out of countenance.

Nar. What signifies talking to *me*, when you have such opposition from others? Why hover about the city, instead of boldly attacking the guard? Wheel about, captain! face the enemy! March! Charge! Rout 'em!—Drive 'em before you, and then—

Camp. And then—

Nar. Lud ha' mercy on the poor city!

Song—Rondeau[48]

[Since 'Tis Vain to Think of Flying][49]

> *Mars would oft, his conquest over,*
> *To the Cyprian Goddess[50] yield;*
> *Venus gloried in a lover,*
> *Who, like him, cou'd brave the field.*
> > > *Mars wou'd oft, &c.*

48. *Song—Rondeau* Narcissa's song was omitted by Mrs. Inchbald. The rondeau (as represented in the Larpent manuscript and the 1787 text) conventionally employs the opening line to provide the refrain at the end of each of its three quatrains. From Samuel Arnold's vocal score, it is evident that in performance the song contained a more complex recapitulation: "Venus gloried in a lover who like him cou'd brave the field . . . cou'd brave the field cou'd brave the field cou'd brave the skies."

49. *Since . . . flying.* I have not been able to identify the source of this tune.

50. *Cyprian Goddess* Venus, for whom the island of Cyprus was considered sacred in ancient times, conducted an illicit relationship with Mars.

In the cause of battles hearty,
    Still the god wou'd strive to prove,
He who fac'd an adverse party,
    Fittest was to meet his love.

                    Mars wou'd oft, &c.

Hear then, Captains, ye who bluster,
    Hear the gods of war declare,
Cowards never can pass muster,
    Courage only wins the fair.

                    Mars wou'd oft, &c.

Enter Patty, hastily.

Patty.   Oh lud, ma'am, I'm frightened out of my wits! sure as I'm alive, ma'am, Mr. Inkle is not dead; I saw his man, ma'am, just now, coming ashore in a boat, with other passengers, from the vessel that's come to the island.

                    [*Exit.*]

Nar.   Then one way or other I must determine.—[*To Campley.*] Look'ye, Mr. Campley, something has happened which makes me waive cere-monies.—If you mean to apply to my father, remember, that delays are dangerous.

Camp.   Indeed!

Nar.   [*Smiling.*] I mayn't be always in the same mind, you know.

                    [*Exit.*]

Camp.   Nay, then—Gad, I'm almost afraid too—but living in this state of doubt is torment. I'll e'en put a good face on the matter; cock my hat; make my bow; and try to reason the Governor into compliance. Faint heart never won a fair lady.[51]

Song[52]

Why should I vain fears discover,
    Prove a dying, sighing swain?
Why turn shilly-shally lover,
    Only to prolong my pain?

51. *Faint heart . . . fair lady.* Proverbial; *ODEP,* 238.

52. *Song* Not in Larpent manuscript and therefore probably composed ex tempore. For reasons not explained, the acting text omits the final quatrain, which is supplied here from the first edition of 1787.

> *When we woo the dear enslaver,*
>   *Boldly ask, and she will grant;*
> *How should we obtain a favour,*
>   *But by telling what we want?*
>
> *Should the nymph be found complying,*
>   *Nearly then the battle's won;*
> *Parents think 'tis vain denying,*
>   *When half our work is fairly done.*

[Exeunt.]

Enter Trudge and Wowski, (as from the ship), with
a dirty runner[53] *to one of the inns.*

Run. This way, sir; if you will let me recommend—

Trudge. Come along, Wows! Take care of your furs, and your feathers, my girl!

Wows. Iss.

Trudge. That's right.—Somebody might steal 'em, perhaps.

Wows. Steal!—What that?

Trudge. Oh Lord! see what one loses by not being born in a Christian country.

Run. If you would, sir, but mention to your master, the house that belongs to my master; the best accommodations on the quay.—

Trudge. What's your sign, my lad?

Run. The Crown, sir.—Here it is.

Trudge. Well, get us a room for half an hour, and we'll come: and harkee! let it be light and airy, d'ye hear? My master has been used to your open apartments lately.

Run. Depend on it.—Much obliged to you, sir.

[Exit.]

Wows. Who be that fine man? He great prince?

Trudge. A prince—Ha! ha!—No, not quite a prince—but he belongs to the Crown.[54] But how do you like this, Wows? Isn't it fine?

Wows. Wonder!

Trudge. Fine men, eh?

---

53. *dirty runner* A runner is "one whose business it is to solicit custom for a hotel" (*OED*, definition 3e). Colman's use of the word in this context considerably predates *OED*'s examples, which incorrectly limit the term to American usage.

54. *he belongs to the Crown* Trudge puns on the name of the inn.

Wows.   Iss! all white; like you.

Trudge.   Yes, all the fine men are like me. As different from your people as powder and ink, or paper and blacking.

Wows.   And fine lady—Face like snow.

Trudge.   What! the fine lady's complexions? Oh, yes, exactly; for too much heat very often dissolves 'em! Then their dress, too.

Wows.   Your countrymen dress so?

Trudge.   Better, better a great deal. Why, a young flashy Englishman will sometimes carry a whole fortune on his back. But did you mind the women? All here—and there; [*Pointing before and behind.*] they have it all from us in England.—And then the fine things they carry on their heads, Wowski.

Wows.   Iss. One lady carry good fish—so fine, she call every body to look at her.

Trudge.   Pshaw! an old woman bawling flounders. But the fine girls we meet, here, on the quay—so round and so plump!

Wows.   You not love me now?

Trudge.   Not love you! Zounds, have not I given you proofs?

Wows.   Iss. Great many: but now you get here, you forget poor Wowski!

Trudge.   Not I: I'll stick to you like wax.

Wows.   Ah! I fear! What make you love me now?

Trudge.   Gratitude, to be sure.

Wows.   What that?

Trudge.   Ha! this it is, now, to live without education. The poor dull devils of her country are all in the practice of gratitude, without finding out what it means; while we can tell the meaning of it, with little or no practice at all.—Lord, Lord, what a fine advantage Christian learning is! Hark'ee, Wows!

Wows.   Iss.

Trudge.   Now we've accomplished our landing, I'll accomplish you. You remember the instructions I gave you on the voyage?

Wows.   Iss.

Trudge.   Let's see now—What are you to do, when I introduce you to the nobility, gentry, and others—of my acquaintance?

Wows.   Make believe sit down; then get up.

Trudge.   Let me see you do it. [*She makes a low courtesy.*][55] Very well! and

55. *courtesy* Curtsy.

how are you to recommend yourself, when you have nothing to say, amongst all our great friends?

Wows.   Grin—show my teeth.

Trudge.   Right! they'll think you've lived with people of fashion. But suppose you meet an old shabby friend in misfortune, that you don't wish to be seen speak to—what would you do?

Wows.   Look blind—not see him.

Trudge.   Why would you do that?

Wows.   'Cause I can't see good friend in distress.

Trudge.   That's a good girl! and I wish every body could boast of so kind a motive for such cursed cruel behaviour.—Lord! how some of your flashy bankers' clerks have *cut* me in Threadneedle-street.—But come, though we have got among fine folks, here, in an English settlement, I won't be ashamed of my old acquaintance: yet, for my own part, I should not be sorry, now, to see my old friend with a new face.—Odsbobs! I see Mr. Inkle—Go in, Wows; call for what you like best.

Wows.   Then I call for you—ah! I fear I not see you often now. But you come soon—

Song

> *Remember when we walked alone,*
>   *And heard, so gruff, the lion growl:*[56]
> *And when the moon so bright it shone,*
>   *We saw the wolf look up and howl;*
> *I led you well, safe to our cell,*
>   *While tremblingly,*
>   *You said to me,*
> *—And kiss'd so sweet—dear Wowski tell,*
>   *How could I live without ye?*
>
> *But now you come across the sea,*
>   *And tell me here no monsters roar;*
> *You'll walk alone, and leave poor me,*
>   *When wolves, to fright you, howl no more.*
> *But ah! think well on our old cell,*

---

56. *lion growl* Fiske, *English Theatre Music,* 479, notes that the song has a musical "accompaniment . . . that suggests a lion roaring."

7. James Gillray, *Wouski*. Engraving, 23 January 1788 (BM Cat. no. 7260). After it was reported that Prince William Henry (later King William IV) had dallied with a pretty African woman on a voyage from Jamaica in December 1787, Gillray caricatured her as Wouski, naming her after Yarico's black maid in Colman's comic opera. The print, with its verse caption, "Free as the forest birds we'll pair together, / Without rememb'ring who our fathers were," humorously matches miscegenation with royal duty. (Courtesy of the Department of Prints and Drawings, British Museum, London.)

> *Where tremblingly,*
> *You kiss'd poor me—*
> *Perhaps you'll say—dear Wowski tell,*
> *How can I live without ye?*
>
> [*Exit Wowski*]

Trudge.   Who have we here?
                    Enter First Planter.

Plant.   Hark'ee, young man! Is that young Indian of yours going to our market?

Trudge.   Not she—she never went to market in all her life.

Plant.   I mean, is she for our sale of slaves? Our black fair?

Trudge.   A black fair, ha! ha! ha! You hold it on a brown green, I suppose.

Plant.   She's your slave, I take it?

Trudge.   Yes; and I'm her humble servant, I take it.

Plant.   Aye, aye, natural enough at sea.—But at how much do you value her?

Trudge.   Just as much as she has saved me—My own life.

Plant.   Pshaw! you mean to sell her?

Trudge.   [*Staring.*] Zounds! what a devil of a fellow! Sell Wows!—my poor, dear, dingy, wife!

Plant.   Come, come, I've heard your story from the ship.—Don't let's haggle; I'll bid as fair as any trader amongst us. But no tricks upon travellers,[57] young man, to raise your price.—Your wife, indeed! Why she's no Christian!

Trudge.   No; but I am; so I shall do as I'd be done by:[58] and, if you were a good one yourself, you'd know, that fellow-feeling for a poor body, who wants your help, is the noblest mark of our religion.—I wouldn't be articled clerk to such a fellow for the world.

Plant.   Hey-day! the booby's in love with her! Why, sure, friend, you would not live here with a black?

Trudge.   Plague on't; there it is. I shall be laughed out of my honesty, here.—But you may be jogging, friend; I may feel a little queer, perhaps, at showing her face—but, dam'me, if ever I do any thing to make me asham'd of showing my own.

Plant.   Why, I tell you, her very complexion—

Trudge.   Rot her complexion.—I'll tell you what, Mr. *Fair-trader*, if your head and heart were to change places, I've a notion you'd be as black in the face as an ink-bottle.

Plant.   Pshaw! the fellow's a fool—a rude rascal—he ought to be sent back to the savages again. He's not fit to live among us Christians.

[*Exit Planter.*]

Trudge.   Oh, here comes my master, at last.

---

57. *no tricks . . . travellers* Proverbial, *ODEP,* 657.

58. *do as I'd be done by* Proverbial; *ODEP,* 191; cf. Luke 6:31: "And as ye would that men should do to you, do ye also to them likewise."

Enter Inkle, and a second Planter.

Inkle.   Nay, sir, I understand your customs well; your Indian markets are not unknown to me.

2nd Plant.   And, as you seem to understand business, I need not tell you, that dispatch is the soul of it. Her name you say is—

Inkle.   Yarico: but urge this no more, I beg you; I must not listen to it: for, to speak freely, her anxious care of me demands, that here,—though here it may seem strange—I should avow my love for her.

Plant.   Lord help you for a merchant!—It's the first time I ever heard a trader talk of love; except, indeed, the love of trade, and the love of the *Sweet Molly,* my ship.

Inkle.   Then, sir, you cannot feel my situation.

Plant.   Oh yes, I can! we have a hundred such cases just after a voyage; but they never last long on land. It's amazing how constant a young man is in a ship! But, in two words, will you dispose of her, or no?

Inkle.   In two words, then, meet me here at noon, and we'll speak further on this subject: and lest you think I trifle with your business, hear why I wish this pause. Chance threw me, on my passage to your island, among a savage people. Deserted,—defenceless,—cut off from my companions,—my life at stake—to this young creature I owe my preservation;— she found me, like a dying bough, torn from its kindred branches; which, as it drooped, she moistened with her tears.

Plant.   Nay, nay, talk like a man of this world.

Inkle.   Your patience.—And yet your interruption goes to my present feelings; for on our sail to this your island—the thoughts of time mis-spent—doubt—fears—for call it what you will—have much perplexed me; and as your spires arose, reflections still rose with them; for here, sir, lie my interests, great connexions, and other weighty matters—which now I need not mention—

Plant.   But which her presence here will mar.

Inkle.   Even so—And yet the gratitude I owe her—

Plant.   Pshaw! So because she preserved your life, your gratitude is to make you give up all you have to live upon.

Inkle.   Why, in that light indeed—This never struck me yet, I'll think on't.

Plant.   Aye, aye, do so—Why, what return can the wench wish more than taking her from a wild, idle, savage people, and providing for her, here, with reputable hard work, in a genteel, polished, tender, Christian country?

Inkle.　Well, sir, at noon—

Plant.　I'll meet you—but remember, young gentleman, you must get her off your hands—you must indeed.—I shall have her a bargain, I see that—your servant!—Zounds, how late it is—but never be put out of your way for a woman—I must run—my wife will play the devil with me for keeping breakfast.

[Exit.]

Inkle.　Trudge.

Trudge.　Sir!

Inkle.　Have you provided a proper apartment.

Trudge.　Yes, sir, at the Crown here; a neat, spruce room they tell me. You have not seen such a convenient lodging this good while, I believe.

Inkle.　Are there no better inns in the town?

Trudge.　Um—Why there is the Lion, I hear, and the Bear, and the Boar— but we saw them at the door of all our late lodgings, and found but bad accommodations within, sir.

Inkle.　Well, run to the end of the quay, and conduct Yarico hither. The road is straight before you: you can't miss it.

Trudge.　Very well, sir. What a fine thing it is to turn one's back on a master, without running into a wolf's belly! One can follow one's nose on a message here, and be sure it won't be bit off by the way.

[Exit].

Inkle.　Let me reflect a little. Part with her!—My interest, honour, engagements to Narcissa, all demand it. My father's precepts too—I can remember, when I was a boy, what pains he took to mould me.—School'd me from morn to night—and still the burden of his song was—Prudence! Prudence, Thomas, and you'll rise. His maxims rooted in my heart, and as I grew—*they* grew; till I was reckoned, among our friends, a steady, sober, solid, good young man; and all the neighbours call'd me *the prudent Mr. Thomas.* And shall I now, at once, kick down the character which I have raised so warily?—Part with her.—sell her!—The thought once struck me in our cabin, as she lay sleeping by me; but, in her slumbers, she passed her arm around me, murmured a blessing on my name, and broke my meditations.

Enter Yarico and Trudge.

Yar.　My love!

Trudge.　I have been showing her all the wigs and bales of goods we met on the quay, sir.

Yar. Oh! I have feasted my eyes on wonders.

Trudge. And I'll go feast on a slice of beef, in the inn, here.

[*Exit.*]

Yar. My mind has been so busy, that I almost forgot even you. I wish you had stayed with me—You would have seen such sights!

Inkle. Those sights have become familiar to me, Yarico.

Yar. And yet I wish they were not—You might partake my pleasures— but now again, methinks, I will not wish so—for, with too much gazing, you might neglect poor *Yarico.*

Inkle. Nay, nay, my care is still for you.

Yar. I am sure it is: and if I thought it was not, I would tell you tales about our poor old grot—bid you remember our palm-tree near the brook, where in the shade you often stretched yourself, while I would take your head upon my lap, and sing my love to sleep. I know you'll love me then.

Song

Our grotto was the sweetest place!
The bending boughs, with fragrance blowing,
Would check the brook's impetuous pace,
Which murmur'd to be stopp'd from flowing.
'Twas there we met, and gaz'd our fill:
Ah! think on this, and love me still.

'Twas then my bosom first knew fear,
—Fear to an Indian maid a stranger—
The war-song, arrows, hatchet, spear,
All warn'd me of my lover's danger.
For him did cares my bosom fill:—
Ah! think on this, and love me still.

For him, by day, with care conceal'd,
To search for food I climb'd the mountain;
And when the night no form reveal'd,
Jocund we sought the bubbling fountain.
Then, then would joy my bosom fill;
Ah! think on this and love me still.

[*Exeunt.*]

SCENE II

An Apartment in the House of Sir Christopher Curry.

Enter Sir Christopher and Medium.

Sir Chr.   I tell you, old Medium, you are all wrong. Plague on your doubts! Inkle *shall* have my Narcissa. Poor fellow! I dare say he's finely chagrined at this temporary parting—Ate up with the blue devils,[59] I warrant.

Med.   Eat up by the black devils, I warrant; for I left him in hellish hungry company.

Sir Chr.   Pshaw! he'll arrive with the next vessel, depend on't—besides, have not I had this in view ever since they were children? I must and will have it so, I tell you. Is not it, as it were, a marriage made above? They *shall* meet, I'm positive.

Med.   Shall they? Then they must meet where the marriage was made; for hang me, if I think it will ever happen below.

Sir Chr.   Ha!—and if that is the case—hang me, if I think you'll ever be at the celebration of it.

Med.   Yet, let me tell you, Sir Christopher Curry, my character is as unsullied as a sheet of white paper.

Sir Chr.   Well said, old fool's-cap![60] and it's as mere a blank as a sheet of white paper. You are honest, old Medium, by comparison, just as a fellow sentenced to transportation is happier than his companion condemned to the gallows—Very worthy because you are no rogue; tender hearted, because you never go to fires and executions;[61] and an affectionate father and husband, because you never pinch your children, or kick your wife out of bed.

59. *the blue devils* Despondency. Colman later titled one of his farces *Blue Devils* (1798).
60. *fool's-cap* In deprecating Medium, Sir Christopher refers humorously to the cap garnished with bells worn by fools and jesters, while also punning on *foolscap*, a long folio sheet of paper.
61. *fires and executions* Possibly an oblique reference to the Gordon riots of 1780 during which many buildings in London were set on fire by the mob and numbers of the supposed ringleaders were executed. Because it was felt that a public display would only incite the crowd, the location of the hangings was widely dispersed. The last public execution by hanging (that of Ryland, a forger) took place at Tyburn in 1783. "Thenceforth," writes Peter Linebaugh, "the exemplary and spectacular cross-city procession of the condemned was abolished, and hangings took place within the more easily controlled confines of Newgate" (*The London Hanged,* 363). Sir Christopher Curry's allusion here is sardonic, since a person of Medium's social background would hardly have been expected to join the mob.

Med.   And that, as the world goes, is more than every man can say for himself. Yet, since you force me to speak my positive qualities—but, no matter,—you remember me in London; didn't I, as member of the Humane Society,[62] bring a man out of the New River,[63] who, it was afterwards found, had done me an injury?

Sir Chr.   And, dam'me, if I would not kick any man into the New River that had done me an injury. There's the difference of our honesty. Oons! if you want to be an honest fellow, act from the impulse of nature. Why, you have no more gall than a pigeon.[64]

Med.   And you have as much gall as a turkey cock, and are as hot into the bargain—You're always so hasty; among the hodge-podge of your foibles, passion is always predominant.

Sir Chr.   So much the better.—Foibles, quotha? foibles are foils that give additional lustre to the gems of virtue. You have not so many foils as I, perhaps.

Med.   And, what's more, I don't want 'em, Sir Christopher, I thank you.

Sir Chr.   Very true; for the devil a gem have you to set off with 'em.

Med.   Well, well; I never mention errors; that, I flatter myself, is no disagreeable quality.—It don't become me to say you are hot.

Sir Chr.   'Sblood! but it does become you: it becomes every man, especially an Englishman, to speak the dictates of his heart.

Enter Servant.

Serv.   An English vessel, sir, just arrived in the harbour.

Sir Chr.   A vessel! Od's my life!—Now for the news—If it is but as I hope—Any dispatches?

62. *the Humane Society* The Humane Society had been founded as recently as 1774 by Dr. William Hawes (1736–1806) and Dr. Thomas Cogan (1736–1818) with the specific purpose of attempting to resuscitate victims of drowning. Oliver Goldsmith, a personal friend of Hawes, was one of its founding members, and David Garrick was one of its earliest supporters. It became known as the Royal Humane Society in 1787, the year when Colman's comic opera was first performed. Its main function today is to award medals and testimonials for bravery and skill in saving human life. See Bishop, *Short History of the Royal Humane Society.*

63. *the New River* An artificial channel of approximately thirty-six miles completed in the early seventeenth century for the purpose of bringing fresh water to the metropolis. Its course was cut from Ware in Hertfordshire to reservoirs in Hornsea and Stoke Newington in London.

64. *no more . . . pigeon* A coward. *OED* (*pigeon*, 3a) cites Thomas Dekker, *The Honest Whore* (1604), 1.1: "Sure he's a pigeon, for he has no gall."

Serv.   This letter, sir, brought by a sailor from the quay.

[*Exit.*]

Sir Chr.   [*Opening the letter*] Huzza! here it is. He's safe—safe and sound at Barbadoes.

[*Reading.*]—*Sir, My master, Mr. Inkle, is just arrived in your harbour,* Here, read, read! old Medium—

Med.   [*Reading.*] Um'—*Your harbour;—we were taken up by an English vessel, on the 14th ult°. He only waits till I have puffed his hair, to pay his respects to you, and Miss Narcissa: In the mean time, he has ordered me to brush up this letter for your honour, from   Your humble Servant, to command,*   Timothy Trudge.

Sir Chr.   Hey day! Here's a style! the voyage has jumbled the fellow's brains out of their places; the water has made his head turn round. But no matter; mine turns round, too. I'll go and prepare Narcissa directly, they shall be married slap-dash, as soon as he comes from the quay. From Neptune to Hymen: from the hammock to the bridal bed—Ha! old boy!

Med.   Well, well; don't flurry yourself—you're so hot!

Sir Chr.   Hot! blood, aren't I in the West Indies? Aren't I Governor of Barbadoes? He shall have her as soon as he sets foot on shore. But, plague on't, he's so slow.—She shall rise to him like Venus out of the sea.[65] His hair puffed? He ought to have been puffing, here, out of breath, by this time.

Med.   Very true; but Venus's husband is always supposed to be lame,[66] you know, Sir Christopher.

Sir Chr.   Well, now do, my good fellow, run down to the shore, and see what detains him. [*Hurrying him off.*]

Med.   Well, well; I will, I will.

[*Exit.*]

Sir Chr.   In the mean time I'll get ready Narcissa, and all shall be concluded in a second. My heart's set upon it.—Poor fellow! after all his rumbles, and tumbles, and jumbles, and fits of despair—I shall be re-

---

65. *Venus out of the sea* Venus was believed to have sprung from the foam of the sea. She is so depicted in Botticelli's *Birth of Venus*.

66. *Venus's husband . . . lame* Venus's husband, Vulcan, became lame when he was hurled from heaven to earth by his father, Jupiter, after a quarrel. Vulcan was the Roman god of fire and, as a consequence of the amour between Venus and Mars, was often depicted as a cuckold.

joiced to see him. I have not seen him since he was that high.—But, zounds! he's so tardy!

Enter Servant.

Serv.   A strange gentleman, sir, come from the quay, desires to see you.

Sir Chr.   From the quay? Od's my life!—'Tis he—'Tis Inkle! Show him up directly.

[*Exit Servant.*]

The rogue is expeditious after all.—I'm so happy.

Enter Campley.

My dear fellow! [*Shakes hands.*] I'm rejoiced to see you. Welcome; welcome here, with all my soul!

Camp.   This reception, Sir Christopher, is beyond my warmest wishes— Unknown to you—

Sir Chr.   Aye, aye; we shall be better acquainted by and by. Well, and how, eh! tell me!—But old Medium and I have talked over your affair a hundred times a day, ever since Narcissa arrived.

Camp.   You surprise me! Are you then really acquainted with the whole affair?

Sir Chr.   Every tittle.

Camp.   And, can you, sir, pardon what is past?—

Sir Chr.   Pooh! how could you help it?

Camp.   Very true—sailing in the same ship—and—But when you consider the past state of my mind—the black prospect before me.—

Sir Chr.   Ha! ha! Black enough, I dare say.

Camp.   The difficulty I have felt in bringing myself face to face to you.

Sir Chr.   That I am convinced of—but I knew you would come the first opportunity.

Camp.   Very true: yet the distance between the Governor of Barbadoes and myself. [*Bowing.*]

Sir Chr.   Yes—a devilish way asunder.

Camp.   Granted, sir: which has distressed me with the cruellest doubts as to our meeting.

Sir Chr.   It was a toss up.

Camp.   [*Aside.*] The old gentleman seems devilish kind.—Now to soften him. Perhaps, sir, in your younger days, you may have been in the same situation yourself.

Sir Chr.   Who? I! 'sblood! no, never in my life.

Camp.   I wish you had, with all my soul, Sir Christopher.

Sir Chr.   Upon my soul, sir, I am very much obliged to you. [*Bowing.*]

Camp.   As what I now mention might have greater weight with you.

Sir Chr.   Pooh! pr'ithee! I tell you I pitied you from the bottom of my heart.

Camp.   Indeed! if, with your leave, I may still venture to mention Miss Narcissa—

Sir Chr.   An impatient, sensible young dog! like me to a hair! Set your heart at rest, my boy. She's yours; yours before to-morrow morning.

Camp.   Amazement! I can scarce believe my senses.

Sir Chr.   Zounds! you ought to be out of your senses: but dispatch— make short work of it, ever while you live, my boy. Here she is.

Enter Narcissa and Patty.

[*To Narcissa*] Here girl: here's your swain.

Camp.   I just parted with my Narcissa, on the quay, sir.

Sir Chr.   Did you! Ah, sly dog—had a meeting before you came to the old gentleman.—But here—Take him, and make much of him—and, for fear of further separations, you shall e'en be tacked together directly. What say you, girl?

Camp.   Will my Narcissa consent to my happiness?

Nar.   I always obey my father's commands, with pleasure, sir.

Sir Chr.   Od! I'm so happy, I hardly know which way to turn; but we'll have the carriage directly; drive down to the quay; trundle old Spintext[67] into church, and hey for matrimony!

Camp.   With all my heart, Sir Christopher; the sooner the better.

[Song—] *Sir Christopher, Campley, Narcissa, Patty*

Sir Chr.[68]   *Your Colinettes, and Arriettes,*
            Your Damons[69] *of the grove,*
        Who like fallals,[70] *and pastorals,*
            Waste years in love;
        But modern folks know better jokes,

---

67. *Spintext* Traditionally a humorous name for "a clergyman or parson, especially one who preaches long or weak sermons" (*OED*); cf. Congreve, *The Old Bachelor* (1693), 1.1.83– 85: "*talks of sending for* Mr. Spintext *to keep me Company . . . Spintext!* Oh, the Fanatick one- ey'd Parson!" (*Complete Plays,* 39).

68. *Sir Chr.* In the vocal score to the opera, the first part of the song is sung by Campley.

69. *Colinettes . . . Damons* Colin and Damon are among the more typical names of naive shepherds and rustic goatherds in English pastoral poetry. Arriette was most probably sug- gested to Colman by Steele's employment of Arietta as the narrator of "the history of Inkle and Yarico" in *Spectator,* no. 11. An *ariette* is a musical term for a short air (*OED*).

70. *fallals* Showy adornments, fripperies.

> *And, courting once begun,*
> *To church they hop at once—and pop—*
> *Egad, all's done!*

All.   *In life we prance a country dance,*
           Where every couple stands;
     Their partners set—a while curvet—[71]
           But soon join hands.

Nar.   *When at our feet, so trim and neat*
           The powder'd lover sues,
     He vows he dies, the lady sighs,
           But can't refuse.
     Ah! how can she unmov'd e'er see
           Her swain his death incur?
     If once the squire is seen expire,
           He lives with her.

All.   *In life we prance, &c. &c.*

Patty.   *When John and Bet are fairly met,*
           John boldly tries his luck;
     He steals a buss,[72] *without more fuss,*
           The bargain's struck.
     Whilst things below are going so,
           Is Betty pray to blame?
     Who knows up stairs; her mistress fares
           Just, just the same.

All.   *In life we prance, &c. &c.*

           [Exeunt.]

ACT THE THIRD

SCENE I

The Quay

Enter Patty.

Patty.   Mercy on us! what a walk I have had of it! Well, matters go on swimmingly at the Governor's—The old gentleman has ordered the carriage, and the young couple will be whisked here, to church, in a quar-

71. *curvet* Leap about.   72. *buss* Kiss.

ter of an hour. My business is to prevent young sobersides, young Inkle, from appearing, to interrupt the ceremony.—Ha! here's the Crown, where I hear he is housed: So now to find Trudge, and trump up a story, in the true style of a chambermaid. [*Goes into the house.*] [*Patty within.*] I tell you it don't signify, and I will come up.

Trudge.   [*within.*] But it does signify, and you can't come up.

Re-enter Patty with Trudge.

Patty.   You had better say at once, I shan't.

Trudge.   Well then, you shan't.

Patty.   Savage! Pretty behaviour you have picked up amongst the Hotty-pots! Your London civility, like London itself, will soon be lost in smoke, Mr. Trudge: and the politeness you have studied so long in Threadnee-dle-street, blotted out by the blacks you have been living with.

Trudge.   No such thing; I practised my politeness all the while I was in the woods. Our very lodging taught me good manners; for I could never bring myself to go into it without bowing.

Patty.   Don't tell me! A mighty civil reception you give a body, truly, after a six weeks parting.

Trudge.   Gad, you're right; I am a little out here, to be sure. [*Kisses her.*] Well, how do you do?

Patty.   Pshaw, fellow! I want none of your kisses.

Trudge.   Oh! very well—I'll take it again. [*Offers to kiss her.*]

Patty.   Be quiet. I want to see Mr. Inkle: I have a message to him from Miss Narcissa. I shall get a sight of him, now, I believe.

Trudge.   May be not. He's a little busy at present.

Patty.   Busy—ha! Plodding! What he's at his multiplication table again?

Trudge.   Very likely; so it would be a pity to interrupt him, you know.

Patty.   Certainly—[*Aside.*] and the whole of my business was to prevent his hurrying himself—Tell him, we shan't be ready to receive him, at the Governor's, till to-morrow, d'ye hear?

Trudge.   No?

Patty.   No. Things are not prepared. The place isn't in order; and the servants have not had proper notice of the arrival. Sir Christopher intends Mr. Inkle, you know, for his son-in-law, and must receive him in public form, (which can't be till to-morrow morning) for the honour of his governorship: why the whole island will ring of it.

Trudge.   The devil it will!

Patty.   Yes; they've talked of nothing but my mistress's beauty and fortune for these six weeks. Then he'll be introduced to the bride you know.

Trudge.   O, my poor master!

Patty.   Then a breakfast; then a procession; then—if nothing happens to prevent it, he'll get into church, and be married, in a crack.

Trudge.   Then he'll get into a damn'd scrape, in a crack.

Patty.   Hey-day! a scrape! How!

Trudge.   Nothing, nothing—It must out—Patty!

Patty.   Well!

Trudge.   Can you keep a secret?

Patty.   Try me.

Trudge.   Then [*Whispering.*] My master keeps a girl.

Patty.   Oh, monstrous! another woman?

Trudge.   As sure as one and one make two.

Patty.   [*Aside.*] Rare news for my mistress!—Why I can hardly believe it: the grave, sly, steady, sober Mr. Inkle, do such a thing!

Trudge.   Pooh! it's always your sly, sober fellows, that go the most after the girls.

Patty.   Well; I should sooner suspect *you.*

Trudge.   Me? Oh Lord! he! he! [*Conceitedly.*] Do you think any smart, tight, little, black eyed wench, would be struck with my figure?

Patty.   Pshaw! never mind your figure. Tell me how it happened?

Trudge.   You shall hear: when the ship left us ashore, my master turned as pale as a sheet of paper. It isn't every body that's blest with courage, Patty.

Patty.   True.

Trudge.   However, I bid him cheer up; told him, to stick to my elbow: took the lead, and began our march.

Patty.   Well?

Trudge.   We hadn't gone far, when a damn'd one-eyed black boar, that grinned like a devil, came down the hill in jog trot! My Master melted as fast as a pot of pomatum![73]

Patty.   Mercy on us!

Trudge.   But what does I do, but whips out my desk knife, that I used to cut the quills with at home; met the monster, and slit up his throat like a pen—The boar bled like a pig.

Patty.   Lord! Trudge, what a great traveller you are!

Trudge.   Yes; I remember we fed on the flitch for a week.

Patty.   Well, well; but the lady.

---

73. *pomatum* Pomade; a scented ointment for the skin or hair.

Trudge. The lady! Oh, true. By and by we came to a cave—a large hollow room, under ground, like a warehouse in the Adelphi.[74]—Well; there we were half an hour, before I could get him to go in; there's no accounting for fear, you know. At last, in we went, to a place hung round with skins, as it might be a furrier's shop, and there was a fine lady, snoring on a bow and arrows.

Patty. What, all alone?

Trudge. Eh!—No—no.—Hum—She had a young lion, by way of a lap-dog.

Patty. Gemini;[75] what did you do?

Trudge. Gave her a jog, and she opened her eyes—she struck my master immediately.

Patty. Mercy on us! with what?

Trudge. With her beauty, you ninny, to be sure: and they soon brought matters to bear. The wolves witnessed the contract—I gave her away— The crows croaked amen; and we had board and lodging for nothing.

Patty. And this is she he has brought to Barbadoes?

Trudge. The same.

Patty. Well; and tell me, Trudge;—she's pretty, you say—Is she fair or brown? or—

Trudge. Um! she's a good comely copper.

Patty. How! a tawny?

Trudge. Yes, quite dark; but very elegant; like a Wedgwood tea-pot.[76]

74. *the Adelphi* Completed in 1774, the Adelphi was designed by Robert and James Adam on a site overlooking the Thames in Westminster. The edifice consisted of a terrace of houses enjoying spectacular views of the river and, beneath them, a wharf with capacious warehousing. The project almost bankrupted the Adam brothers. The Adelphi was demolished in 1936, though the building containing the Royal Society of Arts was spared.

75. *Gemini* A mild exclamation, perhaps a vulgar corruption of *Jesu domine*.

76. *a Wedgwood tea-pot* Sutcliffe, *Plays by George Colman the Younger*, 98, notes that the potter "Josiah Wedgwood is known to have produced, at this time, a range of staple wares, such as teapots, in an inexpensive unglazed earthenware of dark red to chocolate colour, which he called 'rosso antico.'"

However, it seems as likely that Colman has in mind here Wedgwood's black basalt ware, which he may have learned the potter was about to employ as a visible iconographic link with the antislavery movement. Thomas Clarkson (*History of the Rise, Progress, and Accomplishment of the Abolition of the African Slave-Trade,*) records that in 1787 Wedgwood, a committed abolitionist, made his manufactory produce "a beautiful cameo [of] the Negro . . . imploring compassion . . . in his own native colour" (2:191). The design showed "an African . . . in chains in a supplicating posture, kneeling with one knee upon the ground,

Patty.   Oh! the monster! the filthy fellow! Live with a black-a-moor!

Trudge.   Why, there's no great harm in't, I hope?

Patty.   Faugh! I wou'dn't let him kiss me for the world: he'd make my face all smutty.

Trudge.   Zounds! you are mighty nice all of a sudden; but I'd have you to know, Madam Patty, that Black-a-moor ladies, as you call 'em, are some of the very few whose complexions never rub off![77] 'Sbud, if they did, Wows and I should have changed faces by this time—But mum; not a word for your life.

Patty.   Not I! [*Aside.*] except to the Governor and family. But I must run—and, remember, Trudge, if your master has made a mistake here, he has himself to thank for his pains.

Song[78]

Tho' lovers, like marksmen, all aim at the heart,
  Some hit wide of the mark, as wenches all know;
But of all the bad shots, he's the worst in the art
  Who shoots at a pigeon and kiils a crow[79]*—O ho!*
  Your master has kill'd a crow.

When younkers[80] *go out, the first time in their lives,*
  At random they shoot, and let fly as they go;
So your master unskill'd how to level at wives,
  Has shot at a pigeon, and killed a crow—O ho!
  Your master has kill'd a crow.

---

and with both his hands lifted up to Heaven, and round the seal was observed the following motto, as if he were uttering the words himself—'Am I not a Man and a Brother?'" (1:450). Clarkson remarks that these black cameos became so much the vogue that "some had them inlaid in gold on the lid of their snuff-boxes. Of the ladies, several wore them in bracelets, and other had them fitted up in an ornamental manner as pins for their hair" (2:191–92). See figure 4 and Oldfield, *Popular Politics and British Anti-slavery,* 155–59; also Edwards, *Black Basalt,* 75.

On the practice of employing black boys as servants at the tea table, see note 34 above.

77. *Black-a-moor . . . rub off!* See introduction, pp. 20–21.

78. *Song* Omitted by Mrs. Inchbald, but present in the Larpent manuscript, the 1787 text, and the vocal score.

79. *Who shoots . . . a crow* Possibly a loose reworking of the Juvenalian motto to Steele's *Spectator,* no. 11, *Dat veniam corvis, vexat censura columbas* ("judgment acquits the ravens and condemns the doves"): see [2], note 1.

80. *younkers* Young men.

> *Love and money thus wasted, in terrible trim!*
> *His powder is spent, and his shot running low:*
> *Yet the pigeon he miss'd, I've a notion with him*
> *Will never, for such a mistake, pluck a crow.*[81]—*No! No!*
> *Your master may keep his crow.*

[Exit Patty.]

Trudge. Pshaw! these girls are so plaguy proud of their white and red! but I won't be shamed out of Wows, that's flat.—

Enter Wowski.

Ah! Wows, I'm going to leave you.

Wows. For what you leave me?

Trudge. Master says I must.

Wows. Ah, but you say in your country, women know best; and I say you not leave me.

Trudge. Master, to be sure, while we were in the forest, taught Yarico to read, with his pencil and pocket-book. What then? Wows comes on fine and fast in her lessons. A little awkward at first, to be sure.—Ha! ha!—She's so used to feed with her hands, that I can't get her to eat her victuals, in a genteel, Christian way, for the soul of me; when she has stuck a morsel on her fork, she don't know how to guide it, but pops up her knuckles to her mouth, and the meat goes up to her ear. But, no matter—After all the fine, flashy London girls, Wowski's the wench for my money.

Song

> *A clerk I was in London gay,*
> *Jemmy linkum feedle,*
> *And went in boots to see the play,*[82]
> *Merry fiddlem tweedle.*
> *I march'd the lobby, twirl'd my stick,*
> *Diddle, daddle, deedle;*
> *The girls all cry'd, "He's quite the kick."*
> *Oh, Jemmy linkum feedle.*

81. *pluck a crow* Proverbial; "have a crow to pluck," i.e., have a fault to find, *ODEP,* 157.
82. *boots . . . play* Sutcliffe remarks that "a particular source of chagrin to the employers of servants at this time was to see them in public places, such as the theatre, dressed in extravagant outfits and aping the affectations of high society" (*Plays by George Colman the Younger,* 99).

Hey! for America I sail,
   Yankee doodle, deedle;
The sailor-boys cry'd, "Smoke his tail!"
   Jemmy linkum feedle.
On English belles I turn'd my back,
   Diddle, daddle, deedle;
And got a foreign fair, quite black,
   O twaddle, twaddle, tweedle!

Your London girls, with roguish trip,
   Wheedle, wheedle, wheedle,
May boast their pouting under lip,
   Fiddle, faddle, feedle.
My Wows would beat a hundred such,
   Diddle, daddle, deedle,
Whose upper lip pouts twice as much,
   O, pretty double wheedle!

Rings I'll buy to deck her toes;
   Jemmy linkum feedle;
A feather fine shall grace her nose,
   Waving siddle seedle.
With jealousy I ne'er shall burst;
   Who'd steal my bone of bone-a?
A white Othello, I can trust
   A dingy Desdemona.[83]

                                               [*Exeunt.*]

SCENE II

A Room in the Crown.

[*Enter Inkle.*]

Inkle.   I know not what to think—I have given her distant hints of parting; but still, so strong her confidence in my affection, she prattles on

---

83. *A white . . . Desdemona.* The reference in Trudge's song to Shakespeare's *Othello* highlights not only the reversal of racial roles ("*A dingy Desdemona*") but also the consciously antiheroic nature of Colman's comic opera. Joan Hamilton comments that "Wowski becomes desirable because Trudge need never worry about becoming jealous like a white Othello" ("Inkle and Yarico and the Discourse of Slavery," 26).

without regarding me. Poor Yarico! I must not—cannot quit her. When I would speak, her look, her mere simplicity disarms me: I dare not wound such innocence. Simplicity is like a smiling babe; which, to the ruffian that would murder it, stretching its little naked, helpless arms, pleads, speechless, its own cause. And yet, Narcissa's family—

Enter Trudge.

Trudge. There he is; like a beau bespeaking a coat—doubting which colour to choose—Sir—

Inkle. What now?

Trudge. Nothing unexpected, sir:—I hope you won't be angry; but I am come to give you joy, sir!

Inkle. Joy!—of what?

Trudge. A wife, sir! a white one.—I know it will vex you, but Miss Narcissa means to make you happy, to-morrow morning.

Inkle. To-morrow!

Trudge. Yes, sir; and as I have been out of employ, in both my capacities, lately, after I have dressed your hair, I may draw up the marriage articles.

Inkle. Whence comes your intelligence, sir?

Trudge. Patty told me all that has passed in the Governor's family, on the quay, sir. Women, you know, can never keep a secret. You'll be introduced in form, with the whole island to witness it.

Inkle. So public, too!—Unlucky!

Trudge. There will be nothing but rejoicings, in compliment to the wedding, she tells me; all noise and uproar! Married people like it, they say.

Inkle. Strange! that I should be so blind to my interest, as to be the only person this distresses.

Trudge. They are talking of nothing else but the match, it seems.

Inkle. Confusion! How can I, in honour retract?

Trudge. And the bride's merits—

Inkle. True!—A fund of merits!—I would not—but from necessity—a case so nice as this—I—would not wish to retract.

Trudge. Then they call her so handsome.

Inkle. Very true! so handsome! the whole world would laugh at me: they'd call it folly to retract.

Trudge. And then they say so much of her fortune.

Inkle. O death! it would be *madness* to retract. Surely, my faculties have slept, and this long parting from my Narcissa, has blunted my sense of her accomplishments. 'Tis this alone makes me so weak and wavering. I'll see her immediately. [*Going.*]

Trudge. Stay, stay, sir; I am desired to tell you, the Governor won't open his gates to us till to-morrow morning.

Inkle. Well, be it so; it will give me time, at all events, to put my affairs in train.

Trudge. Yes; it's a short respite before execution; and if your honour was to go and comfort poor Madam Yarico—

Inkle. Damnation! Scoundrel, how dare you offer your advice?—I dread to think of her!

Trudge. I've done, sir, I've done—But I know I should blubber over Wows all night, if I thought of parting with her in the morning.

Inkle. Insolence! begone, sir!

Trudge. Lord, sir, I only—

Inkle. Get down stairs, sir, directly.

Trudge. [*Going out.*] Ah! you may well put your hand to your head; and a bad head it must be, to forget that Madam Yarico prevented her countrymen from peeling off the upper part of it. [*Aside.*]

[*Exit.*]

Inkle. 'Sdeath, what am I about? How have I slumbered! Is it I?—I—who, in London, laughed at the younkers of the town—and, when I saw their chariots, with some fine, tempting girl, perked in the corner, come shopping to the city, would cry—Ah!—there sits ruin—there flies the greenhorn's money! then wondered with myself how men could trifle time on women; or, indeed, think of any women without fortunes. And now, forsooth, it rests with *me* to turn romantic puppy, and give up all for love.—Give up!—Oh, monstrous folly!—thirty thousand pounds!

Trudge. [*Peeping in at the door.*]

Trudge. May I come in, sir?

Inkle. What does the booby want?

Trudge. Sir, your uncle wants to see *you.*

Inkle. Mr. Medium! show him up directly.

[*Exit Trudge.*]

He must not know of this. To-morrow! I wish this marriage were more distant, that I might break it to her by degrees: she'd take my purpose better, were it less suddenly delivered.

Enter Medium.

Med.   Ah! here he is! Give me your hand, nephew! welcome, welcome to Barbadoes, with all my heart.

Inkle.   I am glad to meet you here, uncle!

Med.   That you are, that you are, I'm sure. Lord! Lord! when we parted last, how I wished we were in a room together, if it was but the black hole![84] I have not been able to sleep o'nights for thinking of you. I've laid awake, and fancied I saw you sleeping your last, with your head in the lion's mouth, for a night-cap; and I've never seen a bear brought over to dance about the street, but I thought you might be bobbing up and down in its belly.[85]

Inkle.   I am very much obliged to you.

Med.   Aye, aye, I am happy enough to find you safe and sound, I promise you. But, you have a fine prospect before you now, young man. I am come to take you with me to Sir Christopher, who is impatient to see you.

Inkle.   To-morrow, I hear, he expects me.

Med.   To-morrow! directly—this moment—in half a second.—I left him standing on tip-toe, as he calls it, to embrace you; and he's standing on tip-toe now in the great parlour, and there he'll stand till you come to him.

Inkle.   Is he so hasty?

Med.   Hasty! he's all pepper—and wonders you are not with him, before it's possible to get at him. Hasty, indeed! Why, he vows you shall have his daughter this very night.

Inkle.   What a situation!

Med.   Why, it's hardly fair just after a voyage. But come, bustle, bustle, he'll think you neglect him. He's rare and touchy, I can tell you; and if he once takes it into his head that you show the least slight to his daughter, it would knock up all your schemes in a minute.

84. *the black hole* A reference to the notorious Black Hole of Calcutta, into which in 1756 Surajah Dowlah, the nawab of Bengal, is supposed to have pressed 146 English prisoners. Of these only 23 emerged alive; the rest suffocated. The term *black hole* soon after came into more general use among soldiers to describe "the punishment cell or lock-up in a barracks" (*OED*).

85. *head in the lion's . . . in its belly* Altick, *Shows of London*, 35–40, records the popularity in seventeenth- and eighteenth-century London of exhibiting such wild animals in itinerant street shows and at fairs. "Performing animals," he writes, "especially dancing bears, had been staples of London entertainment as early as Tudor times" (40).

Inkle.   [*Aside.*] Confusion! If he should hear of Yarico!

Med.   But at present you are all and all with him; he has been telling me his intentions these six weeks; you'll be a fine warm husband, I promise you.

Inkle.   [*Aside.*] This cursed connexion!

Med.   It is not for me, though, to tell you how to play your cards; you are a prudent young man, and can make calculations in a wood.

Inkle.   [*Aside.*] Fool! fool! fool!

Med.   Why, what the devil is the matter with you?

Inkle.   [*Aside.*] It must be done effectually, or all is lost; mere parting would not conceal it.

Med.   Ah! now he's got to his damn'd square root again, I suppose, and Old Nick[86] would not move him.—Why, nephew!

Inkle.   [*Aside.*] The planter that I spoke with cannot be arrived—but time is precious—the first I meet—common prudence now demands it. I'm fixed, I'll part with her.

[*Exit.*]

Med.   Damn me, but he's mad! The woods have turned the poor boy's brains; he's scalped, and gone crazy! Hoho! Inkle! Nephew! Gad, I'll spoil your arithmetic, I warrant me.

[*Exit.*]

SCENE III

The Quay.

Enter Sir Christopher Curry.

Sir Chr.   Ods, my life! I can scarce contain my happiness. I have left them safe in church, in the middle of the ceremony. I ought to have given Narcissa away, they told me; but I capered about so much for joy, that Old Spintext advised me to go and cool my heels on the quay, till it was all over. Od, I'm so happy; and they shall see, now, what an old fellow can do at a wedding.

Enter Inkle.

Inkle.   Now for dispatch! [*To the Governor.*] Hark'ee, old gentleman!

Sir Chr.   Well, young gentleman?

Inkle.   If I mistake not, I know your business here.

86. *Old Nick* The devil.

Sir Chr. 'Egad, I believe half the island knows it, by this time.

Inkle. Then to the point—I have a female, whom I wish to part with.

Sir Chr. Very likely; it's a common case, now a-days, with many a man.

Inkle. If you could satisfy me you would use her mildly, and treat her with more kindness than is usual—for I can tell you she's of no common stamp—perhaps we might agree.

Sir Chr. Oho! a slave! Faith, now I think on't, my daughter may want an attendant or two extraordinary; and as you say she's a delicate girl, above the common run, and none of your thick-lipped, flat-nosed, squabby, dumpling dowdies, I don't much care if—

Inkle. And for her treatment—

Sir Chr. Look ye, young man; I love to be plain: I shall treat her a good deal better than you would, I fancy; for though I witness this custom every day, I can't help thinking the only excuse for buying our fellow creatures is to rescue them from the hands of those who are unfeeling enough to bring them to market.

Inkle. Fair words, old gentleman; an Englishman won't put up an affront.

Sir Chr. An Englishman! more shame for you! Let Englishmen blush at such practices. Men, who so fully feel the blessings of liberty, are doubly cruel in depriving the helpless of their freedom.

Inkle. Let me assure you, sir, it is not my occupation; but for a private reason—an instant pressing necessity—

Sir Chr. Well, well, I have a pressing necessity too; I can't stand to talk now; I expect company here presently; but if you'll ask for me to morrow, at the Castle—

Inkle. The Castle!

Sir Chr. Aye, sir, the Castle; the Governor's Castle; known all over Barbadoes.

Inkle. [Aside.] 'Sdeath this man must be on the Governor's establishment: his steward, perhaps, and sent after me, while Sir Christopher is impatiently waiting for me. I've gone too far; my secret may be known—As 'tis, I'll win this fellow to my interest. [*To him.*]—One word more, sir: my business must be done immediately; and, as you seem acquainted at the Castle, if you should see me there—and there I mean to sleep to night—

Sir Chr. The devil you do!

Inkle. Your finger on your lips; and never breathe a syllable of this transaction.

Sir Chr.   No! Why not?

Inkle.   Because, for reasons, which, perhaps, you'll know to-morrow, I might be injured with the Governor, whose most particular friend I am.

Sir Chr.   [*Aside.*] So! here's a particular friend of mine, coming to sleep at my house, that I never saw in my life. I'll sound this fellow. [*To him.*] I fancy, young gentleman, as you are such a bosom friend of the Governor's, you can hardly do any thing to alter your situation with him?

Inkle.   Oh! pardon me; but you'll find that hereafter—besides, you, doubtless, know his character?

Sir Chr.   Oh, as well as I do my own. But let's understand one another. You may trust me, now you've gone so far. You are acquainted with his character, no doubt, to a hair?

Inkle.   I am—I see we shall understand each other. You know him too, I see, as well as I.—A very touchy, testy, hot old fellow.

Sir Chr.   [*Aside.*] Here's a scoundrel! I hot and touchy! Zounds! I can hardly contain my passion!—But I won't discover myself. I'll see the bottom of this—[*To him.*] Well now, as we seem to have come to a tolerable explanation—let's proceed to business—Bring me the woman.

Inkle.   No; there you must excuse me. I rather would avoid seeing her more; and wish it to be settled without my seeming interference. My presence might distress her—You conceive me?

Sir Chr.   Zounds! what an unfeeling rascal!—The poor girl's in love with him, I suppose. No, no, fair and open. My dealing is with you and you only: I see her now, or I declare off.

Inkle.   Well then, you must be satisfied: yonder's my servant—ha—a thought has struck me. Come here sir.

Enter Trudge.

I'll write my purpose, and send it her by him—It's lucky that I taught her to decipher characters; my labour now is paid. [*Takes out his pocket book, and writes.*]

[*To himself.*]—This is somewhat less abrupt; 'twill soften matters. [*To Trudge.*] Give this to Yarico; then bring her hither with you.

Trudge.   I shall, sir. [*Going.*]

Inkle.   Stay; come back. This soft fool, if uninstructed, may add to her distress. When she has read this paper, seem to make light of it; tell her it is a thing of course, done purely for her good. I here inform her that I must part with her. D'ye understand your lesson?

Trudge.   Pa—part with Ma—madam Ya-ric-o!

Inkle.   Why does the blockhead stammer! I have my reasons. No muttering—And let me tell you, sir, if your rare bargain were gone too, 'twould be the better: she may babble our story of the forest and spoil my fortune.

Trudge.   I'm sorry for it, sir; I have lived with you a long while; I've half a year's wages too due the 25th ult. for dressing your hair, and scribbling your parchments; but take my scribbling; take my frizzing; take my wages; and I, and Wows, will take ourselves off together—she saved my life, and rot me, if any thing but death shall part us.

Inkle.   Impertinent! Go, and deliver your message.

Trudge.   I'm gone, sir. Lord, Lord! I never carried a letter with such ill will in all my born days.

[Exit.]

Sir Chr.   Well—shall I see the girl?

Inkle.   She'll be here presently. One thing I had forgot: when she is yours, I need not caution you, after the hints I've given, to keep her from the Castle. If Sir Christopher should see her, 'twould lead you know, to a discovery of what I wish concealed.

Sir Chr.   Depend upon *me*—Sir Christopher will know no more of our meeting, than he does at this moment.

Inkle.   Your secrecy shall not be unrewarded; I'll recommend you, particularly, to his good graces.

Sir Chr.   Thank ye, thank ye; but I'm pretty much in his good graces, as it is; I don't know any body he has a greater respect for.—

Re-enter Trudge.

Inkle.   Now, sir, have you performed your message?

Trudge.   Yes, I gave her the letter.

Inkle.   And where is Yarico? did she say she'd come? didn't you do as you were ordered? didn't you speak to her?

Trudge.   I couldn't, sir, I couldn't—I intended to say what you bid me—but I felt such a pain in my throat, I couldn't speak a word, for the soul of me; and so, sir, I fell a crying.

Inkle.   Blockhead!

Sir Chr.   'Sblood, but he's a very honest blockhead. Tell me, my good fellow—what said the wench?

Trudge.   Nothing at all, sir. She sat down with her two hands clasped on her knees, and looked so pitifully in my face, I could not stand it. Oh, here she comes. I'll go and find Wows: if I must be melancholy, she shall keep me company.

[Exit.]

Sir Chr.   Ods my life, as comely a wench as ever I saw!
>   *Enter Yarico, who looks for some time in Inkle's face,*
>   *bursts into tears, and falls on his neck.*

Inkle.   In tears! nay, Yarico! why this?

Yar.   Oh do not—do not leave me!

Inkle.   Why, simple girl! I'm labouring for your good. My interest, here, is nothing: I can do nothing from myself, you are ignorant of our country's customs. I must give way to men more powerful, who will not have me with you. But see, my Yarico, ever anxious for your welfare, I've found a kind, good person who will protect you.

Yar.   Ah! why not you protect me!

Inkle.   I have no means—how can I?

Yarico.   Just as I sheltered you. Take me to yonder mountain, where I see no smoke from tall, high houses, filled with your cruel countrymen. None of your princes, there, will come to take me from you. And should they stray that way, we'll find a lurking place, just like my own poor cave; where many a day I sat beside you, and blessed the chance that brought you to it—that I might save your life.

Sir Chr.   His life! Zounds! my blood boils at the scoundrel's ingratitude!

Yar.   Come, come, let's go. I always feared these cities. Let's fly and seek the woods; and there we'll wander hand in hand together. No cares shall vex us then—We'll let the day glide by in idleness; and you shall sit in the shade, and watch the sun beam playing on the brook, while I sing the song that pleases you. No cares, love, but for food—and we'll live cheerily I warrant—In the fresh, early morning, you shall hunt down our game, and I will pick you berries—and then, at night I'll trim our bed of leaves and lie me down in peace—Oh! we shall be so happy!—

Inkle.   Hear me, Yarico. My countrymen and yours differ as much in minds as in complexions. We were not born to live in woods and caves—to seek subsistence by pursuing beasts—We Christians, girl, hunt money; a thing unknown to you—But, here, 'tis money which brings us ease, plenty, command, power, every thing; and, of course, happiness. You are the bar to my attaining this; therefore 'tis necessary for my good—and which, I think, you value—

Yar.   You know I do; so much, that it would break my heart to leave you.

Inkle.   But we must part: if you are seen with me I shall lose all.

Yar.   I gave up all for you—my friends—my country: all that was dear to me: and still grown dearer since you sheltered there.—All, all was left for you—and were it now to do again—again I'd cross the seas, and follow you, all the world over.

Inkle. We idle time; sir, she is yours. See you obey this gentleman; 'twill be the better for you.

[*Going.*]

Yar. O barbarous! [*Holding him.*] Do not, do not abandon me!

Inkle. No more.

Yar. Stay but a little. I shan't live long to be a burden to you: your cruelty has cut me to the heart. Protect me but a little—or I'll obey this man, and undergo all hardships for your good; stay but to witness 'em.—I soon shall sink with grief; tarry till then; and hear me bless your name when I am dying; and beg you now and then, when I am gone, to heave a sigh for your poor Yarico.

Inkle. I dare not listen. You, sir, I hope, will take good care of her.

[*Going.*]

Sir Chr. Care of her!—that I will—I'll cherish her like my own daughter; and pour balm into the heart of a poor, innocent girl, that has been wounded by the artifices of a scoundrel.

Inkle. Hah! 'Sdeath, sir, how dare you!—

Sir Chr. 'Sdeath, sir, how dare you look an honest man in the face?

Inkle. Sir, you shall feel—

Sir Chr. Feel!—It's more than ever you did, I believe. Mean, sordid wretch! dead to all sense of honour, gratitude, or humanity—I never heard of such barbarity! I have a son-in-law, who has been left in the same situation; but, if I thought him capable of such cruelty, dam'me if I would not return him to sea, with a peck-loaf, in a cockle shell—Come, come, cheer up, my girl! You shan't want a friend to protect you, I warrant you.—[*Taking Yarico by the hand.*]

Inkle. Insolence! The Governor shall hear of this insult.

Sir Chr. The Governor! liar! cheat! rogue! impostor! breaking all ties you ought to keep, and pretending to those you have no right to. The Governor never had such a fellow in the whole catalogue of his acquaintance—the Governor disowns you—the Governor disclaims you—the Governor abhors you; and to your utter confusion, here stands the Governor to tell you so. Here stands old Curry, who never talked to a rogue without telling him what he thought of him.

Inkle. Sir Christopher!—Lost and undone!

Med. [*Without.*] Holo! Young Multiplication! Zounds! I have been peeping in every cranny of the house. Why, young Rule of Three![87] [*Enters from the inn.*] Oh, here you are at last—Ah, Sir Christopher! What are you there! too impatient to wait at home. But here's one that will make you easy, I fancy. [*Clapping Inkle on the shoulder.*]

Sir Chr.   How came you to know him?

Med.   Ha! ha! Well, that's curious enough too. So you have been talking here, without finding out each other.

Sir Chr.   No, no; I have found him out with a vengeance.

Med.   Not you. Why this is the dear boy. It's my nephew; that is, your son-in-law, that is to be. It's Inkle!

Sir Chr.   It's a lie; and you're a purblind old booby,—and this dear boy is a damn'd scoundrel.

Med.   Hey-day! what's the meaning of this? One was mad before, and he has bit the other, I suppose.

Sir Chr.   But here comes the dear boy—the true boy—the jolly boy, piping hot from church, with my daughter.

Enter Campley, Narcissa, and Patty.

Med.   Campley!

Sir Chr.   Who? Campley?—It's no such thing.

Camp.   That's my name, indeed, Sir Christopher.

Sir Chr.   The devil it is! And how came you, sir, to impose upon me, and assume the name of Inkle? A name which every man of honesty ought to be ashamed of.

Camp.   I never did, sir.—Since I sailed from England with your daughter, my affection has daily increased: and when I came to explain myself to you, by a number of concurring circumstances, which I am now partly acquainted with, you mistook me for that gentleman. Yet had I even then been aware of your mistake, I must confess, the regard for my own happiness would have tempted me to let you remain undeceived.

Sir Chr.   And did you, Narcissa, join in—

Nar.   How could I, my dear sir, disobey you?

Patty.   Lord your honour, what young lady could refuse a captain?

Camp.   I am a soldier, Sir Christopher. Love and war is the soldier's

---

87. *Rule of Three* "A method of finding a fourth number from three given numbers, of which the first is in the same proportion to the second as the third is to the unknown fourth" (*OED*). Medium is, of course, alluding to Inkle's preoccupation with ready reckoning.

motto;[88] though my income is trifling to your *intended* son-in-law's, still the chance of war has enabled me to support the object of my love above indigence. Her fortune, Sir Christopher, I do not consider myself by any means entitled to.

Sir Chr.   'Sblood! but you must though. Give me your hand, my young Mars, and bless you both together!—Thank you, thank you for cheating an old fellow into giving his daughter to a lad of spirit, when he was going to throw her away upon one, in whose breast the mean passion of avarice smothers the smallest spark of affection or humanity.

Nar.   I have this moment heard a story of a transaction in the forest, which I own, would have rendered compliance with your former commands very disagreeable.

Patty.   Yes, sir, I told my mistress he had brought over a Hottypot gentlewoman.

Sir Chr.   Yes, but he would have left her for you [*To Narcissa.*] and you for his interest; and sold you, perhaps, as he has this poor girl to me, as a requital for preserving his life.

Nar.   How![89]

Enter Trudge and Wowski.

Trudge.   Come along, Wows! take a long last leave of your poor mistress: throw your pretty, ebony arms about her neck.

Wows.   No, no;—she not go; you not leave poor Wowski. [*Throwing her arms about Yarico.*]

Sir Chr.   Poor girl! A companion, I take it!

Trudge.   A thing of my own, sir. I couldn't help following my master's example in the woods—*Like master, like man,*[90] sir.

Sir Chr.   But you would not sell her, and be hang'd to you, you dog, would you?

Trudge.   Hang me, like a dog, if I would, sir.

Sir Chr.   So say I to every fellow that breaks an obligation due to the feelings of a man. But, old Medium, what have you to say for your hopeful nephew?

Med.   I never speak ill of my friends, Sir Christopher.

88. *Love . . . motto* Not in *ODEP* but sufficiently commonplace to be proverbial.

89. *How!* From this point Colman altered the play's original ending, of which only a fragment is extant in the Larpent manuscript (see introduction, p. 25).

90. *Like master . . . man* Proverbial; *ODEP,* 517.

Sir Chr. Pshaw!

Inkle. Then let me speak: hear me defend a conduct—

Sir Chr. Defend! Zounds! plead guilty at once—it's the only hope left of obtaining mercy.

Inkle. Suppose, old gentleman, you had a son?

Sir Chr. 'Sblood! then I'd make him an honest fellow; and teach him, that the feeling heart never knows greater pride than when it's employed in giving succour to the unfortunate. I'd teach him to be his father's own son to a hair.

Inkle. Even so my father tutored me: from my infancy, bending my tender mind, like a young sapling, to his will—Interest was the grand prop round which he twined my pliant green affections: taught me in childhood to repeat old sayings—all tending to his own fixed principles, and the first sentence that I ever lisped, was—*Charity begins at home.*[91]

Sir Chr. I shall never like a proverb again, as long as I live.

Inkle. As I grew up, he'd prove—and by example—were I in want, I might e'en starve, for what the world cared for their neighbours; why then should I care for the world? Men now lived for themselves. These were his doctrines: then, sir, what would you say, should I, in spite of habit, precept, education, fly in my father's face, and spurn his councils?

Sir Chr. Say! why, that you were a damn'd honest, undutiful fellow. O curse such principles! Principles, which destroy all confidence between man and man—Principles which none but a rogue could instil, and none but a rogue could imbibe.—Principles—

Inkle. Which I renounce.

Sir Chr. Eh!

Inkle. Renounce entirely. Ill-founded precept too long has steeled my breast—but still 'tis vulnerable—this trial was too much—Nature, 'gainst habit combating within me, has penetrated to my heart; a heart, I own, long callous to the feelings of sensibility; but now it bleeds—and bleeds for my poor Yarico. Oh, let me clasp her to it, while 'tis glowing, and mingle tears of love and penitence. [*Embracing her.*]

Trudge. [*Capering about.*] Wows, give me a kiss! [*Wowski goes to Trudge.*]

Yar. And shall we—shall we be happy?

Inkle. Aye; ever, ever, Yarico.

Yar. I knew we should—and yet I feared—but shall I still watch over

91. *Charity . . . home* Proverbial; *ODEP,* 115.

you? Oh! love, you surely gave your Yarico such pain, only to make her
feel this happiness the greater.

Wows. [*Going to Yarico.*] Oh Wowski so happy!—and yet I think I not
glad neither—

Trudge. Eh, Wows! How!—why not!

Wows. 'Cause I can't help cry—

Sir Chr. Then, if that's the case—curse me, if I think I'm very glad either.
What the plague's the matter with my eyes?—Young man, your hand—
I am now proud and happy to shake it.

Med. Well, Sir Christopher, what do you say to my hopeful nephew now?

Sir Chr. Say! Why, confound the fellow, I say, that is ungenerous enough
to remember the bad action of a man who has virtue left in his heart to
repent it—As for you, my good fellow, [*To Trudge.*] I must, with your
master's permission, employ you myself.

Trudge. O rare!—Bless your honour!—Wows! you'll be lady, you jade, to
a governor's factotum.

Wows. Iss—I Lady Jactotum.

Sir Chr. And now, my young folks, we'll drive home, and celebrate the
wedding. Od's my life! I long to be shaking a foot at the fiddles, and I
shall dance ten times the lighter, for reforming an Inkle, while I have it
in my power to reward the innocence of a Yarico.

Finale[92]

[La Belle Catharine][93]

Campley
Come, let us dance and sing,
While all Barbadoes bells shall ring:[94]

92. *Finale* Fiske, *English Theatre Music*, 478–79, points out that the main tune of "the
Vaudeville-Finale . . . is the original of our children's song, 'Have you seen the muffin
man?'"

93. *La Belle Catharine The Catalogue of Printed Music in the British Library* records several later examples of this tune. In 1814, John Freckleton Burrowes the Elder published "a
Sonatina for the Piano Forte, in which is introduced the air of "La Belle Catherine," as a
Rondo" (9:224). There is also an 1824 arrangement of "Come, Let Us Dance and Sing,"
described as "a French air" by R. Williams (61:226).

94. *Barbadoes bells . . . ring* Church bells, though bells were also used to summon slaves
to work. Darnell Davis records playfully that "when Mr. Colman read his Opera . . . to the
late Dr. Mosely, . . . every body else had been delighted with it," but upon being asked his
opinion, the doctor responded by citing this song and complaining "Stuff—nonsense . . .

8. "Come, Let Us Dance and Sing." Wood engraving cut by George Wilmot Bonner (1796–1836) "from a Drawing taken in the Theatre" by Robert Cruikshank (1789–1856), showing Trudge and Wowski making merry. Frontispiece to an edition of Colman's *Inkle and Yarico,* Cumberland's British Theatre, no. III, n.d., c. 1827. (Private collection.)

Love scrapes the fiddle string,
*   And Venus plays the lute;*
Hymen gay, foots away,
Happy at our wedding-day,
Cocks his chin, and figures in,
*   To tabor, fife, and flute.*
                Chorus
Come then dance and sing,
While all Barbadoes bells shall ring, &c.
                Narcissa
Since thus each anxious care
Is vanished into empty air,
Ah! how can I forbear
*   To join the jocund dance?*
To and fro, couples go,
On the light fantastic toe,
While with glee, merrily,
*   The rosy hours advance.*
                Chorus
Come then, &c.
                Yarico
When first the swelling sea
Hither bore my love and me,
What then my fate would be,
*   Little did I think—*
Doom'd to know care and woe,
Happy still is Yarico;
Since her love will constant prove,
*   And nobly scorns to shrink.*
                Chorus
Come then, &c.
                Wowski
Whilst all around, rejoice,
Pipe and tabor raise the voice,

It won't do—there is but one bell in all the island!" ("The *Spectator's* Essays," 8). Dr. Benjamin Moseley (1742–1819) was author of *A Treatise on Tropical Diseases and the Climate of the West Indies* (1787).

It can't be Wowski's choice,
* Whilst Trudge's to be dumb.*
No, no, dey blithe and gay,
Shall like massa, missy play.
Dance and sing, hey ding, ding,
* Strike fiddle and beat drum.*
                    Chorus
Come then, &c.
                    Trudge
'Sbobs! now, I'm fix'd for life,
My fortune's fair, tho' blacks my wife.
Who fears domestic strife—
* Who cares now a souse!*[95]
Merry cheer my dingy dear
Shall find with her Factotum here;
Night and day, I'll frisk and play
* About the house with Wows.*
                    Chorus
Come then, &c.
                    Inkle
Love's convert here behold,
Banish'd now my thirst of gold,
Bless'd in these arms to fold
* My gentle Yarico.*
Hence all care, doubt, and fear,
Love and joy each want shall cheer,
Happy night, pure delight,
* Shall make our bosoms glow.*
                    Chorus
Come then, &c.
                    Patty
Let Patty say a word—
A chambermaid may sure be heard—
Sure men are grown absurd,

---

95. *a souse* A small coin of little or no value (cf. French *sou*); cf. "not worth a brass farthing" (*ODEP*, 81).

Thus taking black for white;
To hug and kiss a dingy miss,
Will hardly suit an age like this,
Unless, here, some friends appear,
Who like this wedding night.
                    Chorus
Come then, &c.
            The End

13

Jean-François Arnould-Mussot,

The American Heroine: A Pantomime

in Three Acts

Originally performed by the Théâtre de l'Ambigu-Comique,
Paris, 1786. Translated from the French by
Samuel Chandler (Philadelphia, 1797).

Only a few of the very many adaptations and renditions into French and German of the story of Inkle and Yarico came to be translated into English. Arnould's pantomime is one such example. It was originally put on in Paris as a piece of street theater at the Saint-Germain fair on 16 March 1786 and transferred to the Théâtre de Boulevard (boulevard du Temple) on 24 April. It was performed by a troupe of young children accompanied by a few adult players. The French edition of the text (*L'héroïne américaine: Pantomime en trois actes,* two editions [Paris, 1786]) includes an authorial commendation of "la Demoiselle *Julie*" for her outstanding performance as "la jeune Indienne" (Yarico). In all likelihood the printed text would have been on sale as a program at the performance.

The Théâtre de l'Ambigu-Comique had been created in 1769 by Nicolas Audinot (1732–1801) and began by using marionettes to exhibit on stage a compelling mix of song, dance, parody, and comic drama. The employment of children aged seven to sixteen followed soon after. As its title indicates, the company thrived on exploiting dramatic ambiguity, deliberately flouting traditional generic boundaries in favor of irregularity and lack of unity. Its helter-skelter and anarchic spirit proclaims it as the forerunner of nineteenth-century vaudeville. As a writer of pantomime, melodrama, and other such spectacles, Jean-François Arnould-Mussot (1734–95) was a prolific contributor to the theater, being for a considerable period its codirector. Although inevitably many of his works were seasonal, *L'héroïne améri-*

caine was still being revived as an entertainment as late as 1808, when it was reprinted (Price, *Inkle and Yarico Album,* 72).

We cannot be absolutely certain that Arnould's pantomime ever achieved a performance in Great Britain, though there is strong likelihood that it did on at least one occasion. An afterpiece containing dancing, titled *The American Heroine,; or Ingratitude Punished,* followed a performance of *The Rivals* at the King's Theatre in Drury Lane on 19 March 1792. It is supposed to have been "Founded on the Tale of Inkle & Yarico" and was advertised as being "in three Parts" (Hogan, *London Stage,* pt. 5, 1438; *Times,* no. 2258 [Monday, 19 March 1792]). According to Price, 71, it was received with disapprobation (perhaps because of its anti-English slant), and it was never published in this form. Five years later, however, Samuel Chandler's translation of Arnould was published in Philadelphia and in all likelihood was staged simultaneously. Since Great Britain was then at war with the French Republic and the United States had sided with France, the pantomime's incipient anglophobia may have gone down well with an American audience.

Little is known about the pantomime's translator, though in the same function his name appears on the title page of an English edition of C. C. Tanguy de la Bossière's *Observations on the Dispatch Written the 16th. January 1797, by Mr. Pickering,* also published in Philadelphia the same year. As Price politely remarks, his English translation of *L'héroïne américaine* is "painfully faithful" (69), though by way of compensation it at least gives us the chance to visualize its performance. Within the pantomime, gesture and mime will have taken the place of dialogue. In all probability, the outline to each scene or paragraph as represented in the text would have been spoken aloud by a narrator before it was enacted. The performance would have been accompanied by music and sometimes dancing. A stage direction at the end of the French text of 1786 states: "Un divertissement général termine la Pantomime." For some further remarks, see introduction, pp. 31–32.

The subject of the following pantomime is taken from a passage in the Philosophical and Political History of the European settlements, and commerce in the East and West-Indies.*[1]

*Vide vol. V, page 271.

1. *Philosophical . . . West-Indies.* Arnould found the story in the Abbé Raynal's *Histoire philosophique et politique des etablissements et du commerce des Européens dans les Deux Indes* (1770). The work was frequently reprinted. The quoted extract in its English translation by

"A party of Englishmen having landed on the continent, with a view of taking slaves were discovered by the Caribbees. These savages fell upon the enemy's troops, which were either put to death or flight. A young man, after being pursued a long time, betook himself to a thicket of woods. An Indian woman having met him, saved his life, fed him privately, and conducted him again to the sea-shore. His companions were waiting on board the vessel at anchor, for those who had gone on shore. The boat went to take him; his benefactress accompanied him to the vessel. As soon as they arrived at Barbadoes, this monster sold her, who had preserved his life, and given him her heart, filled with the tenderest sentiments of love. One of the English poets, to retrieve the honor of his nation, dedicated this infamous monument of avarice and perfidy to the horror of posterity.[2] It has been held up [to] the detestation of nations, in different languages."

This historical subject has been pursued as near the original as possible: such changes only have been made as were necessary for theatrical representation.

The American Heroine: A Pantomime

DRAMATIS PERSONÆ

Yarico	Inkle
An Indian Chief	A company of English soldiers.
Captain of an English vessel	A company of savages.

The Scene is in America

ACT I

*The theatre represents a forest: on the left side of which,
towards the end, is a cottage.*

J. Justamond, *A Philosophical and Political History* . . . , appears on 4:311. As a controversial writer whose works were banned in the France of the ancien régime, Guillaume Thomas François Raynal (1713–96) was widely admired for his outspoken exposure of the cruelties of the transatlantic slave trade. As Price has pointed out (*Inkle and Yarico Album,* 61), the abridged account of Inkle and Yarico that appears in his *Histoire* seems to have been based on Ligon (whose work had appeared in French) rather than on Steele.

2. *One of . . . posterity.* Raynal appears to be alluding to the "Argument" to the anonymous *Yarico to Inkle: An Epistle* (1736) [6], in which the poet states that "the story of *Inkle and Yarico* . . . will as long as either lasts, be mention'd in competition with the blackest, most incredible piece of ingratitude, that history, or romance can furnish."

9. *Un Anglais de la Barbade vend sa maitresse.* Engraved frontispiece by Philibert-Benoît de la Rue (1718–80). From Abbé Raynal, *Histoire philosophique et politique,* vol. 7 (Geneva, 1783). (Courtesy of the Brotherton Collection, University of Leeds.)

Inkle, at the head of a company of soldiers, is conducting two of the Caribbees in chains: they are passing through the forest towards the sea-shore.

Yarico goes cautiously out of her cottage, trying to find out the occasion of the noise she heard: she perceives Inkle stopped from going on by the savages, and returns hastily to her cottage.

Inkle, with his hair in disorder, and his broken sword in his hand, returns back, crossing the forest with precipitation, pursued by a company of savages.

Yarico goes out of her cottage, keeping her eyes fixed on the English officer, in whose fate she appears by degrees warmly interested. Her gesture expresses the fearful apprehensions she entertains of his falling into the enemy's hands. She avails herself of the first favorable opportunity, to get into the forest, in order to liberate him.

The savages, who were in pursuit of Inkle, return, and appear enraged that the enemy had escaped them. After visiting Yarico's cottage and its environs, they disappear and continue their pursuit.

Yarico advances, watching the savages; she shews the highest satisfaction in having saved the life of the person she loves. She returns immediately, conducting Inkle by the hand.

Captivated with the beauty of the young American, and impressed with grateful sentiments for the service she had rendered him, Inkle gives her testimonies of the tenderest love. Yarico is enchanted to see her tenderness returned by her lover: she takes him by the hand, and conducts him to her cottage, where she invites him to repose himself, while she goes into the woods to procure some refreshment for him. She takes her bow and goes into the forest, recommending to her lover not to expose himself to the fury of the savages, by going out before her return, from the place she left him in.

SCENE VIII

Inkle seems to forget the fate he is threatened with, and is wholly taken up with the pleasure of beholding again the object of his tenderness; finally, exhausted with fatigue, he lies down on some rushes, and tries to take repose.

SCENE IX

Yarico returns in a hurry, bringing her game and fruits: as she comes to the cottage she suddenly perceives Inkle asleep: she approaches him, making as little noise as possible, for fear of disturbing his repose; sits down at his feet, and fixes her eyes upon him with the most affectionate attention.

Inkle awakes by degrees. Yarico is transported with joy, hastens to present him the fruit, and persuades him in the tenderest manner to eat them. She runs afterwards to a neighbouring rivulet, and brings some water for him to drink.

A confused noise is heard at a distance. Yarico trembling for the life of her lover, and seeing the savages advance, quickly conducts Inkle into a neighbouring grotto, to conceal him from their pursuit.

SCENE X

The savages appear, incensed at the enemy's escaping them, and persuaded that the young American had concealed him, they seize her, and threaten her with death, if she does not tell where the stranger is secreted. Yarico is not intimidated by their threats. The savages brandish their swords over her head: ready to receive the mortal blow, rather than betray her lover, she falls on her knees, covers her eyes with her hands, and courageously awaits the fate that is preparing for her.

Inkle appears at the entrance of the grotto. Frightened at the sight, he re-enters into the hollow of the rock.

SCENE XI

The Indian chief [3] advances, and forbids them to strike. He orders them to withdraw. They obey.

SCENE XII

He approaches Yarico, assuring her that she has nothing more to fear. He views her, declares he thinks her beautiful, and requests her to attach herself to him. She answers with candor, that her heart is engaged, and that nothing can ever change her sentiments.

SCENE XIII

More savages run up quickly, and announce to the chief the arrival of a second vessel. He leaves Yarico, telling her that he is going to try by his courage to merit the happiness of pleasing her, and proceeds with his companions to the coast, where they perceived the enemy.

SCENE XIV

Yarico hastens to the place where her lover was concealed, and informs him of the arrival of a vessel from his nation, requests him to accompany her to the sea-shore, and earnestly desires the favor of going with him. Inkle consents with pleasure. They both withdraw, on the side opposite the savages.

End of the First Act.

ACT II

The theatre represents a barren landscape, terminated by a chain of rocks, against which the waves are constantly dashing. At a distance is seen an English vessel at anchor.

SCENE I

Yarico is conducting Inkle by the hand, taking every possible precaution not to be seen by the savages. As soon as they come to the sea-shore, she shows him the vessel that had just come in sight. Inkle knowing it to be an English vessel, is transported with the liveliest joy, and expresses his gratitude to Yarico for the signal services she had rendered him.

3. *The Indian chief* In Arnould's French original, he is described as "le Chef des Sauvages" (2d ed. [1786], 11). Whenever Chandler employs the term "Indian" in *The American Heroine*, it is his rendering of "Sauvage."

A confused noise is heard, from the savages who came to reconnoitre the enemy. Yarico conceals Inkle amongst the rocks.

SCENE II

The Indian chief orders his companions to follow him, and prepare for battle, for fear of being surprised by the English, who had just landed.

SCENE III

An English regiment advances in good order. The captain forms three divisions, which he sends to make discoveries in different places.

SCENE IV

The Indian chief, who perceives the enemy's manoeuvres, orders his companions to advance, with which he also forms three divisions, ordering them to take the same rout[4] with the English.

SCENE V

One of the English divisions returns to observe the enemy's motions, and soon after lays in ambuscade, waiting for a favorable moment to fall upon the enemy.

SCENE VI

Inkle, who in his flight, had been met by the savages, appears pursued by five of them, who surround him, unable to defend himself against them.

SCENE VII

Yarico falls into a violent passion, rushes upon one of the savages, takes away his tomahawk, and joins Inkle, whom she screens with her body. Inkle's courage is animated by this brave and generous action, and uniting his efforts to hers, they two put the five savages to flight.

SCENE VIII

Two English divisions come up, closely pursued by the savages; the division which was lying in ambuscade springs up, falls furiously upon them and takes them in the flank. They attack and defend themselves on both sides.

---

4. *rout* Route, path.

The victory, after remaining some time in suspense, declares in favor of the English. The savages betake themselves to flight, and retreat, pursued by the English.

An English detachment returns, conducting a company of savages, made prisoners, chained two and two. The captain orders them to be conducted to the vessel.

Inkle makes himself known to the captain; introduces Yarico to him as a person who had rendered him the most signal services. Captivated with the beauty of this young American, the captain grows jealous of Inkle's happiness: he orders his troops to prepare for a second expedition against the savages. They march different ways, and the captain, Inkle and Yarico retire to repose themselves.

End of the Second Act.

The same scenery as in the second act.

Yarico is lying asleep at the foot of a tree; Inkle, setting[5] by her side, appears to be lost in a profound reverie.

The noise of cannon is heard at a distance from the vessel.

Inkle rises, taking care to make as little noise as possible, for fear of awaking Yarico, and advances towards the sea-shore.

The captain, accompanied by some soldiers, comes to inform Inkle, that the vessel is ready to set sail: he casts his eyes on Yarico who is sleeping; he approaches her and appears undecided what step to take. A soldier who perceives what is pressing in his mind, proposes to put Yarico in chains and carry her on board. The captain hesitates.

5. *setting* Sitting.

SCENE III

Inkle returns; astonished at the proceedings of the soldier, acquaints the captain with his resentment. The captain presents him a purse, desiring him to sell him Yarico as a slave. Inkle hesitates; the captain perceives it, and availing himself of the opportunity, puts a second purse into his hands. Dazzled by the quantity of gold contained in these two purses, and led on by the captain's importunities, Inkle consents, at last, to abandon her who had saved his life, several times, by exposing hers.

The soldier cautiously ties a chain round Yarico's arms for fear of awaking her.

SCENE IV

The Indian chief appears on the top of a rock, and observes, with strict attention, what is passing.

Yarico awakes, perceives Inkle at some distance from her, rises quickly, and runs to the object of her tender affections; she tries to embrace him; at last she beholds the chain that is put upon her; dismayed she casts her eyes upon Inkle's, who in an instant turns them,[6] and is stealing away from her sight.

The unfortunate heroine cannot believe that her lover could be base enough to sell her to his friend. She falls at his knees; but Inkle quits her, declaring that all is over between them, and that she belongs to the captain. She stretches out her arm to her lover, trembling, her eyes bathed with tears; so excessive is her grief that she can hardly support herself. She tries to excite his compassion, but Inkle is inflexible; and the captain orders Yarico to prepare to follow him.

The Indian chief, shocked at this cruelty, retires, promising to take immediate vengeance on him.

SCENE V

They[7] announce to the captain, that he is not safe in that place; and that the Caribbees are taking up their arms and preparing to renew the battle. He commits the heroine to the care of some soldiers, ordering them to take her immediately on board the vessel, and retires with Inkle.

6. *them* His own eyes.   7. *They* The English soldiers.

SCENE VI

The Indian chief appears; his companions advance: he animates them, draws them up in companies, heads them, and marches against the enemy, who are preparing for their departure.

SCENE VII

A company of savages return, pursued by an English detachment. They hide in the forest.

SCENE VIII

Some savages return, and appear in a cruel agitation.

The chief arrives, holding the young American in one hand and a sabre in the other; he takes off her chains, generously restores her her liberty, and puts her into the hands of some savages, to keep her safe.

SCENE IX

Inkle runs and takes Yarico again: he falls violently upon the Indian chief: the savages retire, carrying away Yarico against her inclinations.

A brisk and obstinate combat is fought between Inkle and the chief; the latter is on the point of coming off victorious. Inkle begins to fail.

SCENE X

The captain immediately comes up, and joining with Inkle, they become too powerful for the chief, who is no longer able to resist. He is just going to be sacrificed, when a party of Indians advance, rescue him, and surround Inkle, who is made prisoner and dragged off.

SCENE XI

The captain, who escaped from them, appears again at the head of a detachment of troops; but finding an obstinate resistance in the chief and his companions, is obliged to take to flight.

SCENE XII

The savages remaining masters of the field of battle, draw up in order.

Immediately after, the noise of cannon is heard, which announces the vessel's departure.

One of the savages brings news that the enemy have disappeared, and that their vessel had set sail.

The savages request their chief to put Inkle to death, to revenge the incursions and cruelties of the English; he promises to do it, and retires with them.

SCENE XIII

Yarico, reduced to despair, by the perfidy of her lover, leaves the savages, who try to soothe her sorrows, and seeks a private place where she may more freely vent her grief.

A clamorous feast, which is announced at a distance, and approaches by degrees, obliges her to retire.

SCENE XIV

A march of savages; they advance, dancing; they set up the stake, to which the prisoner is to be fastened.

Inkle is conducted in chains by four savages, two of whom are armed, the one with a scalping knife and the other with a tomahawk.

The usual ceremonies of the savages, when they prepare to put a prisoner to death, being performed, he is brought forward, and tied to the stake. The fire is kindled; the chief is on the point of giving the signal for commencing the torments, that they usually make their prisoners suffer, when Yarico, in despair, runs to him, and stops his arm. She intreats him in the most suppliant manner, to pardon her perfidious lover. The chief, after a moment's hesitation, refuses to comply. Seeing that her prayers are vain, she retires, draws a poignard,[8] and threatens to plunge it into her breast, if he does not grant her request. The chief, terrified at this action, runs up to her, disarms her, and reproaches her with her love to a traitor, who in return for her tenderness, had the cruelty to sell her as a slave. Yarico, without making answer, falls at his knees and redoubles her entreaties. The chief, moved with compassion, by the generosity of Yarico, for whom he conceives the tenderest passion, grants her request.

All the savages are filled with indignation: but the chief with a single look, awes them into silence.

Yarico is transported with joy: she flies to her lover, and hurries off his chains: she stares at them for a moment: she sighs at the thought of their being the same she wore when he sold her to the captain, and throws them away with horror.

---

8. *poignard* Dagger.

Inkle, confused and ashamed to find so much generosity in a woman, that he had so cruelly abused, falls at her knees to embrace them. She pushes him away with disdain, letting him see what difference she makes between his infamous conduct and the noble generosity of the Indian chief. She vows an eternal hatred to him, and offers her hand to the chief, who receives it with a glow of gratitude, and coldly orders Inkle to begone: he tries to move her compassion, but some savages advance and force him to retire: he departs with a heart full of remorse.

The savages express by their gestures, their approbation of Yarico and their chief. They give themselves up to joy, and prepare to celebrate their union.

Finis

14

Charles James Fox, "Yarico to Inkle"

From Maria Riddell, ed., *The Metrical Miscellany:*
Consisting Chiefly of Poems Hitherto Unpublished
(London, 1802), 206–9.

The celebrated Whig politician Charles James Fox (1749–1806) was from
the outset of the British parliamentary campaign a passionate champion for
the abolition of slavery, which he deemed "a practice so enormous, so savage, so repugnant to all laws, human and divine" and a "wholesale sacrifice
of a whole order and race of our fellow creatures" (Wright, *Speeches of the*
*Rt. Hon. C. J. Fox,*4:183, 186: speech of 19 April 1791). Between 1788 and
1796, when the abolitionist lobby laid down an annual motion to the House
of Commons in favor of their cause, Fox was at the forefront of those who
spoke fervently against the iniquities of slavery. He contended that "a trade
in human flesh was so scandalous, that it was to the last degree infamous
to let it be openly carried on by the government of any country" (4:15: speech
of 12 May 1789). "The African trade," he argued, "was a system of injustice
and cruelty, which degraded every man who practised, and every legislature
which sanctioned it" (5:385: speech of 26 February 1795). For Fox, it was to
be understood as "a question not of political, but of personal freedom. Political freedom was undoubtedly as great a blessing as any people under
Heaven—considered collectively as a people—could pant after, or seek to
possess; but political freedom, when it came to be compared with personal
freedom, sank to nothing, and became no blessing at all in comparison."
"Personal freedom," he added, "must be the first object of every human being; and it was a right, of which he who deprives a fellow-creature is absolutely criminal in so depriving him" (4:182–83: speech of 19 April 1791).

After his marriage to Elizabeth Armistead in 1795, Fox took a less active
part in British politics, spending much time at his country house, St. Anne's
Hill in Surrey, where he devoted himself to literary pursuits. In that situa-

tion the author Maria Riddell (1772?–1808), an early patron of Robert Burns, sought out Fox to contribute some of his verse to her anthology *The Metrical Miscellany* (1802). In a prefatory note to the volume she writes: "No Poem, hitherto confined to Manuscript, has been inserted in this Miscellany, without the Concurrence of the respective Writers, whose Names, where the Editor has obtained Permission to make them public, are affixed to their Poems in the following Table of Contents." "Yarico to Inkle" is the second of a cluster of three poems that are attributed in the list of contents to the "*Hon. Charles F**.*" (A poem that appears earlier in the miscellany is listed as the work of the "*Right Hon. C. J. Fox.*") There seems little reason to believe that the author could be anybody other than Fox, whose enduring friendship with Mrs. Riddell is attested elsewhere (see MacNaughten, *Burns' Mrs. Riddell*).

The appeal of "Yarico to Inkle" is considerably enhanced by our awareness of its author. Fox's classical education at Eton may have encouraged him to write within the conventions of Ovidian heroic epistle in which the forsaken heroine laments the turn of her fate (see headnote to selection 3B), yet the whole tenor of the poem seems predicated upon his ardent conviction that personal freedom should be seen as the most basic of human rights. As a critique of slavery, the poem is at its most effective whenever Yarico (whose exact racial ancestry is tellingly left unspecified) berates her former lover for the heartless ease with which he could cash in her body for personal gain. Yet Yarico's powerful denunciation of Inkle as one who had been willing to "barter love for gold" (54) and leave her life forever "polluted" (69) is more than counterbalanced by her artless inability to conceal her own sexual and emotional love for him and by her mental need to believe that, through her forgiveness, he will ultimately recognize the error of his ways. In its contradictory impulses, the poem exemplifies well the extent to which the whole abolitionist ethos was so deeply affected by and ingrained in the prevalent sensibility of the age.

Four years after the publication of Mrs. Riddell's *Miscellany*, it was Charles James Fox who proposed the successful parliamentary motion that legislated the abolition of the slave trade in Great Britain. Addressing the Commons, Fox spoke of "the vast importance of . . . my motion . . . that *if, during the almost forty years that I have had the honour of a seat in parliament, I had been so fortunate as to accomplish that, and that only, I should think that I had done enough, and could retire from public life with comfort, and the conscious satisfaction, that I had done my duty*" (*Speeches*, 6:659: 10

June 1806). It was to prove his final speech to the House, for Fox died a few weeks later. According to a recent biographer, "prominent among the figures represented on Fox's monument in Westminster Abbey is that of a weeping Negro looking up to the couch on which the statesman lies dying" (Mitchell, *Charles James Fox,* 249). His Yarico had been hardly less lachrymose in mourning the injustice of her enslavement.

Yes, perjur'd Man! my passion must have way;
Too long conceal'd within my breast it lay;
Why should my rage in secret thus remain?
Wrongs such as mine[1] concealment should disdain;
Away with tears and unavailing moan,
Since tears nor pray'rs can melt thy heart of stone.
Thy heart, where sordid Interest reigns supreme,
Rules through the day, and gilds the nightly dream;
Where every thought is but to swell your hoards,
Nor start at any crime that wealth affords: 10
Obdurate wretch! and could'st thou then behold
These limbs in shackles for the sake of gold?
So sad a sight could'st thou endure to see,
Nor drop one tear, nor heave one sigh for me?
Alas! for thee I've wept, for thee I've shed
Unceasing torrents o'er my sleepless bed,
When for thy safety, anxious as my own,
In caves I hid thee, from the world unknown;
Fancy has oft, with idle terror fraught,
Shewn murder'd Inkle to my troubled thought,   20
Heard him with well known accents, true in death,
Call on lov'd Yarico with latest[2] breath;
Frantic with fear, from off my couch I start,
Seek the known cavern with a throbbing heart,
With tottering step the deep recess invade,
Wishing to know the truth, yet still afraid:

1. *Wrongs such as mine* Wrongs committed against me.
2. *latest* Last, dying.

Determin'd now I cast around my eye,
"My love is safe, my love is safe!" I cry;—
And wild with joy, my raptur'd bosom burns,
By turn I kiss thee, and I weep by turns.   30
Nor you my love disdain'd; your tender breast
An equal flame for Yarico confest.
Oft in my circling arms entranc'd you lay,
And curs'd the coming of th'unwelcome day.
For you no beauties had the rising Sun,
The day was night when Yarico was gone.
Oft, with reluctant steps when forced to go,
I left you fixt in attitude of woe;
And, slow retreating, saw your fearful eye
Pursue my steps, and heard the bursting sigh;   40
Saw you, 'till now no more my aching sight,
With sudden darkness seiz'd, could bear the light.
When night return'd, it still beheld my flame,
And found our mutual ardor still the same;
Another night appear'd—another past,³
Renewing each our raptures like the last.
Blest in thy love, time wing'd with pleasure flew,
To interrupt my joys no care I knew:
And judging of thy passion by my own,
Resign'd all thought but confidence alone: 50
Trusting in thee, what could'st not thou persuade?
Gave all I had—and am by thee betray'd;
By thee to fierce barbarians vilely sold—
Oh! impious Man, to barter love for gold!
Was it for this I strew'd thy leafy bed?
Was it for this with various fruits I fed?
Was it for this I every want supplied,⁴
And hung thy cavern with the Tyger's hide?
Fool that I was, in dangers thus to run,
And take, alas! such pains to be undone.   60
Hast thou so soon forgot how oft I led

3. *past* Passed.
4. Cf. Jerningham [10], lines 151–53 and note 27.

Thy weary footsteps to the fountain's head?
"Sweet stream," said I, "whose waves so purely glide
Thro' the smooth herbage, with unsullied tide,
O may my happy life as purely flow,
Its waves untainted with the taste of woe!"
In vain I said, tho' gently glides the rill,
Pure and unsullied its meanders⁵ still,
With woe, alas! my life polluted flows,
For slighted love is sure the worst of woes.   70
For thee did I ambitious gifts reject,
Saw humbled princes kneeling with neglect;
Yes Inkle, yes, I saw them bend the knee,
And I despis'd them all, despis'd for thee!
Oh! canst thou think on this, nor inward feel
The stings of conscience worse than sharpen'd steel;
Will not remorse force out the lab'ring sigh,
Throb in your heart, and tremble in your eye?
It will, it will; methinks I see thee now,
By frenzy driv'n to yonder mountain's brow,   80
Calling on me you leave the airy steep,
And headlong plunge into the roaring deep.
O stay my love! my dear repentant, live!
My wrongs, however great, I still forgive.
All may be well, alas! I rave, I burn,
He boasts his crimes, and views my grief with scorn;
Unhappy wretch! what torments do I prove,
Condemn'd to hate him, still, oh! still I love!
From Heaven I call no furious vengeance down,
Wounding his breast, I should but wound my own;   90
Be every blessing show'rd upon his head,
Oh may he live, when I, alas! am dead.
And when his ashes sleep within the grave,
May Heaven forgive as Yarico forgave!

5. *meanders* "Sinuous windings (of a river)" (*OED*).

15

Anna Maria Porter, "Epistle from Yarico to Inkle" (Extract)

From Anna Maria Porter, *Ballad Romances, and Other Poems* (London, 1811).

Without the public attention that preceded the abolition of slavery in the British Isles in 1807, the story of Inkle and Yarico lost much of its imme- diate topicality and verve. Though faithful to the style and tone of heroic epistle, Anna Maria Porter shuns any direct reference to the slave trade, an omission that would have been inconceivable just a few years earlier. In- stead she domesticates "the jetty Yarico" (line 164) into an Indian angel in the house, confiding to her faithless lover that *his* homeland was the place "I hop'd to spend my blissful life, / Thy docile pupil, and exulting wife" (156–57). The poem reads as an extended exhibition of "pictur'd grief" (29) that is often more a rant against man's infidelity to woman than in any real sense a reworking of the traditional tale. In its final lines, Yarico imagines her own imminent death but incongruously assumes an Inkle full of "Chris- tian sorrow" (336) rising to join her in heaven. The extract given here, which begins with self-recrimination, captures the ranting mood of the poem. The sale of Yarico is briefly delineated as a kind of horrific gang rape.

Better known as a popular novelist, Anna Maria Porter (1780–1832) was a prolific writer in a family that was devoted to literature. Her elder sister, Jane (1776–1850), was also well known as a novelist, and her brother, Sir Robert Kerr Porter (1777–1842), was an accomplished artist. Anna Maria showed a precocious ability, revealing a poetic talent even in childhood. A biographical sketch written some years after her death praises the Christ- ian virtue of her works and describes her as one who "has shown herself the friend of religion and humanity" (Elwood, *Memoirs of the Literary Ladies of England,* 2:301). Her *Ballad Romances, and Other Poems* contained a number of pieces that had already appeared in her novels. A presentation copy of the volume to her sister Jane is at Princeton. The work was reprinted in Philadelphia in 1816. Miss Porter never married. See also *DNB.*

O fool![1] to trust to words, or think the face
(Where goodness seemed to wear the dress of grace)
Was bond enough for faith! O fool, to read
Mere sense of right, for virtue's actual deed!   200
Weak wretch! to think his worth and love secure,
Whose selfish feeling made such honour sure;
When no temptation rose, no danger lay,
Save in base wandering from the faithful way!
Alas! by circumstance is virtue tried;—
Proof, proof alone, should be affection's guide.
I had not learnt in those untutor'd days,
Such bitter lore, nor trod deception's maze.
I thought thee all perfection, found thee kind,
Nor knew guilt's lurking seed in man to find;   210
Cold selfishness, which, like the deadly tree,
Poisons all things in its vicinity.
Heavens! had a sordid interest power to move?
Or did thy breast no longer glow with love!
Had my prais'd beauties lost with time their charms?
Or love been surfeited in love's true arms?—
Thy sex by art and calculation won,
From truth and humbleness, disdainful run:—
Yes! when we love too well, with careless ease
Our dearest aim we lose, the power to please;   220
Fond and bewilder'd, all around us seems
Like things unreal, strange, fantastic dreams;
We dread to fail where most we would succeed,
And when we fear, alas, we fail indeed!—
Thus haply ruined by my love's excess,

1. *O fool!* Yarico herself.

Thou more hadst priz'd, if I had worshipped less.
Yet, when did look or speech of thine declare,
That I no longer to thy sense was fair?—
Each day that fled, by new endearments filled,
With livelier confidence my bosom thrilled;   230
Thy passion spoke in sighs, and on thy tongue
Still bliss and gratitude enamoured hung.
O! there are hours, which when by thought renewed,
Leave all my soul to tenderness subdued,
In haste from later scenes I turn mine eye,
Leap their dark gulph,[2] and spring again to joy!
How could I doubt that flush of raptured red
Which o'er thy face expressive beauty spread;
That pulse which throbbed all visible and high,
At my admiring glance, or tender sigh!   240
O! who that had that gracious aspect seen,
Had guessed a vain and selfish soul within?—
Those gentle eyes with thought and sweetness filled,
That voice whose tones e'en careless hearers thrilled,
That finished form, whose very turn defined
The graceful movements of a polish'd mind;
Were these so soon to blast my startled eye
With words and looks of thankless apathy!—
All on that altered brow was stern and chill,
All in that ruthless bosom, cold and still,   250
When on Barbadoes' shore, thy mandate gave
The trusting Indian to a living grave.—
O moment of despair! my ear received
The sound, but not the sense at first believed;
Till scared by frightful men, who rudely grasped
That tender waist which oft thine arms had clasped,
I shrieked, I flew, I sought thy well-known breast,
And looked at once for safety and for rest.
O dire remembrance! from thy bosom cast,
Again before my sight wild phrenzy past,   260
Rooted I stood my dreadful doom to hear,

2. *gulph* Gulf.

No breath my pale lips gave, mine eyes no tear;
Still silence reigned, and thy departing step
Roused my lost spirit from its torpid sleep;
Then, my wild cry resounded thro' the air;
It called thee not, to pity, or to spare,
No, 'twas the cry of madness and despair.

AMERICAN VERSIONS

Its proximity to the Native American tale of Pocahontas perhaps accounts for the fact that Inkle and Yarico never became so ubiquitous or deep rooted a myth in the United States as it had been in western Europe and in parts of the Caribbean. Price (*Inkle and Yarico Album,* 25–26) came upon several secondary allusions to a long poetical adaptation of the tale published in London in 1799 by "Mr. C. Brown" and ascribed to the American writer, Charles Brockden Brown (1770–1810). I have tracked down a copy of this at Northwestern University and regret having to report that, despite being still so listed in contemporary bibliographies, it is categorically *not* the work of the illustrious American to whom it has been casually attributed (see this book's chronology).

The success of George Colman's comic opera on the American stage probably did more than anything else to popularize the tale for a period. S. Foster Damon ("Negro in Early American Songsters," 139, 157) records an additional solo for Yarico, published in *A Choice Collection of Admired Songs* (Baltimore, 1805), 46–47, the first stanza of which "show[s] how the American knowledge of the negro influenced the English text":

> O Inkle, tink how griev'd my heart;
> Say, is it true that we must part?
> Oh! tink, when first my grot you spied,
> How danger lurk'd on ev'ry side;
> And when you saw the daring foe,
> Who save you but poor Yarico?

As might be expected at this time, new versions of the tale published in America for the most part show a greater indebtedness to European models than to native impulses.

16

"Amicus," "Yarico to Inkle"

From *The American Museum, or Universal Magazine*
11 (1792), appendix, "Poetry," 25–27.

There is little at first to indicate that the following verse epistle may have been the work of an American author except that it was published by Matthew Carey at Philadelphia in his journal the *American Museum*. Although Carey frequently reprinted pieces from London and Dublin periodicals (of which the poem may still turn out to be one), he also included some American writing. The pseudonym Amicus remains unidentified.

This is one of two poems contained in the same issue on the topic of Inkle and Yarico, the other probably being the work of a different writer (see chronology). If more sentimental than radical, the primary interest of the poem is its antislavery stance. Yarico writes from shortly after her captivity, having delivered a stillborn child. Implicit to her pathetic plea that Inkle buy her back and allow her to return to her native land is the sense that, if only he had not abandoned her, their baby would have lived.

Unlike other versions of the tale, the poem is not geographically specific in pinpointing Barbados as the point of sale. In fact something of a reversal is evident. Yarico is depicted as by birth an islander (100) rather than from the mainland, so that her enslavement—after sailing away from home with Inkle—could be visualized as taking place on the coast of North America where tobacco ("baneful plants," line 45) was grown. Whatever its origin, the appearance of the poem in the *American Museum* reflects nascent abolitionist tendencies in the early years of the United States.

If that great Power you taught me to adore,
Has blest your passage to your native shore,
And, 'scap'd the dangers of the wat'ry main,
You see your country, and your friends again—
Oh! if my Inkle, (heaven grant it so!)
Remembers still the once-lov'd Yarico—
If in the silent hour she claims one thought,
And if you feel¹ the virtues you have taught—
When these sad lines to you shall be convey'd,
(The mournful story of too fond a maid!)   10
Then, then, perhaps, your melting heart may spare
One sigh, one wish, to snatch her from despair;
Perhaps a tear of penitence may fall,
And one good action recompence for all.
Could you, fair ingrate,² now behold the maid
You once enamour'd, and alas! betray'd;
Ah! could you know all, all the slave has felt,
Your soul must shudder, and your heart must melt:
What fiend infernal could your bosom steel?
O, heart of stone! that could refuse to feel,   20
When agoniz'd, my pow'rs, my reason fled,
By barb'rous hands you saw me captive led;
By horrid chains you saw me rudely bound,
While savage monsters taunted all around.—
Monsters, I say, (though born of savage race)
Yet, by your precepts taught, of heaven and grace,
My rising soul detests this hideous crew,
And yet for these refinements³ curses you.
When call'd to life by some barbarian's stroke,
From the kind trance⁴ to misery I 'woke,   30
On thee I call'd, to loose⁵ me from my chain,
To soothe my anguish, and to share my pain:

1. *feel* The 1792 text reads "fell."   2. *ingrate* Ungrateful one.

   3. *refinements* "Improvement or advance towards something more . . . perfect" (*OED*)—
said, of course, ironically here.

   4. *the kind trance* Sleep.   5. *loose* The 1792 text reads "lose."

In vain I call'd—far, far was Inkle fled,
And thus (dread news) my horrid keepers said:—
"The man you call, in yonder vessel flies,
Whose top now seems to touch the distant skies;
In vain, fond fool, you threaten, and you rave,
We paid the purchase, and he sold you, slave."
"Unfeeling man," (with bursting heart I cry'd)
"Unfeeling man," the sounding beach reply'd.   40
Ah! was it thus, unkind, I dealt by you,
When from the shipwreck, to our shades you flew?
When in the wood I saw you breathless lay,
Did Yarico thus treacherously betray?
For baneful plants,[6] or still more baneful gold,
Was false, unkind, ungrateful Inkle sold?
Ah no!—far different passions touch'd my breast,
Love, pity, joy, my actions all confest.—
Amaz'd I saw the whiteness of your skin,
Your eyes of azure, and your lips so thin,   50
Your various coverings, and your breast so fair,
Your cheeks of crimson, and your auburn hair,
Pleas'd I beheld, and pleas'd you saw me smile,
I smil'd, and yet I felt for you the while,
Lest to the place, where tir'd and faint you lay,
In search of fruits, my countrymen should stray;
For had my Indian lovers[7] found you there,
The crew's sad fate had you been forced to share:
Your fears to quiet, and your life to save,
I softly led you to my secret cave;   60
The choicest fruits I cull'd thee, and to drink
I led thee to the crystal fountain's brink;
All the gay spoils my lovers gave to me,
I brought to deck thy cave, or share with thee.
Oft when the sun had hid his sultry rays,
Or the pale moon her silver lamp displays,

6. *baneful plants* Presumably tobacco. On the relation of the tobacco trade to slavery in America, see Kulikoff, *Tobacco and Slaves.*
    7. *lovers* Wooers.

To some lone glade, or unfrequented grove,
(Where the fierce Indian never learnt to rove)
Thro' pathless vallies, and thro' forests rude,
To some delightful, secret solitude,   70
I gently led you, and upon my breast
Pleas'd have beheld you sink to balmy rest,
While falls of water lent their soothing sound,
And night-birds sang from all the shades around;
Thus liv'd I—lov'd I—thus I watch'd for you;
To perjur'd[8] Inkle faithful, fond, and true.
Thus did I guard you, while secure you staid,
The captive only of a faithful maid.—
While you with golden fables, charm'd my ear,
Of happier climes, and vow'd to be sincere: 80
Can you forget, how oft you told the tale,
By the clear stream that murmur'd thro' the vale,
How on the poor, believing maid you hung,
While soft persuasion dwelt upon your tongue;
Would I, you cry'd, but leave those lone retreats,
And fly with you to happier, fairer seats,
What joys, what blessings, should attend my days,
Where pleasure spread her stores a thousand ways;
In your fair country, what fine things were seen,
Suns ever temperate, meads for ever green,   90
Such spacious houses, such delightful shows,[9]
Such arts, such manners, and such splendid clothes,
All these, you said, shou'd Yarico enjoy,
Without the fears of Indians to alloy.—[10]
Then wou'd you sing my praises in the grove,
Tell how you lov'd, and would forever love.
But ah! when once I left my native shore,
(Those peaceful shades I must behold no more)
And, lost in love, believ'd you must be true,
And left our isle[11] without one friend but you;   100

8. *perjur'd* "Characterized by perjury; perjurious" (*OED*).
9. *shows* Displays, entertainments.   10. *alloy* impair or debase.
11. *our isle* The author seems to view Yarico as a native of one of the Caribbean islands rather than of the American mainland.

How chang'd the man! no more you talk'd of truth,
Nor vow'd, nor lov'd;—oh, false, inconstant, youth!
No more in raptures clasp'd me in your arms,
But scorn'd my kindness, and despised my charms;
No tears could melt you, and no words could move,
(Rebel to truth, to nature, and to love,)
But hard, unfeeling, as the ore you gain'd,
You saw me weeping, trembling, captive chain'd,
While each gay vision, which you taught to rise,
Each dear delusion, vanish'd from my eyes: 110
Joy from this breast for ever forc'd to part,
And ev'ry hope was banished from my heart.
This was my lot,—still is, while now I write,
Toils fill the day, and misery the night;
Each night renews my mournful task to weep,
And long my sorrows banish'd gentle sleep.
And oh! thus wretched, friendless, and forlorn,
The pangs of childbirth, helpless have I borne;
But to the babe, (I thank indulgent heaven)
A happier fate, than Yarico's was given;   120
Clos'd are its eyes in everlasting sleep—
It never knew to sigh, nor liv'd to weep;
In peace it rests, beneath the grass green sod,[12]
And its pure spirit, flies to meet its God.
Thrice happy lot! oh, had propitious heav'n,
A fate like this to me as timely given;
Ere I saw you, had laid me in the grave,
A harmless virgin, not a wretched slave!
—A wretched slave, for ever must I be,
And will no pitying mortal set me free?   130
Will no kind hand the least assistance give,
But e'en in age must I a captive live?
Yet, yet, I hope—nor let that hope be vain,
That Inkle may commiserate my pain;—

12. *grass green sod* Poetic; cf. William Shenstone, "Elegy XXII," lines 11–12, in *The Works in Prose and Verse,* 2 vols. (Edinburgh, 1765)1:73: "she that, in the morning of her day, / Intomb'd beneath the grass-green sod was laid."

Yet, yet, I hope, that bosom may relent,
And for the slave a ransom may be sent;
The generous boon for once in pity send,
I ask not of the lover, but the friend.
Then thankful will I seek my native shore,
Nor shall you hear of my sad story more;   140
But in those distant shades, (can you forget)
Those peaceful shades, where first we met;
With grateful heart I'll beg of heaven to shed
Its choicest blessings on my Inkle's head.
Oh! grant but this! 'tis all a captive prays,
And peace attend and plenty crown your days.

17

Rufus Dawes, "Yarico's Lament"

From Rufus Dawes, *Geraldine, Athenia of Damascus,
and Miscellaneous Poems* (New York, 1839).

The work of the Boston-born poet Rufus Dawes (1803–59) has long been neglected. "Yarico's Lament" made its first appearance in his *The Valley of the Nashaway, and Other Poems* (Boston, 1830) and was collected into *Geraldine, Athenia of Damascus, and Miscellaneous Poems* (New York, 1839), from which it is reprinted here. As with other short lyric poems on the theme (e.g., selections 11A and 11B), the narrative has undergone considerable elision. However, Dawes shares with "Amicus" [16] the assumption that Yarico is a native not of the American mainland but of her "father's isle" (9), upon which Inkle had been wrecked. As with several other versions of the tale, he also imagines that Yarico nurtures a baby boy, the product and only remaining joy of her union with Inkle. Lacking any direct reference to her bondage, the poem concentrates on Yarico's abandonment by her "Christian" lover and the contrast between her breaking heart and his callous indifference.

Thy bark is on the midnight wave,
   Thy thoughts are far from love and me,
And hope has found a cheerless grave,
   Within a heart still true to thee.

Thy babe is on my aching breast,
   Where passion breathed a father's sigh,
When that cold cheek I fondly prest,
   And wet with tears I could not dry.

I found thee on my father's isle—
   My father!—nay fond memory, cease—   10
I would not think of one whose smile
   Can only light the wreck of peace!

I found thee friendless and alone,
   No hand to soothe thy bed of pain;
Oh, Inkle, did my bosom own
   No joy to see thee live again!

I led thee where the lemon grew,
   Where waterfalls and fountains played,
And where the kind banana threw
   Her arms to comfort thee with shade.   20

And thou didst swear to love me then,
   And teach me how the Christians pray;
And tears were on thine eyelids, when
   I gave my virgin heart away.

My heart! oh, do not break so soon,
   Throb yet awhile to cheer my boy;
Kind heaven, but grant the simple boon,
   Nor thus my life's poor hold destroy.

Forgive the wrong! his heart is mild,
   And did not mean to give me pain;   30
Blest image! come, my tearless child,
   And let me dream the past again!

CARIBBEAN VERSIONS

The popularity of Inkle and Yarico in England did not long outlast the abolition of the slave trade in the British Isles in 1807. However, the story was appropriated into the culture of the Caribbean, most particularly of course in Barbados, where Yarico had become enslaved. Nineteenth-century historians of the West Indies invariably tarry over her fate, some even pinpointing Yarico's pond on the Kendal plantation as the place where she had given birth to the child of her union. Today that pond is no longer in existence, though another nearby has been allowed to preserve the name. Barbadian versions of the tale surface frequently enough to suggest that it remained well known, even if its more common expression in the form of poetry has been frowned upon by some as being an elite importation rather than belonging to an indigenous *folk* culture (see headnote to selection 20). N. Darnell Davis's fine account, "The *Spectator*'s Essays relating to the West Indies," published in Demerara (British Guiana) in 1885, indicates that "the famous story . . . that . . . has moved many a heart to compassionate for the forlorn and cruel fate of *Yarico*" (3, 7) was probably appreciated more widely across the English-speaking Caribbean.

18

Matthew James Chapman,

Barbadoes (Extracts)

From Matthew James Chapman, *Barbadoes, and Other Poems* (London, 1833), 23–27, 28–31.[1]

The story of Inkle and Yarico takes up only a short section of M. J. Chapman's lengthy two-part poem *Barbadoes,* written in rhyming couplets. The opening part of the work is conceived as an elegiac record of the island's history, in which Chapman traces the extinction (among others) of the Carib:

> The nut-brown warrior long has left the scene,
> And dim the traces where his step has been;
> Hunted from every spot he called his own,
> The Charib perished, and his race is gone. (7)

The poet's inclusion here of the story of Yarico is primarily meant to exemplify the former cruelty of the slave trade. Though fully aware that the tale has been widely retold elsewhere, Chapman distinguishes his version by locating it specifically within a Barbadian context, claiming of the poem as a whole that "in all that relates to local objects, . . . the Author has scrupulously adhered to the literal truth" (vii). His stated preference is for the "inimitable simplicity" of Ligon over what he sees as "a great deal of embellishment, by Steele . . . in the Spectator" (96). His omission of Inkle's name may be read as implicit acknowledgment of Ligon as his primary source.

Though of Barbadian birth, Matthew James Chapman (1796–1865) was

1. Unlike the other selections, in which the line numbers are those of the original works, in this text I have begun the numbering with the extracted portion. Numbers cited in the headnote, however, are pages in Chapman's book.

raised in Britain, where he went to school in Macclesfield, Cheshire, before qualifying as a doctor at Edinburgh in 1820. Later he entered Trinity College, Cambridge, graduating in 1832 (M.A., 1835). Returning to the West Indies, he lived for some time in British Guiana but eventually settled in London, where he is said to have practiced medicine with distinction. The significance of the particular year in which *Barbadoes* was published should be apparent when we recognize that it was in 1833 that Parliament extended the Emancipation Act to include all the British colonies. Chapman's poem is a rearguard attempt to preserve the status quo. While decrying what he views as ancient iniquities, the poet argues that the humanely managed West Indian slaves of his own era would be far more likely to remain contented under the existing paternalistic system than if granted instant freedom. In his preface he writes that it "is not unbecoming the patriot or the poet" to protest against the impending legislation, describing his intention as "to stop the current of frantic innovation, that threatens with almost instant ruin both colonies and empire" (vii–viii). His poem, as Paula Burnett comments, paints "a descriptive picture of his society on the old pastoral model, giving a landscape in which the happy negroes are picturesque additions to the sylvan scene; watched over by a paternalistic planter" (*Penguin Book of Caribbean Verse in English,* xlviii). If misguided in its conservatism, the poem reflects contemporary fears shared by many slaveholders (and even some slaves) in the colonies. No less than earlier versions, this first recorded Barbadian rendition of Inkle and Yarico reveals itself to be inextricably linked with white European attitudes toward the larger question of slavery. On Chapman, see also Fraser, Carrington, Forde, and Gilmore, *A–Z of Barbadian Heritage,* 36; J. A. Venn, *Alumni Cantabrigiensis,* part 2 (London, 1944), 2:13.

Near yonder copse, in olden days, a wood,
In its embrowned primeval horror, stood;
Within it was a sheltered, heaven-fed pool,
Untroubled, limpid, shade-embowered, and cool.
There came the hapless gentle Yarico,
In nature's travail, vexed with many a wo—[2]

2. *wo* Woe.

Thither she fled from man's unpitying gaze,
And bore the pang of her accomplished days.
Alone, unaided, in the friendly wild,
The new-made mother on her infant smiled;   10
And while she gently clasped him to her breast,
Thus to his listless ear her hopes addressed:
"Fed from my breast, my hope, my only joy!
Thou wilt not trample me, desert, destroy.
Thy faithless father brought me o'er the wave,
And sold his fond preserver as a slave;
But thou, my boy! art all the world to me—
Parents and brethren, home and liberty.
Yes! thou shalt bid thy mother not to mourn,   20
Kiss off my tears, and all my love return;
While I to thee the fondest care will give—
Content for thee to suffer and to live."

    In a deep bay of the Colombian shore,
Where mighty streams their torrent waters pour,
Where yet the fire-tube's volley[3] was unfelt,
An Indian tribe in fearless freedom dwelt.
Their well-spun hammocks[4] from the trees they slung,
While overhead innumerous songsters sung:
They feared not danger, and they knew not care—   30
Alas! the dark-souled pale-face found them there!
On the dark wave a gallant ship was seen—
Its band of robbers sought their home of green.
Not all escaped the suffering Indian's wrath;
Some fell beleagured in the tangled path;
Some bit the dust, and others fled away,
But one was left to curse his natal day.[5]

    Threatened with famine, or the vengeful foe,
The lingering torture, or the sudden blow—   40
Starting at every sound and passing shade,
Him, coward hind![6] surprised an Indian maid—

3. *fire-tube's volley* Gunshots.   4. *hammocks* See selection 1, note 12.
5. *his natal day* The day he [Inkle] was born.
6. *coward hind* Cowardly boor.

A bright-limbed Hebe[7] of the ancient wood,
A shape to love in holy solitude;
Whose eyes, quick-rolling, seemed to dance in dew;
Whose laugh was music, and whose footstep flew:
A brighter Venus of a darker hue
Than sculptor e'er designed, or painter drew.
Her rounded arms—her bosom's graceful swell—
Her twinkling ankles, with their wreaths of shell—   50
Her limbs' proportion, and their wavy line,
Instinct[8] with beauty, breathing and divine—
Her glorious form, complete in every part,
Shewed nature's triumph over colder art.

   The gentle creature to the white man came;
She saw and loved him, and she felt no shame.
She loved the stranger, cherished him and saved—
For him her father's dreaded frown she braved;
For him she left her careful mother's side;
For him the dangers of the deep she tried.   60
She knew not what his moving lips might say—
His earnest gesture beckoned her away:
She read his love-suit in his pleading eye;
Her bosom heaved in answer to his sigh—
She shrunk not from his arms, his bosom, side—
The Indian Dryad[9] was the white man's bride.
Him whom she fed by day and watched by night,
Could she refuse, fond girl! to share his flight?
'Tis true she would not hear her sister's voice,
Whose soft low accents made her soul rejoice;   70
Her infant brother needs must miss her arm;
Her father's hut would lose its dearest charm:
But she had found a treasure in the wood—
Her own white man was gentle, kind, and good.
Though, as they left the shore, her eyes were dim,
How could she fear to trust herself to him?

7. *Hebe* Classical goddess of youth.   8. *Instinct* Imbued.
9. *Dryad* Wood nymph.

To leave her kindred grieved her gentle heart,
But from her lover it were death to part—
He was her all, and in his loving days,
The child of nature imaged thus his praise: 80
"All persons, things, that ever pleasured me,
All met in one, methinks I find in thee—
The swift canoe in which I urged my way;
The bird that waked me up to joy and day;
The tree that gave me shelter in the night;
My mother's smile, so pleasant to my sight;
The dance by moonlight, when the day was done;
After long rains, the bright and gladsome sun."

   To this fair island[10] came they: then she found
The white man's honour was an empty sound;   90
The white man's plighted faith a scornful lie,
His love a dream, his oath a perjury.
For him the Indian would have gladly died,
And to the wingéd death opposed her side—[11]
Deceit, and broken vows, and chains repaid
The fond devotion of the Indian maid—
He left her there to sicken or to die;
And for her love she lost her liberty.[12]

   Accursed slavery! dire thirst of gold,
That makes the tender heart obdure[13] and cold;   100
At whose chill touch ethereal Mercy flies,
And shrieks, and groans, and curses fret the skies:
At whose fierce bidding comes the armed band,
And tears the peasant from his native land;
Steals on the village in the hour of sleep,
And leaves the absent—to return and weep.
Curst avarice! that makes and mocks distress;

10. *this fair island* Barbados, the subject of Chapman's poem.
11. *the wingéd death . . . her side* Used her body to shield him from Indian arrows.
12. *And for . . . her liberty.* The line echoes Ligon [1], 74: "And so poor *Yarico* for her love, lost her liberty."
13. *obdure* Obdurate.

For gold puts out the light of happiness;
That forges tortures for its human kind,
Chains for the body, fetters for the mind. . . .   110

[Chapman links Inkle and Yarico to broader questions of slavery, main-
taining that the poor in England ("nerveless children, wo-begone, and pale,
/ Whose limbs seem wire-hung, and whose sinews fail") are worse off than
"the happier negro" slave in the Caribbean. The section continues here by
considering the history of plantation labor in Barbados.]

The English serf,[14] allured by hope of gain,
Here toiled and found his golden hopes were vain;
Then, dying, homeward turned his failing eye,
And murmured "England!" with his latest[15] sigh.
Unused to slavery, and unapt for toil,
The Indian savage tilled the virgin soil;
But in his fetters still for freedom sighed,
And lived unwilling, and rejoicing died.[16]
Long since the Indian slave and English serf
Slept their last sleep beneath the verdant turf;   120
Then Libya's[17] sons supplied their vacant place,
Bound by the curse entailed upon their race.[18]

    From Congo's swamps, and wide-extended plains—
From Coromantee,[19] where the demon reigns,
Who speaks in thunder and who shakes the sky,

14. *The English serf* Chapman is referring here to the seventeenth-century practice of
employing white indentured servants, a system that was eventually superseded in Barbados
and elsewhere by the enslavement of blacks. See Ligon [1].
    15. *latest* Last, dying.   16. *rejoicing died* Rejoiced to die.
    17. *Libya's* Africa's.
    18. *the curse . . . their race.* In Gen. 9:21–27, Noah cursed his youngest son, Ham, who
had seen him drunk and naked. In occidental cultures, blacks were commonly believed to be
the descendants of Ham. According to John Brown of Haddington, *Dictionary of the Holy
Bible,* 330, Ham "mocked at his father's shame, and had his posterity cursed on that account.
. . . His posterity peopled Africa, and part of the west of Asia. They have been generally most
wicked and miserable, and few of them have hitherto enjoyed the light of the gospel." The
belief was uncritically employed as a justification for the enslavement of blacks.
    19. *Coromantee* Possibly Coromane, in present-day Mozambique.

And scares the nations with his evil eye—
From Whiddaw,[20] and Angola, and the coast
Whose streams and barren sands the gold-dust boast—
From Ebo, and Mondingo, and the plain
Of Minnah,[21] came the captived negro-train: 130
They changed their country, but their life the same—
In wide-spread Libya freedom is a name.

   Yet mourned they long their own dear village-tree,
Their loved and pleasant home of infancy;
The orphaned cradle, and the widowed bed;
The sacred ground that kept their happy dead:
And oft, their exile and their grief to end,
They, wilful, sought in death a guide and friend;
Through the free ether to o'erleap the main,
And see their rice-fields and their loved again.[22]   140

   But, now the race has vanished from the land,
Whose hopes lie buried in far Guinea's sand;
Now that a brighter faith[23] their children warms,
And hope delights them in a thousand forms;
Now that brute force and cruelty are gone,
Their hearths are sacred and their store their own;
Now that the brand, the torture, and the chain,
The sharp wild shriek of agonizing pain,
The sobbing accents that in vain implore,
And slavery's blotch, are seen and heard no more—   150
Change but the name—hunt freedom o'er the waves,
Search through the earth for happier than the slaves;—
Vain is the search! and when their minds shall be
Free as their persons, will the slaves be free?

   20. *Whiddaw* Probably the port of Ouidah (Wida) on the Gulf of Guinea, in present-day Benin.

   21. *Ebo . . . Minnah* Chapman appears to be referring to the Ibo people (of present-day Nigeria), the Mandingo region (present-day Guinea and Mali), and Minna (Nigeria).

   22. *They, wilful . . . loved again.* Chapman's sense is that by taking their own lives, transported Africans believed they would be returned to their native lands. See Ligon [1], 69.

   23. *a brighter faith* Christianity.

Pause, painted Britons! ere ye take away,
By rash injustice, freedom's future day.
Ye, after fifteen ages—scarcely then—
Began to walk in open day as men;
Forgot your manacles, and girths, and bands,
And then forged fetters for earth's new-found lands.   160

Pause, free-born English! by gradations slow,
Freedom, like nations, must have time to grow.
The cry of Africa has reached the skies;
A load of guilt on England's bosom lies.
Think not decrees the damned dye will drench,[24]
Think not to move the load by sudden wrench;
Shut not the door upon the feeble child;
Thrust not the helpless on the howling wild.
O, let not loose rebellion's fiery rage!
Spare woman's sanctity; spare feeble age!   170
Break not in battle-broils the sacred rood![25]
Quench not the light of holy faith in blood!
The parent bird long tends upon her young,
Till all their plumes are grown, their pinions strung;
In their first flight she hovers ever nigh,
Cheers their faint hearts, instructs them how to fly;
Till fully fledged, they need no more her care,
But spread their wings—free denizens of air.
So let your slaves, step after step, grow free,
That they mature may keep their liberty;   180
Lest heavier fetters and a darker fate
The dear-bought children of your guilt await.

24. *Think not . . . drench* Do not suppose that legislation will cleanse the stain.
25. *rood* Cross.

19

"A Barbadian," *Inkle and Yarico, a*
Legend of Barbados (Extract)

Reproduced, by kind permission, from a copy
in the Library of the American Antiquarian Society,
Worcester, Massachusetts.

The text of this four-part narrative poem, randomly composed in a mixture of octosyllabic couplets and pentameters and totaling well over six
hundred lines, was published in Bridgetown, Barbados, about 1840–45 by
Israel Bowen at his bookshop in Broad Street. Little is known about Bowen
except that he was in trade during the 1840s, probably as a printer as well
as bookseller. The exact identity of the poet—"A Barbadian"—remains a
mystery, though it is likely that the writer, whether male or female, would
have claimed British nationality and extraction. Part 3 contains a short
eulogium of "old England's ensign": "Wave on proud flag, may you for ever
be / The tyrants dread, the hope of liberty" (389–90). The rousing tones are
set against the poet's expressed distaste at the iniquity of Inkle's deed of selling Yarico into slavery. Within the narrative, it is never less than implicit
that Inkle's cruel action should be viewed as "un-English" as well as morally
wrong.

Key elements of the familiar story are elided or altered in the poem, suggesting that this rendering owes as much to oral sources as to written versions. The idyll of the cave, so prominent in Steele and others, is omitted
altogether, and rather than being directly described, the transaction of selling Yarico into slavery is only alluded to after the event. This *Legend of Barbados* endeavors to make up in local color what it annuls of the traditional
narrative. Instead of Inkle's party of adventurers being slain by the natives,
he is attacked by a fearsome panther that is shot dead by one of Yarico's
darts. Perhaps the purpose here is to assuage local sensitivities, since the

poet moralizes upon the commonality of mankind. So soon after the abolition of the slave trade from the British Empire, it would have severely undercut the poem's well-meaning didacticism to have depicted native peoples of whatever background as predatory or cannibalistic. The semi-Christian closure, in which the writer imagines the lovers united in forgiveness in a world to come, unconsciously echoes a similar mawkishness at the end of Anna Maria Porter's heroic epistle [15].

The text given here incorporates the whole of part 2 of the poem.

[The scene of part 1 of the poem is "Kendal Plantation" in Barbados, where, sitting by Yarico's pond, the poet contemplates "the primeval forest" (9) that covered the island before it was settled. He imagines Yarico issuing "from the wood, / A dark skinn'd girl . . . / Faultless alike in form and face, / A bright limb'd Venus of some Indian race" (121–24). The questions, "Why left she, her native strand? / Why now a slave in foreign land?" (172–73), lead us to the extracted passage and a different setting.]

Part II

Scene—Coast of Venezuela.[1]

Forced by the winds and adverse tides,
A lofty ship at anchor rides;
Her sickly crew long tempest tost,
With transport view the unknown coast.
The boat is launch'd, they ply the oar,
And soon is gain'd the wooded shore.
The keel grates on the milk white sand,   180
The boisterous crew now leap on land;
They laugh, they run upon the strand,
As only those can understand,
Whose sicken'd soul and wearied eye
Have gaz'd for weeks on sea and sky.
From their ocean prison's narrow bound,
Released, they roam the country round.

1. *Venezuela* Strictly speaking, the locational name is anachronistic, since Venezuela became an independent republic only in 1829.

Some spread the seine² to catch the finney prey—³
Along the winding shore some take their way
With gun in hand, in search of sport and food;   190
Some ply the axe and fell the nodding wood:
With willing hand the empty casks they fill
With purest water from a neighbouring rill,
Which from the rugged hill side dash'd,
In sparkling cascades, whose water's flash'd
And roar'd, and madly tore their way
O'er rugged rocks, while glittering spray
In wreathing mist is tost on high,
And rainbow colours charm the eye,
As glancing through the sun-beams bright,   200
Iris⁴ bends his bow of light.
Fainting from the noontide heat,
Young Inkle seeks this cool retreat;
He sat him down beneath the shade,
A clump of graceful bamboos made;
Whose feathery foliage over head
Like a plumed canopy was spread—
Before him from the rocky steep
The rushing waters wildly leap:
While moistened by the falling spray,   210
The cliffs rich clothed in verdure lay.
The tangled woods on every side,
Unseen, a lurking foe might hide.
Charmed with the spot which to his eyes
Seem'd a fragment left of paradise:
His cunning hand the pencil plies—
The lovely scene is quickly traced,
The sketch-book in his hat replaced:

2. *seine* "A fishing net designed to hang vertically in the water, the ends being drawn together to inclose the fish" (*OED*).

3. *finney prey* Fish, a very common circumlocution in eighteenth-century English poetry, though archaic here.

4. *Iris* Classical messenger of the gods who was believed to use the rainbow as the path from the heavens to earth when appearing before mankind. Traditionally, Iris is represented as a female figure.

He turns to go. Dashed to the ground,
A living tomb had Inkle found   220
In a monstrous panther's maw,
Whose glaring eyes and open jaw
Too late the helpless victim saw.
One wild, one fearful scream he gave
In hopes his friends might hear, and save.
They heard, and ne'er will be forgot
The sight, as rushing to the spot
From whence had come the fearful sound:
Raising their comrade from the ground
As though a feather. One bound   230
The monster made: ha! he drops his prey—
Quick, quick, another moment: he may
Yet be saved; on, for God's sake on—
What is it now which breaks upon
Their wondering eyes? Raised upon his side,
From which now pours a bloody tide,
A panther of enormous size,
Roused by their cries, vain effort makes to rise,
Pierced by an arrow through the heart;
Death-struck he stands. The fatal dart   240
Is drinking his life's blood. Yet his eyes glare
With savage fury on his foes; who dare
Not venture near his gnashing jaws—
Though dying, still his claws
Might deal a grievous wound;
But now, he makes one furious bound—
It is the last. He falls upon the ground
In death's last agony;
The film grows thicker on the glazing eye,
One effort more he makes to rise: 250
In vain, staggering he falls and dies.
Around the dying brute, spell bound they stand,
And wonder whose the friendly hand
So well had aimed the fatal dart,
Yet quivering in the monster's heart.

And Inkle—where can Inkle be?
Look yonder! Inkle there they see
Unhurt, reclining 'neath the shade
By the golden cassia⁵ made,
Amidst whose branches over head   260
A petrea's⁶ lovely blossoms spread;
The beauteous flowers together blending,
In gold and purple wreaths descending
On every side, and from above:
'Twas a fairy bower formed for love.
A dusky form is o'er him bending
And every look and want attending;
'Tis the young warrior, from whose bow
The arrow sped, which laid the savage low;
With clear cool water from a calabash⁷   270
Moistens his lips, and gently tries to wash
With tender hand, the dust from his soil'd cheeks:
Such gentle care a tender heart bespeaks—
With joy young Inkle springs to meet
His friends, with open arms they greet
Him they deem'd lost; the extended hand
Is warmly grasp'd by the kind-hearted band
That round their rescued comrade, gathering stand.
Questions are asked, and answered o'er and o'er,
And now they turn to greet the warrior: 280
Some mighty chief no doubt, tho' few his years;
No! no! it cannot be! a woman's form appears—
And such a form! of such we may have dream'd
In our young love, when all things seem'd

5. *cassia* Ligon, *True and Exact History of the Island of Barbadoes,* 68–69, had described the *Cassia fistula* as "a tree that will grow the most, in the least time, of any that ever I knew. . . . The leaf of this tree is like that of an Ash, but much longer, and of a darker colour; the fruit, when 'tis ripe, just of the colour of a black pudding, and shap'd as like, but longer. . . . the pulp of it is purgative, and a great cooler of the reins."

6. *petrea* A tropical American climbing shrub or vine, also known as purple wreath and queen's wreath.

7. *calabash* The hollow shell of the fruit of the calabash tree was in common use as a drinking vessel in the West Indies.

So fairy like and bright, alas! but too ideal
To bear the world's hard ways, so rough, so coldly real—
And she was young and beautiful; o'er her head
Perhaps some fifteen summers may have shed
Their ripening heat. There was a winning grace
In the sweet smile that played upon her face,   290
Made the heart captive ere it was aware
Of its own danger. 'Twas a beauteous snare,
More potent than the Cestus[8] fabled power;
A priceless gift to beauty's matchless dower—
In her hand, emblem of peace and love
She held a green bough, such as the dove
Bore to the Ark in days of yore,[9]
In token they had reach'd a friendly shore.
And sure 'tis strange, after so many years
Have pass'd away, the emblem still appears.   300
Whatever changes have come o'er man's race,
Yet still one common origin we trace:
Symbol of peace; it marks a common lot,
That ne'er 'mid every change has been forgot;
The skin may vary in its hue; broad oceans sever
Man from his brother man. But for ever
The heart will speak one language—from above
'Twas given; all, all, can understand 'tis love.
What is that deep booming sound
Like thunder, which shook the very ground   310
On which they stood, and which rung
Through the rude rocks, whose echoing tongue
Roll'd back a stern defiance? Hark! every glen
Arousing from its sleep, hurls back again
The unwelcome sound that dares intrude
Upon their long unbroken solitude.
The distant hills take up the note.

8. *Cestus* The girdle or cestus worn by Venus was said to have the power of awakening
love.
9. *the dove . . . yore* As in Gen. 8:11.

Which, echoing from their sides, grows more
And more remote.
The savage panther howls in very fear.   320
Cowering with drooping tail, skulks to his lair.
The stag puts forth his utmost speed,
Madden'd by fear, nor seems to heed
The puma, he must jostle on his way.
The serpent leaves his fascinated prey,
Stealthily seeks some covert where he may
Find shelter, and securely rest—
O'er head the eagle screams, and sails towards her nest.
What has all this sudden fear inspired?
'Twas the first gun they heard—fired   330
From the tall ship, as the strangers knew,
A signal to recall her absent crew.
And what thought Yarico of the strange sound?
As if bewilder'd, starting from the ground
She gazes on the sky, but all is clear—
There is no sign of storm or thunder there.
Now kneels and clasps young Inkle's feet,
And gazes in his eyes, as if their souls could meet,
That earnest, searching look.—Oh! never
On earth unscath'd, can those hearts sever;   340
Their eyes spoke but the language of the heart,
Which said, whate'er betide no more we part—
Then starting to her feet, she grasps her bow,
And quite prepared, expects the unknown foe;
Calmly she takes her stand—her flashing eye
Says plainly, by thy side "I'll do or die."[10]
Then Inkle tries to make her understand—
Points to the dark ship, now takes her hand,
And leads her down to the bright rippling bay,
Beside whose snow white sand the pinnace lay.   350
Embark'd the crew now ply the labouring oar,
And Yarico for ever quits her native shore.

10. *do or die* Proverbial; see *ODEP,* 192.

[In part 3 Inkle sets off home from Barbados, after having sold Yarico into slavery. The poet traces his uneasy conscience and warns of his doom. During the voyage (part 4), Inkle sinks into a delirious fever, fantasizing in his final moments that Yarico has died in captivity and that her spirit has come to guide him to an afterlife, in which his sin against her will be forgiven and their hearts eternally reunited].

20

Anonymous, "The Lament of Yarico"

The memory of Inkle and Yarico flourished in Barbados long after it had waned in Europe and in the United States. The balladic version given here was taken from a collection made by E. G. Sinckler, a well-known local historian of the early years of the twentieth century. As a curiosity that might appeal to visitors to the island, it was reprinted by Flora Spencer in *Inside Barbados: Magazine of the Barbados Hotel Association,* no. 9 (April 1978): 8. The poem is anonymous and, according to an accompanying note, was "published in the *Advocate* about 1810." This dating should be treated with suspicion, since the *Barbadian Advocate,* still the main newspaper on the island, made its first appearance only many years later (1895).

The reprinting of the poem in the 1970s highlights a debate at the time among West Indian folklorists as to the status of a myth that some believed was indigenous but others considered largely extrinsic. In introducing the ballad, Flora Spencer described the story of Yarico as woven "into the tapestry of our Culture," and just such a view was maintained in Jerome S. Handler's confident claim that Yarico's "story of enslavement has become classic in Caribbean lore" ("Amerindians and Their Contribution," 192). Some collectors of folk songs were far less certain, however. They pointed out that surviving songs based on the tale existed only in literary English rather than in the vernacular strains of an oral language. What has been "fairly well bandied about as a Barbadian folk song," they argued, is really "not a slave song or a song of the free coloureds or 'poor whites.'" They ultimately dismissed the story of Yarico as not belonging to the folk heritage but as being "part of the tradition of the élite culture in Barbados" (Marshall, McGeary, and Thompson, *Folk Songs of Barbados,* xiv).

The latter perspective, it must be admitted, was partly informed by an understandable desire among native Barbadians to reclaim their own cultural inheritance after achieving independence from Britain in 1966. A more considered and mature interpretation that has developed in recent years has been to recognize that the richness of Caribbean culture lies in its hybrid qualities and in its complex interplay of literary and oral traditions. Historically, there is little doubt that Inkle and Yarico is a tale that primarily reflects European attitudes; but in its Caribbean context, there is no reason why it should be any less protean and adaptable to fresh impulses. The new attitude toward the tale is reflected by its successful reworking into fiction by the Guyanese novelist Beryl Gilroy (1996) and by the Caribbean re-orchestration of Colman's comic opera at the Holder House Festival in Barbados during the spring of 1997 (see headnote to selection 12).

Ah me! for I'm a wretched slave,
Far from my native shore,
And ne'er shall see my father brave,
Nor tender mother more!
I was their pet and only child,
Free as the humming-bird,
And both to me were ever mild,
I heard no angry word.

As happy as the woodland fawn,
No tear bedimm'd mine eyes.　　　　　10
I rose to greet the early dawn,
And see the sun arise,
With pearly dew I bathed my cheek,
And pluck'd the fairest flower,
Then rowed across the little creek,
To see my favourite bow'r.

'Twas there in hiding I espied
A pale and manly form:—
'Twas there I better then had died,
While yet my heart was warm;　　　　　20
'Tis now as cold as Winter's snow,

On Chimborazo's crest,[1]
And ne'er again will love bestow
The peace that fled my breast.

I see his form still in my mind,
As how I saw it then;
And thought the gods their wisdom join'd,
To make such perfect men.
To me he pleaded for his life,
Should not my people tell,   30
That one surviv'd the deadly strife,
In which his comrades fell.

I hid him in a sylvan cave,
And took him daintly[2] food,
He vowed to me his heart he gave,
And ever would be good.
I deem' him true as Heaven above,
Nor dreamt of future pain;
So home with all its changeless love,
I left to cross the main.   40

And now I suffer for my love,
As though it were a crime:
Adored he was as from above,
With love that was sublime,
For this he sold me as a slave,
To work another's will,—
Oh! that I'd found an early grave!
And yet I love him still.

They say the Indian's God is false,
The pale man's God is true;   50
But 'tis the pale man's God that's false,

---

1. *Chimborazo's crest* An inactive volcano, Chimborazo (20,577 feet) in the Ecuadorian Andes was long believed to be the highest peak on the South American continent. Alexander von Humboldt attempted an ascent in 1802. Chimborazo is also the name given to what was supposed to be the tallest point on the island of Barbados (1,105 feet), though Mount Hillaby reaches higher.

2. *daintly* Perhaps poetic but maybe no more than a misprint for "dainty."

The Indian's God that's true,
For on my own dear native strand
All men are free as air,
In this false-hearted Christian land
The slave must weep and fear.

I had a dream, a vision bright—
I toil'd no more with slaves;
And in a large canoe whose height
Rose far above the waves,   60
My faithless lover by me stood,
Repentant though insane:
And then the scene was in a wood,
And I was home again.

Thou Spirit Great, to whom I pray,
Release thine erring child;
Oh! burst the chains that hold their sway
Where love should be enshrin'd.
The Christian's Christ they say is just
And kind to every man;   70
Then why should slavery, crime, and lust,
Reign in a Christian land?³

Oh! give me back my southern home,
With all its wealth of love!
Among its woods I long to roam,
Where coos the turtle dove.
Oh! give me back my father dear,
My mother's tender heart,
Restore me to their loving care,
For there's no better part.   80

3. *Then why . . . Christian land?* Slavery was abolished in the British colonies only in 1833 (see headnote to selection 18).

APPENDIX A

Petronius, "The Ephesian Matron"

From *The Satyrical Works of Titus Petronius
Arbiter, in Prose and Verse* (London, 1708), 170–75.

Richard Steele [2] devised the tale of Inkle and Yarico as an anecdotal "coun-terpart" to the story of the matron or widow of Ephesus (see introduction, pp. 10–11). The latter, which was exceedingly well known throughout the eighteenth century, has its origin in the *Satyricon* of Petronius, a prose satir-ical fiction interspersed with short verse. In the *Satyricon,* the story is told by Eumolpus, a lecherous poet and raconteur. Its contemporary reputation as an urbane antifeminist libel is well illustrated by the reaction of Mary de la Rivière Manley, who comments: "Can any thing be more unnatural than a beautiful Lady . . . just expiring thro' Grief and Abstinence, tempted to dishonour herself . . . [with] a despicable common sentinel! . . . *Petronius's* Designs were doubtless to expose the Frailty of the Sex" (*Memoirs of Europe,* 272–73). Later, Sarah Fielding is no less severe when she represents the Eph-esian matron as "a known character . . . of inconstancy in women; . . . a pic-ture of the highest hypocrisy and affectation in her apparent affliction; and consequently . . . all the love she is described to have for her husband when living, was equally pretence and affectation" (*The Cry,* 2:103 [pt. 3, scene 7]). The lubricious reputation of the tale enhanced its popularity.

Gaius Petronius, at one time a proconsul, was a close companion of the dissolute emperor Nero, who appointed him director of the pleasures of the Roman court. He is supposed to have taken his own life about A.D. 66 after Nero turned against him. Though in a fragmentary state, Petronius's *Satyri-con* was frequently reprinted and many times translated. The edition from which the present version is taken was (according to its title page) "Made English by Mr. Wilson, Mr. Burnaby, Mr. Blount, Mr. Tho. Brown, Capt. Ayloff, and several others," appearing some three years before *The Specta-tor.* For discussions of the story of the Ephesian matron and its contemporary reputation, see Samuel B. Carleton, "Widow of Ephesus in Restoration England," 51–63, and Runte, "The Matron of Ephesus in Eighteenth-Century France," 361–75. William Arrowsmith's reading that "the symbolism of love-in-the-tomb [is] of life rising phoenix-like from its own ashes" offers a less cynical interpretation of the tale ("Luxury and Death in the *Satyricon*," 328). See also Doody, *True Story of the Novel,* 110–13.

Eumolpus, our advocate, and reconciler, to entertain the company, and keep up the mirth, began to be pleasant on the inconstancy of women: How forward they were to love, and how soon they forgot their sparks![1] And that no woman was chast, but her lust might be rais'd into fury: nor wou'd he bring instances from ancient tragedies, or personages notorious to antiquity, but was ready to entertain us,[2] if we wou'd please to hear, with a story within the circle of his own memory: Upon which, the whole company giving him attention, he began his story in this manner.

"There was at *Ephesus* a lady of so celebrated a reputation, that the women of the neighbouring nations came to pay their respects to her, as a person of an extraordinary virtue: This lady at the death of her husband, not content with tearing her hair, or beating her breast, those common expressions of grief, follow'd him into the vault, where the dead body was plac'd in a monument, and, after the *Grecian* custom, watch'd the corps,[3] and whole nights and days continu'd weeping; the perswasions of parents and relations cou'd neither divert her grief, or make her take any thing to preserve life: The magistrates of the town endeavour'd to perswade her from so severe a mortification; but were oblig'd to retire, having met with no success in their attempt: and thus lamented by all for so singular an example of grief, she liv'd five days without eating.

All left her but a faithful maid,[4] whose tears flow'd as fast as her afflicted lady's, and who when the lamp they had by them began to expire, renew'd

1. *sparks* Lovers, suitors.

2. *nor wou'd he . . . entertain us* Unlike Eumolpus, Steele's commonplace talker lards his argument with "quotations out of plays and songs, which allude to the perjuries of the fair, and the general levity of women" when retelling the tale of the Ephesian matron in *The Spectator* [2].

3. *corps* Corpse.

4. *faithful maid* Seventeenth- and eighteenth-century popular recitations of the tale commonly omit all reference to the maid and to the role assigned to her in the *Satyricon*.

the light; by this time she became the talk of the whole town, and all de-grees of men confest, she was the only true example of love and chastity.

In the mean time there happening a trial of criminals, the condemn'd were order'd to be crucify'd near the vault in which the lady was weeping o'er the corps of her late husband. The soldier that guarded the bodies lest any might be taken from the cross and buried, upon his watch observ'd a light in the vault, and hearing the groans of some afflicted person, prest with a curiosity common to mankind, he desir'd to know who or what it was; Upon which he enter'd the vault, and seeing a very beautiful woman, amaz'd at first, he fancy'd 'twas a spirit, but viewing the dead body, and con-sidering her tears and torn face, he soon guess'd, as the truth was, that the lady cou'd but ill support the loss of her husband: He brings his supper with him into the vault, and began to perswade the mournful lady not to continue her unnecessary grief, nor with vain complaints consume her health: That death was common to all men; and many other things he told her, which use[5] to restore afflicted persons to that calmness they before en-joy'd: But the lady startled at the consolation a stranger offer'd, redoubled her grief and tearing her hair, cast it on the body that lay before her.

The soldier however did not withdraw but with the like invitations offer'd her somewhat to eat, till her maid o'ercome, I presume, by the pleas-ing scent of the wine, no longer cou'd resist the soldier's courtesie. When refresh'd with the entertainment, she began to join her perswasions to win her lady; 'And what advantage,' began she, 'wou'd you reap in starving your self, in burying your self alive? What wou'd it signifie to anticipate your fate?

D'ye think departed souls regard our care?

Will you, Madam, in spight of fate, revive your husband? Or will you shake off these vain complaints, the marks of your sex's weakness, and en-joy the world while you may? The very body, that lies there might advise you to make the best of your life.'

We obey without reluctance when commanded to eat or live.

The lady now dry with so long fasting, suffer'd her self to be o'ercome; nor was she less pleas'd with her entertainment, than her maid that surren-der'd.

You know with what thoughts encouraging meats inspire young persons.

5. *use* Are used.

With the same charms our soldier had won her to be in love with life, he addrest himself to her as a lover; nor did his person appear less agreeable to the chaste lady, than his conversation; and the maid, to raise her opinion of him, thus exprest her self.

And arm'd with pleasing love, dare you ingage,
E're you consider in whose tents you are?

To make short; nor even in this cou'd the lady deny him any thing. Thus our victorious soldier succeeded in both, she receiv'd his embraces: Not only that night they struck up the bargain, but the next and the next night after: Having shut the door of the vault, that if any of her acquaintance or strangers had come out of curiosity to see her, they might have believ'd the most chaste of all women had expir'd on the body of her husband. Our soldier was so taken with his beautiful mistriss, and the privacy of enjoying her, that the little money he was master of, he laid out for her entertainment, and, as soon as 'twas night, convey'd it into the vault.

In the mean time the relations of one of the malefactors, finding the body unguarded, took it from the cross and buried it. The soldier thus robb'd while he was in the vault, the next day, when he perceiv'd one of the bodies gone, dreading the usual punishment, he told the lady what had happen'd; and added, That with his sword he would prevent the judge's sentence, in case she would be so kind to give him burial, and make that place at once the fatal monument of a lover and a husband.

The lady not less merciful than chast, protested, That the gods would never permit her, at one time, to feel the loss of the only two she held most dear; 'I'd rather,' added she, 'hang up the dead body of the one, than be the wicked instrument of the other's death.' Upon which she order'd her husband's body to be taken out of the coffin and fixt to the cross, in the room of that which was wanting: Our soldier pursued the directions of the discreet lady, and the next day the people wonder'd how the dead body was a second time affix'd to the cross."

Jean Mocquet, *Travels and Voyages into Africa, Asia, America, the East and West-Indies* (Extract)

Translated by Nathaniel Pullen (London, 1696), 124–27.

Because of its striking correspondence, this anecdotal record translated from Jean Mocquet's *Voyages en Afrique, Asie, Indes Orientales et Occidentales* (Paris, 1617) has commanded some attention. It has urged several cultural historians to argue that consciousness of the outline story of Inkle and Yarico long predates Ligon and Steele. However, Nathaniel Pullen's English translation of Mocquet is of a much later date than the *History . . . of Barbadoes* [1], and it seems unlikely that Ligon himself would have had ready access to the story in its original French.

Sailing toward Brazil in 1604, Mocquet recounted meeting an English vessel that also put in to land to take on supplies of fresh water. The relationship between the anonymous pilot of the English ship and an Indian woman as imparted by Mocquet pitches together "civilization" and savagery, though the nightmarish barbarity of its ending seems to demand that such a liaison can only be viewed as fatally cursed. The hideous violence of the Indian woman in tearing in two the love child of her union with the pilot leads Wylie Sypher to contend that "Yarico was originally no noble savage, but an Indian girl of barbaric passion that [the eighteenth-century cult of] primitivism was to refine." Mocquet, concludes Sypher, "lays a treacherous foundation upon which to erect a legend of noble savagery" (*Guinea's Captive Kings*, 122–24).

More recently, in a fine critique, Peter Hulme warns against talking "unproblematically about Yarico making her first appearance in this passage," but he simultaneously agrees that there is an "undoubted relationship between Mocquet's story and Ligon's." The presence of the child is, for Hulme, "the living symbol . . . of a potential harmony between European and native American, so callously deserted by the English pilot and so savagely destroyed by the Amerindian woman in unconscious parody of the judgement of Solomon." Mocquet's terrifying anecdote of the severed child, he argues, "is too terrible and potent an image for the more refined sensibilities of the eighteenth century" (*Colonial Encounters,* 257–58).

Jean Mocquet (b. 1575) is described on the title page of the English translation of his *Travels and Voyages* as "Keeper of the *Cabinet of Rarities,* to the King of *France, in the Thuilleries.*" His work was also translated into Dutch (1656) and German (1688). It is highly unlikely that Ligon would have fashioned his narrative on a conscious awareness of Mocquet, but the earlier story, even if providing no more than a strange analogue, remains far too powerful to dismiss. See also Gilbert Chinard, *L'Amérique et le rêve exotique,* 25–27.

Strange History of an English Pilot

Our trumpeter shewed me their pilot, and told me, that he some years before being in an English vessel, as they were upon the coasts of the *West-Indies,* towards *St John de Love* (the first place of the *Indies* to go to *Mexico,* where the Spaniards are, then their sworn enemies) a great storm overtook them, which cast them upon the coast, where they were all lost, except this pilot, who saved himself by swiming to land, carrying with him a little sea-compass, and went thus wandring about to return by land to the *Newfound* countries: Upon that, he had found an Indian-woman, of whom he was enamoured, making her fine promises by signs, that he would marry her; which she believed, and conducted him through these desarts; where she shewed him the fruit and roots good to eat, and served him for an interpreter amongst the Indians, which he found, she telling them that it was her husband. After having been thus 2 or 3 years continually wandering about, and that for above 800 leagues, without any other comfort but this woman; At last they arrived at the *Newfoundland,* guiding himself by his compass: They had a child together; and found there an English ship a fishing: He was very glad to see himself escaped from so many dangers, and gave these English an account of all his adventures: They took him on board their vessel to make him good chear; but being ashamed to take along with him this Indian-woman thus naked, he left her on land, without regarding her any more:

Strange and Cruel Acts of an Indian Woman

But she seeing herself thus forsaken by him, whom she had so dearly loved, and for whose sake she had abandonned her country and friends, and had so well guided and accompanied him through such places, where he would, without her, have been dead a thousand times. After having made some lamentation, full of rage and anger, she took her child, and tearing it into two pieces, she cast the one half towards him into the sea, as if she would say, that belonged to him, and was his part of it; and the other she carried away with her, returning back to the mercy of fortune, and full of mourning and discontent.

The seamen who took this pilot into their boat, seeing this horrible and cruel spectacle, asked him, why he had left this woman; but he pretended she was a savage, and that he did not now heed her; which was an extream ingratitude and wickedness in him: Hearing this, I could not look upon him, but always with horrour and great detestation.

William Wordsworth, "The Mad Mother"

From William Wordsworth and Samuel Taylor Coleridge,
Lyrical Ballads (Bristol, 1798).

Wordsworth's short poem is far better known today than any one of the sundry poetic versions of Inkle and Yarico. Its inclusion here is controversial, since evidence that it takes its inspiration from the same source remains far from conclusive. The arguments in favor of (and against) considering it in this light are closely aired in the introduction, pp. 34–40. Within the poem, the nearest Wordsworth comes to acknowledging the mad mother's possible Indian origin is in lines 53 to 56. Unlike the many heroic epistles from Yarico to Inkle, the mother vents her emotions in direct address not to a lover who has abandoned her but to their newborn child, who is significantly a son. The babe seems to articulate its fragile existence through its suckling of the "tight and deadly band" (37) that is its mother's breast, a movement that is far more eloquent in its pathos than Inkle's textual silence in response to Yarico. A useful test for ascertaining whether the poem may be interpreted in the context of the tale is to read it as though it were from Yarico to Inkle junior, with the babe as the love child through whom the abandoned mother emotionally reiterates her traumatic idolization of the father. Even if the resemblances ultimately break down, the comparison helps to situate Inkle and Yarico as a tale that belongs to the age of sensibility but also possesses tangible links with the nascent Romantic era.

Her eyes are wild, her head is bare,
The sun has burnt her coal-black hair,
Her eye-brows have a rusty stain,

And she came far from over the main.
She has a baby on her arm,
Or else she were alone;
And underneath the hay-stack warm,
And on the green-wood stone,
She talked and sung the woods among;
And it was in the English tongue.   10

"Sweet babe! they say that I am mad,
But nay, my heart is far too glad;
And I am happy when I sing
Full many a sad and doleful thing:
Then, lovely babe, do not fear!
I pray thee have no fear of me,
But, safe as in a cradle, here,
My lovely baby! thou shalt be.
To thee I know too much I owe;
I cannot work thee any woe.   20

A fire was once within my brain;
And in my head a dull, dull pain;
And fiendish faces one, two, three,
Hung at my breasts, and pulled at me.
But then there came a sight of joy;
It came at once to do me good;
I waked, and saw my little boy,
My little boy of flesh and blood;
Oh joy for me that sight to see!
For he was here, and only he.   30

Suck, little babe, oh suck again!
It cools my blood; it cools my brain;
Thy lips I feel them, baby! they
Draw from my heart the pain away.
Oh! press me with thy little hand;
It loosens something at my chest;
About that tight and deadly band
I feel thy little fingers press'd.
The breeze I see is in the tree;
It comes to cool my babe and me.   40

Oh! love me, love me, little boy!
Thou art thy mother's only joy;
And do not dread the waves below,
When o'er the sea-rock's edge we go;
The high crag cannot work me harm,
Nor leaping torrents when they howl;
The babe I carry on my arm,
He saves for me my precious soul.
Then happy lie, for blest am I;
Without me my sweet babe would die.   50

Then do not fear, my boy! for thee
Bold as a lion I will be;
And I will always be thy guide,
Through hollow snows and rivers wide.
I'll build an Indian bower; I know
The leaves that make the softest bed;
And, if from me thou wilt not go,
But still be true 'till I am dead,
My pretty thing! then thou shalt sing
As merry as the birds in spring.   60

Thy father cares not for my breast,
'Tis thine, sweet baby, there to rest:
'Tis all thine own! and, if its hue
Be changed, that was so fair to view,
'Tis fair enough for thee, my dove!
My beauty, little child, is flown;
But thou wilt live with me in love,
And what if my poor cheek be brown?
'Tis well for me, thou canst not see
How pale and wan it else would be.   70

Dread not their taunts, my little life!
I am thy father's wedded wife;
And underneath the spreading tree
We two will live in honesty.
If his sweet boy he could forsake,
With me he never would have stay'd:

From him no harm my babe can take,
But he, poor man! is wretched made,
And every day we two will pray
For him that's gone and far away.   80

I'll teach my boy the sweetest things;
I'll teach him how the owlet sings.
My little babe! thy lips are still,
And thou hast almost sucked thy fill.
—Where art thou gone, my own dear child?
What wicked looks are those I see?
Alas! alas! that look so wild,
It never, never came from me:
If thou art mad, my pretty lad,
Then I must be for ever sad.   90

Oh! smile on me, my little lamb!
For I thy own dear mother am.
My love for thee has well been tried:
I've sought thy father far and wide.
I know the poisons of the shade,
I know the earth-nuts fit for food;
Then, pretty dear, be not afraid;
We'll find thy father in the wood.
Now laugh and be gay, to the woods away!
And there, my babe, we'll live for aye."   100

Chronology

The listing here is limited to main works in English, including translations from other languages. For French and German renditions of the tale, consult Price, *Inkle and Yarico Album*, 139–40. See also Levin, "Inkle and Yarico in Russia," 231–40. An asterisk in the present list indicates a work not recorded in Price's chronology.

1657 Richard Ligon, *A True and Exact History of the Island of Barbados* (London, 1657; reprinted 1673) [1].

1696 *Jean Mocquet, *Travels and Voyages into Africa, Asia, America, the East and West-Indies*, trans. Nathaniel Pullen (London, 1696) [appendix B].
[A memorable analogue that first made its appearance in Mocquet's *Voyages en Afrique, Asie, Indes Orientales et Occidentales* (Paris, 1617).]

1711 Richard Steele, *The Spectator*, no. 11 (13 March 1711) [2].
[The reprints of the volumes of *The Spectator* are too numerous to list. The work was readily available throughout the eighteenth century.]

1719 *Daniel Defoe, *The Life and Strange Surprizing Adventures of Robinson Crusoe, of York, Mariner* (London, 1719).
[According to Moore, "Robinson and Xury and Inkle and Yarico," 24–29, the story of Xury in Defoe's novel may be indebted to Inkle and Yarico.]

1725 Frances Seymour, Countess of Hertford, "The Story of Inkle and Yarico, Taken out of the Eleventh *Spectator*" and "An Epistle from Yarico to Inkle, after He Had Sold Her for a Slave," in *A New Miscellany: Being a Collection of Pieces of Poetry from Bath, Tunbridge, Oxford, Epsom, and Other Places, in the Year 1725* (London, [1726?]) [3A and 3B].
[The two poems were published on their own in 1738, the earliest versions known to Price.]

1727 *William Pattison, "Yarico to Inkle: An Epistle," in *The Poetical Works of Mr. William Pattison, Late of Sidney College Cambridge* (London, 1728), 53–54 [4].

1734 Anonymous, "The Story of Inkle and Yarico, from the Eleventh *Spectator*," *London Magazine* 3 (May 1734): 257–58 [5].

[Price notes that the poem was reprinted in the *Weekly Amusement,* 7 June 1766.]

1735–36 (?) *James Cawthorne, "Inkle and Yarico" (1735) and *The Perjur'd Lover, or Tragical Adventure of Alexis and Boroina; in Heroic Verse, from the Story of Inkle and Yarico* (Sheffield, 1736).
[No copy of either work has been traced; see introduction, note 53.]

1736 Anonymous, *Yarico to Inkle: An Epistle* (London, 1736) [6].
[T. J. Wise's attribution of this poem to Edward Moore is unsafe. Price traces ten later reprints and a complex textual history. There is also a short poem dedicated to the author in the *London Magazine* 5 (1736): 215.]

1736 *Stephen Duck, *Avaro and Amanda: A Poem in Four Canto's, Taken from "The Spectator," Vol. I, No. XI,* in *Poems on Several Occasions* (London, 1736), 85–128 [7].
[Despite the change of names, this is unquestionably an Inkle and Yarico poem.]

1740s John Winstanley, "Yarico's Epistle to Inkle: A Poem, Occasioned by Reading *Spectator,* Vol. I, No. 11," in *Poems Written Occasionally by the Late John Winstanley,* 2 vols. (Dublin, 1751), 2:8–16 [8].

1742 [Mrs. Weddell?], *Incle and Yarico, a Tragedy in Three Acts, as It Was Intended to Have Been Performed at the Theatre Royal in Covent Garden* (London, 1742).
[The play is distinguished only in being the first drama to be written on the theme of Inkle and Yarico. It was never performed. Price, 35–43, includes a synopsis.]

1750 *Robert Paltock, *The Life and Adventures of Peter Wilkins, a Cornish Man* (London, 1750).
[Recently Peter Merchant has argued persuasively that Paltock's exotic novel shows a strong literary indebtedness to Inkle and Yarico ("Robert Paltock and the Refashioning of 'Inkle and Yarico'").]

1766 Edward Jerningham, *Yarico to Inkle: An Epistle.* ("By the Author of the Elegy Written among the Ruins of an Abbey") (London, 1766) [10].
[The poem was frequently republished during its author's lifetime.]

1771 Christian Fürchtegott Gellert, *Inkle and Yariko: A Poetic Tale from the German of Mr. Gellert, Weekly Magazine, or Edinburgh Amusement* 14 (1771): 164–67.
[A prose translation of Gellert's poem, first published in his *Sämmtliche Fabeln und Erzählungen* (Leipzig, 1746).]

1771 Salomon Gessner, *Inkle and Yariko. . . . From the German of Mr. Gessner, Weekly Magazine, or Edinburgh Amusement* 14 (1771): 197–200.
[A superior translation appeared as "Continuation of the Story of Inkle and Yarico," in *The Works of Solomon Gessner, Translated from the German,* 2 vols. (Liverpool, 1802), 2:230–38. It is included here as selection 9.]

1782 Anonymous, "Epistle from Yarico to Inkle," *Lady's Magazine* 13 (1782): 664 [11A].

1787 George Colman the Younger, *Inkle and Yarico: An Opera, in Three Acts* (London, 1787) [12].
[Frequently reprinted and widely performed.]

1792 "A Poetical Version of the Much Admired Story of Inkle and Yarico," *American Museum, or Universal Magazine* (Philadelphia), 11 (1792), appendix "Poetry," 21–24.
[In this version the names of the protagonists have been altered "for poetical reasons" to Mercator and Barsina. The poem was reprinted as an additional piece in *The Secret History and Misfortunes of Fatyma* (Banbury, 1820).]

1792 "Amicus," "Yarico to Inkle," *American Museum, or Universal Magazine* (Philadelphia), 11 (1792), appendix "Poetry," 25–27 [16].

1793 [Peter Pindar], "Yarico to Inkle," *Scots Magazine* 55 (May 1793): 242 [11B].
[Also printed in *The Times*, 10 June 1793, and *Gentleman's Magazine* 63 (June 1793): 560.]

1797 Jean-François Arnould-Mussot, *The American Heroine: A Pantomime in Three Acts*, trans. Samuel Chandler (Philadelphia, 1797) [13].
[Translation of *L'héroïne américaine* (Paris, 1786). The outline of the story is indebted to its retelling by the Abbé Raynal in his frequently reprinted *Histoire philosophique et politique des établissements et du commerce des Européens dans les Deux Indes*, 6 vols. (Amsterdam, 1770).]

1798 *William Wordsworth, "The Mad Mother," in William Wordsworth and Samuel Taylor Coleridge, *Lyrical Ballads* (Bristol, 1798), 141–46 [appendix C].
[Later titled "Her Eyes Are Wild," after the poem's opening line. Possibly indebted to Inkle and Yarico, though more profitably approached as an instructive analogue than as a precise retelling.]

1799 Mr. C. Brown, *Inkle and Yarico: A Poem* (London: Printed for the Author and Sold by W. Glendinning, No. 9, Charles-Street, Hatton-Garden, 1799).
[Dedicated to "Her Grace the Duchess of Beaufort" and personally addressed "To Miranda." The copy of the poem in the Charles Deering McCormick Library of Special Collections at Northwestern University, Evanston, Illinois, has a manuscript inscription above its half-title page: "From the Author Chas. Br. with his Comp^ts." The poem continues to be incorrectly attributed to the American author Charles Brockden Brown.]

1802 *Charles James Fox, "Yarico to Inkle," in *The Metrical Miscellany: Consisting Chiefly of Poems Hitherto Unpublished*, ed. Maria Riddell (London, 1802), 206–9; (London, 1803), 202–5 [14].

1802 W. Smith, "Inkle to Yarico," *Lady's Magazine, or Entertaining Companion for the Fair Sex* 35 (1802): 215–16.

1802 John Webb, "Yarico to Inkle," *Lady's Magazine, or Entertaining Companion for the Fair Sex* 35 (1802): 436–37.

1802 W. Smith, "Inkle to Yarico. Epistle II," *Lady's Magazine, or Entertaining Companion for the Fair Sex* 35 (1802): 495–96.

1802 John Webb, "Yarico to Inkle. Epistle III" [*sic*], *Lady's Magazine, or Entertaining Companion for the Fair Sex* 35 (1802): 714–15.

[The preceding four items constitute an exchange of verse epistles between Inkle and Yarico conducted by two writers. W. Smith writes from "Tooley-street, Southwark," the first of his epistles dated "March 8, 1802," the second "Sept. 7 1802." John Webb's responses (representing Yarico) are from "Haverhill" (Suffolk) and are dated "June 3, 1802" and "November 5, 1802." Although the notion of a correspondence is intriguing, the poems themselves are slight.]

1805 *Sarah Scudgell Wilkinson, *Inkle and Yarico, or Love in a Cave: An Interesting Tale* (London, 1805).
   [A prose retelling of the tale that endeavors to combine Steele's and Colman's versions. Copy in Special Collections, University of Virginia Library, Charlottesville.]

1810 *Paul Methuen, *An Epistle from Yarico to Incle,* title poem in *An Epistle from Yarico to Incle, with Other Poems* (London, 1810).
   [A poem of 544 lines, based on the story from *The Spectator* but in which Yarico writes to Inkle from a dungeon. The poet utilizes his reading of travel works about the Americas, referring to these sources in a series of notes at the end of the poem.]

1811 *Anna Maria Porter, "Epistle from Yarico to Inkle," in *Ballad Romances and Other Poems* (London, 1811), 101–19 [15].

1830 Rufus Dawes, "Yarico's Lament," in *The Valley of the Nashaway* (Boston, 1830), 63–64. Reprinted in *Geraldine, Athenia of Damascus, and Miscellaneous Poems* (New York, 1839), 265–66 [17].

1833 *Matthew James Chapman, *Barbadoes,* in *Barbadoes, and Other Poems* (London, 1833) [18].
   [The story of Yarico is told on 23–26.]

1840s *"A Barbadian," *Inkle and Yarico, a Legend of Barbados.* (Sold by I. Bowen, Bookseller, Broad Street, Bridgetown, Barbados, about 1840–45) [19].

1860 *George Eliot, "Brother Jacob," *Cornhill Magazine,* July 1864.
   [See introduction, note 75.]

Undated (nineteenth or early twentieth century) *Anonymous, "The Lament of Yarico," from a collection made by E. G. Sinkler [20].

[A Barbadian version.]

1996 *Beryl Gilroy, *Inkle and Yarico* ("Being the narrative of Thomas Inkle concerning his shipwreck and long sojourn among the Caribs, his marriage to Yarico, a Carib woman and life on the island of Barbados") (Leeds, 1996).

[An evocative reworking of the tale.]

1999 *Yarico: "The Musical,"* composed by Paul Leigh and James McConel, Holder House Festival, Barbados, premiere 6 March 1999.

[Loosely indebted to Colman's comic opera and announced as "based on the true Barbadian legend of Inkle and Yarico," "a modern-day musical based on the original story."]

Bibliography

Primary Texts

Adolphus, John. *Memoirs of John Bannister, Comedian.* 2 vols. London, 1839.

Aesop. *See* L'Estrange, Roger.

Alexander, William, M.D. *The History of Women.* 2 vols. London, 1779.

Anketell, John. *Poems on Several Subjects.* Dublin, 1793.

Arnould-Mussot, Jean-François. *L'heroïne américaine: Pantomime en trois actes.* 1st and 2d eds. Originally performed at the Théâtre de l'Ambigu-Comique. Paris, 1786. Translated into English by Samuel Chandler as *The American Heroine: A Pantomime in Three Acts.* Philadelphia, 1797.

The British Theatre. Ed. Elizabeth Inchbald. 25 vols. London, 1806–9.

Brown, John, of Haddington. *A Dictionary of the Holy Bible.* New ed. London, 1813.

Burns, Robert. *The Poems and Songs of Robert Burns.* Ed. James Kinsley. 3 vols. Oxford, 1968.

———. *The Letters of Robert Burns.* 2d ed. Ed. G. Ross Roy. 2 vols. Oxford, 1985.

Chalmers, Alexander, ed. *The Works of the English Poets.* 21 vols. London, 1810.

Chamfort, Sébastian-Roch Nicolas. *La jeune Indienne.* Ed. Gilbert Chinard. Princeton, N.J., 1945.

Clarkson, Thomas. *A Summary View of the Slave Trade and of the Possible Consequences of Its Abolition.* London, 1787.

———. *The History of the Rise, Progress, and Accomplishment of the Abolition of the African Slave-Trade by the British Parliament.* 2 vols. London, 1808.

Colman, George, the Younger. *The Dramatic Works of George Colman the Younger.* Ed. J. W. Lake. 4 vols. Paris, 1827.

———. *Random Records.* 2 vols. London, 1830.

———. *Plays by George Colman the Younger and Thomas Morton.* Ed. Barry Sutcliffe. Cambridge, 1983.

Congreve, William. *The Complete Plays of William Congreve.* Ed. Herbert Davis. Chicago, 1967.

Dryden, John. *Secret Love, or The Maiden-Queen.* London, 1668. Reprinted in the California edition of *The Works of John Dryden,* vol. 9. Berkeley, Calif., 1966.

Duck, Stephen. *Poems on Several Occasions.* London, 1736.

Dürer, Albrecht [attrib.]. *A Book of Dravving, Limning, Washing or Colouring of Maps and Prints; and the Art of Painting.* London, 1652 (Wing J662).

Elwood, Anne Katharine. *Memoirs of the Literary Ladies of England.* 2 vols. London, 1843.

Fielding, Sarah. *The Cry: A New Dramatic Fable.* 3 vols. London, 1754.

Gilroy, Beryl. *Inkle and Yarico.* Leeds, 1996.

Hazlitt, William. *The Complete Works of William Hazlitt.* Ed. P. P. Howe. 21 vols. London, 1930–34.

Hoeufft, Jacobus Henricus. *Pericula Poëtica.* N.p., 1783.

Hurd, William. *A New Universal History of the Religious Rites, Ceremonies, and Customs of the Whole World.* London, [ca. 1780].

Jefferson, Thomas. *The Papers of Thomas Jefferson.* Ed. Julian P. Boyd. Vol. 15. Princeton, N.J., 1958.

Juvenal. *Satires, Book I.* Ed. Susanna Morton Braund. Cambridge, 1996.

Lamb, Charles. *The Life, Letters and Writings of Charles Lamb.* Ed. Percy Fitzgerald. 6 vols. London, n.d.

L'Estrange, Roger. *Fables from Aesop.* London, 1692 (Wing A706).

Ligon, Richard. *A True and Exact History of the Island of Barbadoes,* 2d ed. London, 1673.

Locke, John. *An Essay concerning Human Understanding.* Ed. Peter Nidditch. Oxford, 1979.

Manley, Mary de la Rivière. *Memoirs of Europe, towards the Close of the Eighth Century.* London, 1710.

Mocquet, Jean. *Travels and Voyages into Africa, Asia, America, the East and West-Indies. . . .* Trans. Nathaniel Pullen. London, 1696.

Montaigne, Michel de. "Of Cannibals." In *The Complete Essays,* trans. M. A. Screech. London, 1993.

Murphy, Arthur. *The Citizen.* In *The Modern British Drama,* vol. 5. London, 1811.

A New Miscellany: Being a Collection of Pieces of Poetry from Bath, Tunbridge, Oxford, Epsom, and Other Places, in the Year 1725. London, [1726?].

O'Keefe, John. *The World in a Village.* London, 1793.

Pattison, William. *The Poetical Works of Mr. William Pattison, Late of Sidney College Cambridge.* London, 1728.

Peake, Richard Brinsley. *Memoirs of the Colman Family.* 2 vols. London, 1841.

Petronius. *The Satyrical Works of Titus Petronius Arbiter, in Prose and Verse.* London, 1708.

Porter, Anna Maria. *Ballad Romances, and Other Poems.* London, 1811.

Raynal, Abbé. *Histoire philosophique et politique des établissements et du commerce des Européens dans les Deux Indes.* 6 vols. Amsterdam, 1770. English translation by J. Justamond, *A Philosophical and Political History. . . .* 3d ed., 5 vols. London, 1777.

[Riddell, Maria]. *The Metrical Miscellany: Consisting Chiefly of Poems Hitherto Unpublished.* London, 1802.

Sancho, Ignatius. *Letters of the Late Ignatius Sancho, an African.* 5th ed. 1803. Facsimile edition with an introduction by Paul Edwards, London, 1968.

The Spectator. Ed. Donald F. Bond. 5 vols. Oxford, 1965.

Walpole, Horace. *Horace Walpole's Correspondence.* Ed. Wilmarth Lewis. 48 vols. New Haven, Conn., 1937–83.

Wansey, Henry. *The Journal of an Excursion to the United States of North America, in the Summer of 1794.* Salisbury, 1796.

Wilkinson, Tate. *The Wandering Patentee.* 4 vols. York, 1795.

Winstanley, John. *Poems Written Occasionally by the Late John Winstanley.* 2 vols. Dublin, 1751.

Wollstonecraft, Mary. *The Female Reader, or Miscellaneous Pieces, in Prose and Verse; Selected from the Best Writers, and Disposed under Proper Heads; for the Improvement of Young Women* (1789). Reprinted in *The Works of Mary Wollstonecraft,* ed. Janet Todd and Marilyn Butler, vol. 4. London, 1989.

Wordsworth, William, and Samuel Taylor Coleridge. *Lyrical Ballads.* Ed. Michael Mason. London, 1992.

Wright, J., ed. *The Speeches of the Rt. Hon. C. J. Fox in the House of Commons.* 6 vols. London, 1815.

Secondary Texts

Aldridge, A. Owen. "Feijoo and the Problem of Ethiopian Color." *Studies in Eighteenth-Century Culture* 3 (1973): 263–77.

Allsopp, Richard. *Dictionary of Caribbean English Usage.* Oxford, 1995.

Alsop, James. "Richard Steele and Barbados: Further Evidence." *Eighteenth-Century Life* 6, pt. 1 (1981): 21–28.

Altick, Robert. *The Shows of London.* Cambridge, Mass., 1978.

Anstey, Roger. *The Atlantic Slave Trade and British Abolition, 1760–1810.* London, 1975.

Arens, W. *The Man-Eating Myth: Anthropology and Anthropophagy.* New York, 1979.

Arnaud, Claude. *Chamfort: A Biography.* Trans. Deke Dusinberre. Chicago, 1992.

Arrowsmith, William. "Luxury and Death in the *Satyricon.*" *Arion* 5, no. 3 (1966): 304–31.

Ashby, Clifford. "A Black Actor on the Eighteenth Century Boston Stage?" *Theatre Survey: The American Journal of Theatre History* 28, no. 2 (1987): 101–2.

Bagster-Collins, Jeremy F. *George Colman the Younger, 1762–1836.* New York, 1946.

Barker, Anthony J. *The African Link: British Attitudes to the Negro in the Era of the Atlantic Slave Trade, 1550–1805.* London, 1978.

Barker-Benfield, G. J. *The Culture of Sensibility: Sex and Society in Eighteenth-Century Britain.* Chicago, 1992.

Beckles, Hilary McD. *Black Rebellion in Barbados: The Struggle against Slavery, 1627–1838.* Bridgetown, Barbados, 1984.

———. *White Servitude and Black Slavery in Barbados, 1627–1715.* Knoxville Tenn., 1989.

————. *A History of Barbados: From Amerindian Settlement to Nation-State.* Cambridge, 1990.

Beer, Gillian. "'Our Unnatural No-Voice': The Heroic Epistle, Pope, and Women's Gothic." *Yearbook of English Studies* 12 (1982): 125–51.

Bettany, Lewis. *Edward Jerningham and His Friends.* London, 1919.

Beutler, Ernst. *Essays um Goethe.* Leipzig, [1941].

Bewell, Alan. *Wordsworth and the Enlightenment.* New Haven, Conn., 1989.

A Biographical Dictionary of Actors, Actresses, Musicians, Dancers, Managers and Other Stage Personnel in London, 1660–1800. Ed. Philip H. Highfill Jr., Kalman A. Burnim, and Edward Langhans. 16 vols. Carbondale, Ill., 1973–93.

Bishop, P. J. *A Short History of the Royal Humane Society.* London, 1974.

Bissell, Benjamin. *The American Indian in English Literature of the Eighteenth Century.* Yale Studies in English, vol. 68. New Haven, 1925.

Blanchard, Rae. "Richard Steele's West Indian Plantation." *Modern Philology* 39 (1942): 281–85.

Braude, Benjamin. "The Sons of Noah and the Construction of Ethnic and Geographical Identities in the Medieval and Early Modern Periods." *William and Mary Quarterly* 54 (1997): 103–42.

Brewer's Dictionary of Phrase and Fable. 5th ed. London, 1959.

Bridenbaugh, Carl, and Roberta Bridenbaugh. *No Peace beyond the Line: The English in the Caribbean, 1624–1690.* New York, 1972.

Brown, Paula, and Donald Tuzin, eds. *The Ethnography of Cannibalism.* Washington, D.C., 1983.

Burnett, Paula, ed. *Penguin Book of Caribbean Verse in English.* London, 1986.

Campbell, P. F. "Richard Ligon." *Journal of the Barbados Museum and Historical Society* 37, no. 3 (1985): 215–38.

Carleton, Samuel B. "The Widow of Ephesus in Restoration England." *Classical and Modern Literature* 9 (1988): 51–63.

The Catalogue of Printed Music in the British Library. 62 vols. London, 1981–87.

Chinard, Gilbert. *L'Amérique et le rêve exotique dans la littérature française au XVIIIe et au XVIIIe siècle.* Paris, 1913.

Cockrell, Dale. *Demons of Disorder: Early Blackface Minstrels and Their World.* Cambridge, 1997.

Conner, Patrick. *Michael Angelo Rooker, 1746–1801.* London, 1984.

Craton, Michael. *Testing the Chains: Resistance to Slavery in the British West Indies.* Ithaca, N.Y., 1982.

Cro, Stelio. *The Noble Savage: Allegory of Freedom.* Waterloo, Canada, 1990.

Dabydeen, David. *Hogarth's Blacks: Images of Blacks in Eighteenth Century Art.* Mundelstrup, Denmark, 1985.

Dale, Peter Allan. "George Eliot's 'Brother Jacob': Fables and the Physiology of Common Life." *Philological Quarterly* 64 (1985): 17–35.

Damon, S. Foster. "The Negro in Early American Songsters." *Papers of the Bibliographical Society of America* 28 (1934): 132–63.

Davies, K. G. *The Royal African Company.* London, 1957.

Davis, Darnell. "The *Spectator*'s Essays relating to the West Indies." *West Indian Quarterly* (Demerara) 1, pt. 3 (1885): 1–21.

Davis, David Brion. *The Problem of Slavery in Western Culture.* 1966. New York, 1988.

Davis, Jim. *John Liston, Comedian.* London, 1985.

Deane, Seamus, ed. *The Field Day Anthology of Irish Writing.* Vol. 1. Derry, 1991.

Dictionary of National Biography, ed. Leslie Stephen and Sidney Lee, 63 vols. London, 1885–1900.

Dircks, Phyllis T. "London's Stepchild Finds a Home." In *Musical Theatre in America: Papers and Proceedings of the Conference on the Musical Theatre in America*, ed. Glenn Loney, 23–35. Westport, Conn, 1984.

Dobell, Percy. *A Catalogue of Eighteenth Century Verse.* London, 1933.

Doody, Margaret Anne. *The True Story of the Novel.* London, 1996.

Douglas, Mary. *Risk and Blame: Essays in Cultural Theory.* London, 1992.

Dudley, Edward, and Maximilian E. Novak, eds. *The Wild Man Within.* Pittsburgh, 1972.

Dunn, Richard S. *Sugar and Slaves: The Rise of the Planter Class in the English West Indies, 1624–1713.* London, 1973.

Edwards, Diana. *Black Basalt.* London, 1994.

Eighteenth-Century Short-Title Catalogue. [On-line database, now part of the *English Short Title Catalogue.*]

Fagg, William, John Pemberton, and Bryce Holcombe. *Yoruba: Sculpture of West Africa.* London, 1982.

Fairchild, Hoxie Neale. *The Noble Savage: A Study in Romantic Naturalism.* New York, 1928.

Fanon, Frantz. *Black Skin, White Masks.* London, 1952. Trans. Charles Lam Markmann. London, 1986.

Fass, Barbara. *La Belle Dame sans Merci and the Aesthetics of Romanticism.* Detroit, 1974.

Felsenstein, Frank. *Anti-Semitic Stereotypes: A Paradigm of Otherness in English Popular Culture, 1660–1830.* Baltimore, 1995.

Ferguson, Moira. *Subject to Others: British Women Writers and Colonial Slavery, 1670–1834.* London, 1992.

———. *Colonialism and Gender Relations from Mary Wollstonecraft to Jamaica Kincaid* (New York, 1993).

Fischer-Lamberg, Hanna, ed. *Der junge Goethe.* 5 vols. Berlin, 1963–74.

Fiske, Roger. *English Theatre Music in the Eighteenth Century.* Oxford, 1973.

Foxon, D. F. *English Verse, 1701–1750.* 2 vols. Cambridge, 1975.

Francis, Basil. *Fanny Kelly of Drury Lane.* London, 1950.

Fraser, Henry, Sean Carrington, Addinton Forde, and John Gilmore. *A–Z of Barbadian Heritage.* Kingston, Jamaica, 1990.

George, M. Dorothy. *London Life in the Eighteenth Century.* London, 1930.

Gerzina, Gretchen. *Black England: Life before Emancipation.* London, 1995.

Gilberthorpe, Enid. *Books Printed by John Garnet, Sheffield's First Known Printer.* Sheffield City Libraries Local History Leaflets 13. Sheffield, 1969.

Glasby, William, ed. *The Sheffield Miscellany.* 6 pts. Sheffield, 1897.

Grant, Douglas. *The Fortunate Slave: An Illustration of African Slavery in the Early Eighteenth Century.* Oxford, 1968.

Greenblatt, Stephen. *Marvelous Possessions: The Wonder of the New World.* Oxford, 1991.

Greene, D. H. "The Shadow of the Glen and the Widow of Ephesus." *PMLA* 62 (1947): 233–38.

Hamilton, Joan. "Inkle and Yarico and the Discourse of Slavery." *Restoration and Eighteenth Century Theatre Research* 9, no. 1 (1994): 17–33.

Handler, Jerome S. "Amerindians and Their Contribution to Barbadian Life in the Seventeenth Century." *Journal of the Barbados Museum and Historical Society* 35, no. 3 (1977): 189–209.

Hazard, Paul. *European Thought in the Eighteenth Century.* 1946. London, 1973.

Hibberd, John. *Salomon Gessner: His Creative Achievement and Influence.* Cambridge, 1976.

Hill, Errol. *Shakespeare in Sable: A History of Black Shakespearean Actors.* Amherst, Mass., 1984.

Hogan, Charles Beecher, ed. *The London Stage, 1660–1800.* Part 5. *1776–1800.* Carbondale, Ill., 1968.

Hoyos, F. A. *Barbados: A History from the Amerindians to Independence.* London, 1978.

Hughes, Helen Sard. *The Gentle Hertford: Her Life and Letters.* New York, 1940.

Hulme, Peter. *Colonial Encounters: Europe and the Native Caribbean, 1492–1797.* London, 1986.

Jacobus, Mary. *Tradition and Experiment in Wordsworth's Lyrical Ballads (1798).* Oxford, 1976.

———. *Romanticism, Writing and Sexual Difference.* Oxford, 1989.

Kates, Carolyn J. "Chronicling the Heroic Epistle in England: A Study of Its Development and Demise." Ph.D. diss., University of North Carolina at Greensboro, 1991.

Kauffman, Linda S. *Discourses of Desire: Gender, Genre, and Epistolary Fictions.* Ithaca, N.Y., 1986.

Kay, Donald. *Short Fiction in the "Spectator."* Tuscaloosa, Ala., 1975.

Kimball, Jean. "An Ambiguous Faithlessness: Molly Bloom and the Widow of Ephesus." *James Joyce Quarterly* 31 (1994): 455–72.

Kulikoff, Allen. *Tobacco and Slaves: The Development of Southern Cultures in the Chesapeake, 1680–1800.* Williamsburg, Va., 1986.

Langford, Paul. *A Polite and Commercial People: England 1727–1783.* Oxford, 1989.

Layman, C. H., ed. *Man of Letters: The Early Life and Love Letters of Robert Chambers.* Edinburgh, 1990.

Leader, Robert Eadon. *Sheffield in the Eighteenth Century.* Sheffield, 1901.

Legman, G. *The Horn Book: Studies in Erotic Folklore and Bibliography.* New York, 1964.

Lehmann, John. *Ancestors and Friends.* London, 1962.

Levin, Yu D. "Inkle and Yarico in Russia." In *The Perception of English Literature in Russia,* trans. Catherine Phillips, 231–40. Nottingham, 1994.

Ligon, William D. *The Ligon Family and Connections.* New York, 1947.

Linebaugh, Peter. *The London Hanged: Crime and Civil Society in the Eighteenth Century.* Cambridge, 1991.

Lonsdale, Roger. *Eighteenth Century Women Poets: An Oxford Anthology.* Oxford, 1989.

Lowenberg, Alfred. *Annals of Opera.* 3d ed. London, 1978.

MacMillan, Dougald. *Catalogue of the Larpent Plays in the Huntington Library.* San Marino, Calif., 1939.

MacNaughten, Angus. *Burns' Mrs. Riddell.* Peterhead, Scotland, 1975.

Marshall, Trevor G., Peggy L. McGeary, and Grace J. I. Thompson. *Folk Songs of Barbados.* Bridgetown, Barbados, 1981.

Mayo, Robert. "The Contemporaneity of the 'Lyrical Ballads.'" *Publications of the Modern Language Association of America* 69 (1954): 486–522.

Merchant, Peter. "Robert Paltock and the Refashioning of 'Inkle and Yarico.'" *Eighteenth-Century Fiction* 9, no. 1 (1996): 37–50.

Mitchell, L. G. *Charles James Fox.* Oxford, 1992.

Moore, Catherine E. "Robinson and Xury and Inkle and Yarico." *Modern Language Notes* 19 (1981); 24–29.

Morgan, Jennifer L. "'Some Could Suckle over Their Shoulder': Male Travellers, Female Bodies, and the Gendering of Racial Ideology, 1500–1700." *William and Mary Quarterly* 54, no. 1 (1997): 167–92.

Nussbaum, Felicity. "The Politics of Difference." *Eighteenth-Century Studies* 23, no. 4 (1990): 375–86.

O'Donoghue, D. J. *The Poets of Ireland.* 2d ed. Dublin, 1912.

Oldfield, J. R. *Popular Politics and British Anti-slavery.* Manchester, 1995.

Ong, Walter J. *Orality and Literacy: The Technologizing of the Word.* London, 1982.

The Oxford Dictionary of English Proverbs. 3d ed. Ed. F. P. Wilson. Oxford, 1970.

Oxford English Dictionary, 2d ed., 20 vols. Oxford, 1989.

Pratt, Mary Louise. *Imperial Eyes: Travel Writing and Transculturation.* London, 1992.

Price, Lawrence Marsden. *Inkle and Yarico Album.* Berkeley, Calif., 1937.

Rankin, H. D. *Petronius the Artist.* The Hague, 1971.

Rosenfeld, Sybil. *The Georgian Theatre of Richmond Yorkshire.* London, 1984.

Rowland, Beryl. *Birds with Human Souls: A Guide to Bird Symbolism.* Knoxville, Tenn., 1978.

Runte, Roseann. "The Matron of Ephesus in Eighteenth-Century France: The Lady and the Legend." *Studies in Eighteenth-Century Culture* 6 (1977): 361–75.

Said, Edward W. *Culture and Imperialism.* London, 1993.

Sayre, Gordon M. *Les Sauvages Américains: Representations of Native Americans in French and English Colonial Literature* (Chapel Hill, N.C., 1997).

Sheppard, Jill. *The "Redlegs" of Barbados.* London, 1977.

Shevelow, Kathryn. *Women and Print Culture: The Construction of Feminity in the Early Periodical.* London, 1989.

Shyllon, Folarin. *Black Slaves in Britain.* London, 1974.

Simms, Norman. "A Silent Love Affair: Frances Seymour's 'Inkle and Yarico' (1726)." *AUMLA (Journal of the Australian Universities Language and Literature Association)* 85 (1996): 93–101.

Steicher, Henry F. *Elizabeth Rowe, the Poetess of Frome: A Study in Eighteenth-Century Pietism.* Berne, 1973.

Sypher, Wylie. *Guinea's Captive Kings: British Anti-slavery Literature of the Eighteenth Century.* 1942. Reprinted New York, 1969.

Thomson, Peter. "The Early Career of George Colman the Younger." In *Essays on Nineteenth Century British Theatre,* ed. Kenneth Richards and Peter Thomson, 67–82. London, 1971.

Thorne, R. G. *The House of Commons, 1790–1820.* 5 vols. London, 1986.

Tilton, Robert S. *Pocahontas: The Evolution of an American Narrative.* Cambridge, 1994.

Troost, Linda V. "Social Reform in Comic Opera: Colman's *Inkle and Yarico. Studies on Voltaire and the Eighteenth Century* 305 (1992): 1428.

Vries, Ad de. *Dictionary of Symbols and Imagery.* Amsterdam, 1974.

Walsh, T. J. *Opera in Dublin, 1705–1797: The Social Scene.* Dublin, 1973.

Walvin, James. *England, Slaves and Freedom, 1776–1838.* Jackson, Miss., 1986.

Wechselblatt, Martin. "Gender and Race in Yarico's Epistles to Inkle: Voicing the Feminine/Slave." *Studies in Eighteenth-Century Culture* 19 (1989): 197–223.

White, Hayden. *Tropics of Discourse: Essays in Cultural Criticism.* Baltimore, 1978.

Willis, Eola. *The Charleston Stage in the Eighteenth Century.* 1933. Reprinted New York, 1968.

Withycombe, E. G. *The Oxford Dictionary of English Christian Names.* 3d ed. Oxford, 1977.

Wu, Duncan. *Wordsworth's Reading, 1770–1799.* Cambridge, 1993.

Young, Philip. "The Mother of Us All: Pocahontas." In *Three Bags Full: Essays in American Fiction.* New York, 1967.

Index

Library of Congress Cataloging-in-Publication Data

English trader, Indian maid : representing gender, race, and slavery in the New World: an Inkle and
Yarico reader / edited by Frank Felsenstein.
p.   cm.
Includes bibliographical references and index.
ISBN 0-8018-6105-5 (alk. paper). — ISBN 0-8018-6106-3 (pbk. : alk. paper)
1. Indians of the West Indies—Literary collections.   2. Survival after airplane accidents, shipwrecks,
etc.—Literary collections.   3. British—West Indies—History—18th century—Literary collections.
4. West Indies—Race relations—Literary collections.   5. Indian women—West Indies—Literary
collections.   6. Slave trade—Barbados—Literary collections.   7. Carib Indians—Literary
collections.   8. Inkle, Thomas—Literary collections.   9. Yarico—Literary collections.   10. English
literature—18th century.   11. American literature.   I. Felsenstein, Frank.
PR1111.I57E54   1999
820.8'03520397—dc21
99-10538
CIP